About the author

James Leslie Mitchell wrote using his ov[illegible] under which he became famous, Lewis Gr[illegible] is present-day Aberdeenshire, Scotland, [illegible] and worked as a newspaper reporter in Aber[illegible] and Glasgow, then in 1919 joined the Royal Army Service Corps, in which he served mostly in the Middle East. From 1923 to 1929 he was a clerk in the Royal Air Force in southern England, leaving to become a full-time writer. He published seventeen books, fictional and non-fictional, between 1928 and his sudden death in 1935. His most famous work is a trilogy of novels set in the region of his upbringing, which has come to be known as *A Scots Quair*.

About the editor

Macdonald Daly was born in Glasgow and took degrees in English Literature from the Universities of Glasgow and Oxford. He was Lecturer in Modern Literature and then Associate Professor in Culture, Film and Media at the University of Nottingham, from which he retired in 2016. He has also edited works by H. G. Wells, Elizabeth Gaskell, D. H. Lawrence and Ellis Sharp, and co-edited books as various as *Karl Marx and Frederick Engels on Literature and Art* (2006), *The Genres of Post-Conflict Testimonies* (2010) and *"Black and Whites" and Other New Short Stories from Malaysia* (2012). His most recent books are *Reading Radio 4* (Palgrave Macmillan, 2016) and *Politics and the Scottish Language* (New Ventures, 2020).

Lewis Grassic Gibbon
[James Leslie Mitchell]

THE CALENDS OF CAIRO

with an introduction, notes and commentary by
Macdonald Daly

London
***Jet**stone*
2024

A ***Jet**stone* paperback.

ISBN 9781910858288

First published in 1931.

The front cover photograph shows Bab El-Wazir, Cairo, in the 1920s. The rear cover photograph is a likewise contemporary image of the Muhammad Ali Mosque (constructed 1832-48) in the Cairo Citadel.

Cover design by The Ever-Shifting Subject.

CONTENTS

INTRODUCTION by Macdonald Daly

> No, no, a thousand times no. This is a magazine story, sentimental, with bright chatter and a "surprise ending": its epitaph is, "Makes you think, don't it?" – or would be if one had not foreseen from somewhere about the middle the end you are so busily preparing behind your screen of patter. As soon as one knows the end, the story's over: it's one of that kind. I'm sorry, but there's nothing else to be said for it: the story's obvious; the patter poor; yourself, as usual, all over the page (your work's frightfully selfconscious) and in your most sentimental mood.
>
> J. R. Ackerley, in a postcard to Fred Urquhart, 6 December 1938 [1]

The Calends of Cairo appears out of sequence in James Leslie Mitchell's publishing history. The short-story collection was issued in July 1931, six months after the publication of his second novel, *The Thirteenth Disciple*. But in fact all the stories had been published before even Mitchell's first novel, *Stained Radiance*, had appeared in September 1930. Opposite the title page of the latter book's first edition, Mitchell put "POLYCHROMATA, a story cycle" in his two-item list of works "*By the Same Author*", the first being the essay *Hanno, or the Future of Exploration* (1928). "Polychromata" was the name under which twelve of the *Calends* stories had been published monthly by *The Cornhill Magazine* from summer to summer, 1929-30. *The Cornhill* had previously published, also in 1929, the one other story which was to be included in *The Calends*. Thus, while the lightly revised collection was the

[1] Quoted in Peter Parker, *Ackerley: a life of J. R. Ackerley* (New York: Farrar Straus Giroux, 1989), p. 200. Ackerley was editor of *The Listener*, then a weekly magazine published by the BBC. Urquhart became a very successful short-story writer during his lifetime (1912-1995). Once a landworker at Laurencekirk, he was to set many of his narratives in a fictional Mearns town, Auchencairn. The dating is from Parker's textual annotations (p. 442). In the text itself he states that the postcard was written in "December 1936" (p. 200). It does not appear in *The Letters of J. R. Ackerley*, ed. Neville Braybrooke (London: Duckworth, 1975).

third of Mitchell's imaginative writings to appear in book form, it is in fact his first published work of volume-length fiction.

These books represent the apprenticeship of a young man who turned thirty years of age only in February 1931. Mitchell's first two novels, while showing definite promise, are hardly masterpieces, so one might expect work which appeared before them to share their flaws. However, while *The Calends of Cairo* has its inevitable weaknesses, they are not of the same besetting kind as those of *Stained Radiance* or *The Thirteenth Disciple*. Both novels are highly autobiographical, and both seem to suffer from the writer being too close to his protagonist to write him up believably. John Garland in the first and Malcom Maudslay in the second are Mitchell surrogates it is difficult to take too seriously. Mitchell could easily have fallen into such an autobiographical trap in the "Polychromata" stories. After all, he had been in Egypt for a year with the Royal Army Service Corps, which he joined for a second time in January 1921. [2] He did attempt to capture some of this actual Cairo experience briefly in the eighth chapter of *Stained Radiance*, but this was to result in a typically miscalculated monologue in which the hero does little more than utter a bumptious denunciation of the Giza pyramids (while sitting on top of the highest one) and seems, as often, to glory in his own intellectual conceit.

Mitchell avoids this potential problem in the stories simply by absenting himself as implied narrator or protagonist. He hands the narration principally to Anton Saloney, a Russian counter-revolutionary and ex-schoolteacher of English hiding out in Cairo after the Russian Civil War and extemporising a living as a not entirely reliable "dragoman" or tour guide. When not doing that, or even perhaps while doing that, Saloney is an indefatigable raconteur of tales about the cosmopolitan folk he has encountered in 1920s Cairo. Our narrator is thus distanced from his creator linguistically, culturally and politically and, in the stories he tells us, we are invited not to take Saloney's romantic sensibility, occasional bombast, or self-confessedly suspect veracity at face value. This narrative viewpoint relieves Mitchell of the authorial narcissism which can be detected in his autobiographical novels, while permitting the stories to be transmitted via the sentimental medium of Saloney, whose acknowledged unreliability

[2] Mitchell was in Cairo from February 1922 to February 1923. He was stationed at Helmieh Camp in what maps of the period designate El Hilmîya, now a north-eastern suburb of Cairo west of Heliopolis (not to be confused with the neighbourhood on the same maps called El Helmîya, now Al-Helmiya, which is much closer to downtown Cairo). The camp was sometimes called "Helmich", which is how Mitchell referred to it in correspondence, but he is consistent in his usage of "Helmieh" in *The Calends* and the later novel *The Lost Trumpet* (London: Jarrolds, 1932).

legitimises the more fanciful elements in what is to come. It prevents Mitchell from smuggling into the fictions too many of his own hobby-horses, like Diffusionism or archaeology or anthropology, which sometimes blight the longer works. While the kaleidoscopically-rotating nature of events and people in the story-cycle also means that there is no central plot or character that has to bear all the weight of an extended narration, Mitchell's choice of a vast cosmopolitan city in a post-war period also gives him licence to introduce migrant or displaced *dramatis personae* whose eccentricity, madness, political despair, religious extremity or personal catastrophism, as well as their all being able to gather in one place, seem mostly credible.

But what exactly is a "story-cycle"? On 26 May 1929, Mitchell wrote to Alexander and Ellen Gray, "I think I told you I was going to write a story-cycle – 'Polychromata' – for the Cornhill. (Twelve stories about Cairo, linked together by a common narrator, afterwards to be published in book form.)" This makes it clear that he envisaged the stories in a stand-alone collection and thought that what they had in common was Saloney as teller. He later (12 March 1931) expressed the slightly grander view that "'Polychromata' isn't a collection of short stories; it's a story-cycle, an episodic novel". [3] This is a somewhat exaggerated conception with which we need not trouble ourselves overlong. Mitchell was on that occasion attempting to encourage his American publisher, who was leery of the market for short stories. But reading the *Calends* stories in sequence does indubitably immerse one in a larger, more detailed and, yes, colourful world than any single story could possibly evoke, and so Mitchell had some right to claim that linking stories by place and time and teller does differentiate *The Calends* from a typically miscellaneous collection. It may not make a composite novel – even if Mitchell listed it in the front papers of *Three Go Back* (1932) as one of "*four novels*" – but the montage of associated stories can amount to more than the sum of its parts because of the superimpositional effects it manufactures in the overlapping of locations and persons.

It was a quite seasoned genre, the associated-story-cycle, going back as far, most pertinently, as *One Thousand and One Nights*, the accumulation of early Middle-Eastern folk tales, many of which had been available in English since the eighteenth century. [4] These were told, one per night, by

[3] Sources for this and the preceding quotation are, respectively, correspondence TS, National Library of Scotland, and a letter in The Lilly Library, Indiana University. My thanks to William K. Malcolm for drawing these letters to my attention.

[4] Selections and editions often appear under the title *The Arabian Nights* or *The Book of the Thousand Nights and One Night* or similar. It was under the latter title

Scheherazade (as Saloney's were published, one per month). There had also been at least two distinguished recent works in this narrative tradition: James Joyce's *Dubliners* (1914) and Sherwood Anderson's *Winesburg, Ohio: A Group of Tales of Ohio Small-Town Life* (1919). In both modern cases the main unifying features are place and society. Neither Joyce nor Anderson employs a seemingly omnipresent and continuous narrator. One can agree, nevertheless, with William K. Malcolm about the value judgment that would likely follow such comparisons:

> direct comparison with *Dubliners* and *Winesburg, Ohio* reflects badly on Mitchell's work, for while his *Polychromata* is imbued with an admirable sense of the spirit of place [...] the characterisation appears wooden, the narrative mode dated and affected, and the action forced when set against those of Joyce and Anderson. [5]

While Mitchell had a necessarily high estimate of his own writing, it is doubtful if, at this nascent stage in his career, he was hoping to compete with the Irishman or the American. He was at this time a less gifted writer than either; indeed, an almost entirely unpublished one. Rather, he was looking to secure the slippery foothold he had on the literary ladder.

While there is plenty of evidence that Mitchell read a great deal of contemporary writing, a lot of it most likely in periodical or library-book form, it is misleading to think of his early work as "modernist" in any sustained sense. The internal evidence of these texts, and their general style, suggest that he was more at home with rather settled late Victorian or Edwardian literary models than he was with the less easily categorised and stylistically more venturesome modernist writing of the 1920s. The same impression is given by the rather sober tomes in the library he left (now housed at the University of Edinburgh). As for his inclination in the short story in particular, a glance at the pre-1929 contents of this library gives us strong hints that it was hardly his favoured form, or at least shows that what he possessed of it was meagre and lamentable. It contains *The Plattner story and others* (1897), *Tales of Space and Time* (1899) and *Twelve stories and a dream* (1903). All are by H. G. Wells and are notably all volumes in The Essex Edition of the Collected Works of H. G. Wells (London: Ernest Benn, 1927), so Mitchell could have acquired them, at the earliest, only the year before he started work on "Polychromata". But Wells, now in his early

that the first complete and unexpurgated English translation was made by John Payne (9 vols.; London: The Villon Society, 1882-84).

[5] William K. Malcolm, *A Blasphemer & Reformer: A Study of James Leslie Mitchell/ Lewis Grassic Gibbon* (Aberdeen: Aberdeen University Press, 1984), p. 47.

sixties, was hardly at the cutting edge of modernist experimentation: the nearest Mitchell's library gets to that (and it's not very near) is *Little Mexican and other stories* by Aldous Huxley (London: Chatto and Windus, 1928), a hardly remembered collection first published in 1924, and Huxley also just happened to be the son of his *Cornhill* editor. Other pre-1929 short story collections in his possession at death were rather dated Scottish ones by R. B. Cunninghame Graham and John Galt, and *Nash and Some Others* (1928) by the largely forgotten English writer C. S. Evans. [6] As he was a back-office clerk in the army and RAF, and not a front-line operative, so was the young Mitchell relative to the modernist literary avant-garde.

One could elaborate a litany of Wellsian textual habits in the short story to which *The Calends* also resorts: a cast of cosmopolitan characters, each story including usually at least one eccentric, tormented, passionate, obsessed or deluded individual who takes a decidedly unusual course of action; having the story, or large parts of it, told at second-hand by a person reporting what another person has told him; at times making a direct address to the reader as if he or she were present; stressing interpersonal interactions and keeping largely (if not completely) at bay the realms of politics, economics and world events; making an attempt somewhere in the story, often towards the end, to overturn false expectations already created for the reader; and concluding by drawing out a seeming-moral message, or suggesting that a profound question or reflection has been prompted (thus performing a sort of non-narrative final nod towards the "point" of the story). [7] There are other Wellsian tendencies the Mitchell of *The Calends* shares which it is harder to isolate in analysis, as they involve impressions to do with tone, style and implied world-view. There is a knack Wells has of delivering his tales in a boisterous, clubbable register, for example, which undercuts any possibility of the tragic or monumental, and gives the story the air of being "middlebrow" at best, first and foremost an entertainment, an extended pub or tea-shop anecdote, rather than a serious stab at art.

[6] Mitchell's surviving library has other materials pertinent to his interest in Egypt and the romance genre. It includes the ninth (1916) edition of E. A. Reynolds-Ball, *Cairo of to-day: a practical guide to Cairo and its environs* (London: A. and C. Black, 1898) and two Victorian translations of novels by the German writer George Ebers (1837-1898), *An Egyptian Princess* (tr. Eleanor Grove, Leipzig: Tauchnitz, 1871) and *Uarda: a romance of ancient Egypt* (tr. Clara Bell, Leipzig: Tauchnitz, 1877).

[7] Of course, many other short-story writers used these devices too, but one does not need to argue too persuasively that Wells exercised a larger literary influence on Mitchell (as well as his publishing career) than any other writer did. As for many developing authors, Mitchell's better work was arguably done only when he broke free of such models.

There is also a general assumption of a world-view shared by narrator and reader, which is at its least tolerable today in how unmistakably white and colonial in cultural perspective Wells's short stories usually are: the word "nigger", for example, appears gratuitously in many of them, and non-white people in them are routinely killed and beaten by the protagonists, who freely admit to the acts, without consequence or even criticism. As Wells starkly put it in one of his short stories, "The life of a Chinaman is scarcely sacred like a European's." [8]

The N-word appears twice, with the same Wellsian casualness and thoughtlessness, in *The Calends*. Mitchell, himself stationed in Cairo as an instrument of British domination, hardly gives a hint that the Cairo he is describing is thoroughly controlled by a squatting British imperial power, or that there was mounting pressure from Egyptians to get the British out from virtually the day he arrived there. Making the narrator a Russian refugee who struggles to keep body and soul alive obviates the need: Saloney, neither Egyptian nor British, but one who has just fought in two lost wars to defend a defeated empire, cannot be expected to be over-interested in the rights and wrongs of imperialism. His escape to Cairo is what permits him, and Mitchell, to hold such concerns at more than arm's length. Not only is there no seeming wish to talk about colonialism, but the other political and economic concerns which are likely to crop up in most Mitchell/Gibbon novels are here almost entirely ignored. William K. Malcolm does his best to make the case that "[t]he *Polychromata* contains vehement protests against the sexual, religious, racial and social bigotry which Mitchell observed in contemporary life", [9] but challenging mere bigotry is a soft liberal cause, not the class-conscious socialist stuff readers increasingly came to expect from the later writer. [10] Perhaps religious zealotry, racial

[8] H. G. Wells, "The Treasure in the Forest", *The Stolen Bacillus and Other Incidents* (London: Methuen, 1895), p. 262.

[9] Malcolm, *A Blasphemer & Reformer*, p. 47.

[10] Although the Great War does play a significant part in a few stories such as "A Volcano on the Moon" it is in the past, like the Russian Civil War in "He Who Seeks" and the Greco-Turkish War of "The Life and Death of Elia Constantinides": rather, it is the developing geopolitics of the 1920s, including the renewed British occupation of Egypt, that the volume overlooks in favour of the delights of romance, intrigue, vicariously experienced evil and exotic adventure. But even something like "A Volcano in the Moon" is patently Wellsian. Two people examining the moon by telescope is very reminiscent of the opening of Wells's novel *The War of the Worlds* (London: Heinemann, 1898), where the narrator and the astronomer Ogilvy watch Mars from an English observatory and see a "jetting out of gas from the distant planet" (p. 6). Gellion and Freligrath's falling-out is reminiscent of the obnoxious

conflict, social injustice and sexual abuse were included because we get more sensational plots with them than without them. To adapt a metaphor found in "The Epic", Mitchell (when he is in his presumed "oh-dear-how-unjust" mode) repeatedly lifts the veil on the horrifying side of Cairo life so that we can take a good entertaining look at it, then replaces it while intimating how terribly ghastly and abominably unfair it all is. I tend to the view that Mitchell was probably more interested as a writer in the vice than in the virtue, and thought we would be too, and we can be fairly certain from its lists of potboilers that his rather populist publisher (Jarrolds) would not mind it either, even if conventional liberal morality's finger got to wag parentally in the background.

More than any textual social justice crusade, we are presented with Saloney's irrepressible romanticism, indefatigable whimsy and unremitting keenness to poke his nose into the private recesses of other people's business and then go and gossip to all and sundry about them. In "The Epic", the text rather overweeningly claims for itself an "all human life is there" dimension: "If you sit long enough in the Khalig all Cairo will sometime pass by – boyar and beggar, brown man and black, and the men of the shades of white, and all the women of the history of the world, the vile and the fair and the pitiful": the book as parade of assorted human exhibits, one might paraphrase, with Saloney the ringmaster of the circus, assembled primarily to entertain rather than provoke thought, never mind prick the political conscience. If the collection is considered such a *divertissement* then, in fulfilling its modest function, it succeeds. Few readers are likely to feel in these individual stories that they are in the hands of an incompetent writer, which for stretches of the first two novels many surely must.

No wonder Mitchell approached Wells (who had assisted him in getting published in *The Cornhill* in the first place) to help him sell *The Calends* by providing an introductory puff. Wells minimally obliged, in a way that suggests he might not even have read the proofs Mitchell sent with the request. We now tend to see Wells as an exemplar of the "middlebrow" writer in his time: he had enviable capacities in plot concoction and wrote very fluently and copiously, but mostly for popular publications or in popular genres with little to show in the way of artistic flair or aesthetic originality. I think we can be fairly confident that Mitchell in 1928-29 would have been more than pleased to frequent the newspapers and magazines where writers much weaker and workaday than Wells were to be found: *The Cornhill* was one of them. He wanted to be a full-time writer and needed to

battle in learned journals of the lepidopterists Hapley and Pawkins in Wells's "A Moth – Genus Novo" – later retitled simply "The Moth" – in *The Stolen Bacillus and Other Incidents*, pp. 232-256.

make money, and consequently hardly ever wrote without an awareness of the market. And finally – let us be frank – Mitchell's own detectable preferences in fiction, which leave substantial traces in his work, also seem to have been for the romantic, sentimental, remote-or-exotic-locale mode redolent of the boy's classic and the cosmopolitan love story.

A good example of the kind of writing and publishing success Mitchell might have envied or desired at this time is probably that of W. Somerset Maugham. Maugham was twenty-five years older than Mitchell. He had had remarkable early success in the theatre and the novel, and in 1920 turned seriously to writing short stories which were often set in far-flung outposts like southeast Asia or the Pacific Islands or the closer but still romance-inspiring continental Europe. Coincidentally, when he came to collect them in 1951 he "grouped, as well as I conveniently could, stories of which the local (or locale) was in one particular country. In that way I hoped to give the reader a chance to take his bearings in whatever distant land I chose to lead him to." [11] A typical Maugham story comprises a foreign spot you are unlikely to know, a bar for drink that makes tongues wag and leads to tittle-tattle, and a male narrator who listens to or hears of another transplanted foreigner who has gone mad, or gone native, or gone off this mortal coil altogether in controversial circumstances worth recording (controversial, that is, to his white readers: Maugham contrived all kinds of sexual and criminal and irreligious denouements to shock everyday morality, which was often represented by his narrators). Maugham's astounding commercial success said a lot about the kind of thing that pleased the British mainstream short-story market in the 1920s: tales of washed-up characters, often at a climactic point in life or unwittingly in their final days, their plight and its usually sensational circumstances (murder, fornication, suicide, alcoholism, bad finances) related by the inveterately involved Maugham narrators, heightened in intensity by the distant setting, and as hard to look away from as a car-crash.

But wherever it is said to be, the world of Maugham's short stories is always the white man's playground. He made no bones about the fact that he was out to entertain and did not even attempt to describe a real world, never mind depict or criticise actual economic and political relations. The Empire may as well be a feature of nature in his works, like the weather.

[11] W. Somerset Maugham, "Preface", *The Complete Short Stories*, (3 vols., London: Heinemann, 1951), vol. I, p. viii. Maugham published three collections of short stories in the 'twenties: *The Trembling of a Leaf* (1921), *The Casuarina Tree: Six Stories* (1926) and *Ashenden, or the British Agent* (1928). His reputation among the literary has evaporated more radically than Wells's. It is not easy now to find people under a certain (advanced) age who have read him, or sometimes even heard of him.

While there is no reason to think that Mitchell was directly influenced by Maugham, whose politics and social perspective and entire life-experience were alien to his, he could hardly have been unaware of him. Edwin Muir rather liked him: he had written a very positive short notice for *The Casuarina Tree* in 1926 and thought one of its constituents "surely one of the best short stories written in our time". [12] One contemporary review of Maugham's *The Trembling of a Leaf* begins:

> The siren song of the South Sea Islands has never been more alluring than at the present time, when it sounds with musical softness through the harsh discords of a disordered world. They seem a refuge for romance, those islands with their lagoons and flowers and palm trees and splendid tropical skies. There life, we feel, must be simpler and easier; there the struggle for existence is abated, and men have time to dream. [13]

The review went on to claim that "now comes Somerset Maugham, the brilliant and sophisticated, to show us how the dreams may end, to show us that life and love lose none of their ironies when their dramas are played beside a forest pool or in the cabin of a schooner sailing the Pacific", but despite the dire horrors of some of the lives Maugham describes, the "siren song" of the distant setting, one feels, always reaches us like "musical softness through the harsh discords of a disordered world". The Cairo setting of *The Calends* works rather in the same fashion, and many of the individual stories are not far removed in atmosphere and event from those Maugham was publishing in the 'twenties, and which he went on doing long after. Rather like Maugham's, they give a sense of nostalgic anachronism, as if the fictional world they describe is that of the settled pre-War *status quo*, transferred to the decade after the War as if in hope or expectation that it might return (or under the delusion that it has). It would have been impossible to do that successfully if you set your stories in strife-ridden 1920s industrial Britain, as Mitchell was to do in his first two novels, both of which recognise that the War has transformed everything and that political change is both inescapable and needed.

Also like Maugham's, Mitchell's stories are modest successes if we consider them as having been written within certain limited conventions,

[12] Edwin Muir, review, *Nation and Athenaeum* XI, 9 October 1926, p. 30, reprinted in Anthony Curtis and John Whitehead (eds.), *W. Somerset Maugham: The Critical Heritage* (London: Routledge, 1987), p. 170.

[13] Louise Maunsell Field, review, *New York Times*, 20 November 1921, p. 16, reprinted in Curtis and Whitehead (eds.), p. 148.

either by choice or necessity.[14] The first, "For Ten's Sake", is densely detailed, skilfully evocative of environment and adroit in introducing a multitude of characters, showing relatively accomplished handling of transitions from scene to scene, and disclosing its plot details from a welter of differing perspectives. The slight moralising at its end perhaps weakens but hardly ruins it.[15] The concluding hint that a principle can be drawn from the story runs the risk of suggesting that it is no more than a shell yielding this traditional pearl of wisdom, and this didacticism may possibly diminish some readers' engagement. It is one of those now dated conventions. There can be little doubt, however, that the story, set in an obviously biblical landscape, does its best to earn this parable-like quality, and in any case is hardly reducible to it. "For Ten's Sake" is ambitious in the way it parodies the excesses of Calvinism while reversing a specific biblical narrative and taking a very destructive God out of the worldly equation. It is the only story not set in Cairo but, placed as "Proem" in *The Calends*, it quite believably establishes the setting as the dusty Middle East, the cultural differences as mainly those between Europeans and Arabs, and the prevailing mood as potentially catastrophic but, at the same time, salvation (earthly, not religious) is always a possibility. It is with these ignited expectations that we enter upon the "Polychromata" proper.

These terms of reference are quickly amended by the introduction (or imposition) in "He Who Seeks" of Saloney, henceforth our Cairo dragoman narrator. "Long the evenings I sat and puzzled till I knew the Khalig and Life

[14] This was pretty much what D. H. Lawrence said when reviewing Maugham's collection of spy stories, *Ashenden*: "Mr Maugham is a splendid observer. He can bring before us persons and places most excellently. But as soon as the excellently observed characters have to move, it is a fake. Mr Maugham gives them a humorous shove or two. We find they are nothing but puppets, instruments of the author's pet prejudice. The author's pet prejudice being 'humour'"; D. H. Lawrence, "Four Contemporary Books", *Vogue*, 20 July 1928, reprinted in Curtis and Whitehead (eds.), p. 177, which also quotes a lovely extract from one of Lawrence's last letters (from France, 6 January 1930) in which he denounces "Maugham and Wells and Co. rolling their incomes round Nice for Xmas, rich as pigs" (p. 176). Lawrence had for some time been writing literary-critical essays which complained about authors (many of them famous, like Tolstoy) unduly interfering with their characters and plots in order to arrive at some morally or aesthetically orthodox design, and this expressed difference between himself and his predecessors one can see now as an element of his modernism. The early Mitchell, however, was in a pre-modernist groove, and also made his characters do puppet-like things in order to achieve his desired effects.

[15] A similar problem occurred in the concluding section of the *Cornhill* version of "It is Written", and Mitchell deleted it.

for one," Saloney tells us. "Key-colour to the kaleidoscope, master-note in the syncopation – it is Quest." This immediately assimilates Cairo to life itself, something the stories will try to do several times (for example, in "Vernal" we get the blunt sentence, "'Cairo,' I said. 'Life.'"). But it also announces a master theme centring on the oldest plot in literature, the Quest narrative, and simultaneously bounces us into the environs of sagas and romances that have built up around it. The story itself goes on to intimate, however, that the true quester is not done when he achieves his goal, for his nature is to go on questing: "To strive, to seek, to find, and not to yield", as one of Mitchell's favourite poems, Tennyson's "Ulysses", puts it in conclusion. Once more the story is in danger of seeming to exist largely to demonstrate this sentiment, as well as being open to the charge that it merely enlarges prosaically on an idea Tennyson had already exploited with classic poetic brilliance. But in fact these issues arise only at the very beginning and end of the story, almost as a detachable framework.

For the most part it is an engrossing and historically knowledgeable account of how Andrei Bal'mont, like Saloney, escaped the Russian Civil War and came to Cairo. Mitchell's plot wanders a little along with his hero, but he is skilful enough to engineer a powerful reversal of readerly expectations. Such narrational twists, however, were to become largely deprecated in literary evaluation and thought redolent of the popular. One can see why. Overuse of the device by a writer can lead to the plot bulking too large or to ridiculous plot contrivances; it can encourage readers to imagine distractingly in advance what unexpected reversal the author has up his sleeve this time (which is far from desirable, especially if the author has none); and worst of all what one might call the expected unexpected reversal may be correctly predicted by the reader in advance, which takes a lot of the power out of it. But on this occasion I think Mitchell succeeds, not least because the reversal is very quickly done and there is no explicit explanation given for it. There is still that final nut to crack, and the reader has to do it by inference. [16]

So far, so good. Mitchell has within the opening two stories firmly established the scene of the tales yet to unfold, leading us confidently to Cairo via Persia, Transjordan, Palestine, Turkey and post-revolutionary Crimea. He has seated us (or saddled us) with a White Russian expatriate

[16] It should be said that the "infer from what's unspoken" ending could also be seen, by this time, as excessively formulaic. Maugham's most famous story, "Rain" (*The Trembling of a Leaf* [London: Heinemann, 1921], p. 295) ends with the line: "Dr. Macphail gasped. He understood." But what Macphail understands we are not told and have to work out, and when we do we should, mentally at least, gasp too. "Rain" also happens to be a tale of a demonic Calvinist whose maniacal mission is undone.

narrator, and we have now read two stories in which the principal character seeks ardently for something but has a striking change of mind and does not secure it. It has been made very clear that we can expect romance rather than realism, as Saloney has let us know that he considers the Quest a human preoccupation in Cairo as well as life in general.

One can imagine certain anticipatory questions arising for Mitchell's contemporary readers after this reasonable start. Are we simply to have plot modulation in the book hereafter? Is every story to concern some uprooted foreigner as quester who happens to end up in Cairo, his or her story of thwarted or fortunate seeking to be told by another foreigner, Saloney, to yet another foreigner, the reader? One question they are unlikely to have asked generally, however, is, *why a White Russian narrator*? The text itself makes the Cairene Saloney entirely plausible, partly because there was a real Russian refugee enclave in Cairo in the 1920s; and the choice of a non-British speaker allows Mitchell to have gentle fun with Saloney's slightly imperfect English, which in my view regularly enhances the texture of the prose and never allows us to forget who is doing the telling. But some of Mitchell's socialist and Communist friends must have wondered why he, of all people, chose a White, counter-revolutionary Russian as his foreign mouthpiece. When he re-invented Andrei Bal'mont as Andreas Koupa in *Stained Radiance,* Mitchell made him a Red Army Dutchman who becomes disenchanted with the Bolsheviks and flees from them. But then, *Stained Radiance* itself can be read as a satire on 1920s British Communism, and we can surely only conclude that Mitchell, whatever may have been his objective political views, was not in his early writing aiming to offer ideological nutrition to left-wing radicals. Our sense of *that* kind of Mitchell comes only from later work.

But while Saloney is an explicable choice (a literal loser telling us about many other metaphorical losers, with whom he has a great deal of empathy), and no one would surely expect such a collection of stories to be narrated by a Bolshevik, the question can be asked, as it were, from a different angle: *why not an Egyptian narrator*? We simply don't know the answer to this poser, but it becomes increasingly difficult, I would suggest, to refrain from the judgment that the Egyptian perspective simply did not seem to matter. To a Brit stationed in Cairo as part of an occupying force like Mitchell in 1922-23, Egypt was British, in many ways more British than Britain, as a lot of expatriate enclaves seem to be. The indigenous modern Egyptians were a subject people, often represented as a nameless mass (like the residents of the "Warrens" to which the text alludes on a couple of occasions), and could perhaps be presumed not to have interesting stories to tell and/or to have likely too many nationalist axes to grind. In "Vernal", Freeman remarks to Saloney, "Dr Adrian tells me you are reliable, which is not the case with natives." Saloney too is not at all reliable, as he himself frequently indicates. But to have had an Egyptian narrator who is as insouciant about the colonial regime as Saloney and the other Europeans seem to be would, alternatively, have strained credulity. The blunt fact is, Mitchell wants little talk in these stories of imperial repression or socialism or Egyptians, and a White Russian narrator therefore fits the bill. [17] He keeps the European desperadoes to the fore, and the Egyptians in the shadowy background. To maintain the empire of romance, after all, you have to contain the possibly undermining threat of anti-imperialist realism.

In the third story, "The Lost Prophetess", Mitchell goes up a gear in sensationalism: we get abduction, confinement, rape, torture, multiple murder and the founding of a cult religion by a temporarily hysterical woman. It's *News of the World* stuff, but Saloney lets us know frankly that the tale is a thirty-year old "legend of the bazaars ... embroidered and miracle-adorned" of whose likely large fictionality we are constantly warned: "no record but the fragmentary verbal survives". Jane Hatoun is portrayed as a crusading *fin-de-siècle* feminist, not merely a suffragist (and Mitchell deserves some credit for including these radical political notes) but she is also redolent of a more primal protagonist like H. Rider Haggard's Ayesha, in the novel *She* (1887), an immortal sorceress in control of a pre-Egyptian African kingdom, and also something of a prophet. For example, in the thirteenth chapter of the novel Ayesha shows the narrator images in a font of water, as impossibly as Jane conjures up pictures on the curtain. [18] "Magic" such as this, as well as other implausible occurrences, are often integral to the romance genre, and Mitchell does not hesitate in depicting it.

Much depends on the reader's preparedness to accept such conventions which, to my mind, Mitchell deploys quite competently. The problem is not his execution, but that today's readers are much more likely to find such romances absurd or childish. We can be sure that Mitchell's audience of almost a century ago would have been more indulgent towards them, not least because we know that middling literary magazines and potboiler novels were full of these kinds of mystery plots and had been for generations. They were extremely popular. Science fiction was yet to mature

[17] Anti-imperialism had been a Communist rallying-cry at least since Lenin's *Imperialism, the Highest Stage of Capitalism: A Popular Outline* (1917) but there were much earlier home-grown critiques: Lenin himself had somewhat relied on J. A. Hobson's *Imperialism: A Study* (London: Nisbet & Co., 1902). Mitchell could hardly have been unaware that colonialism was increasingly seen as the devil's work by those on the political left.

[18] H. Rider Haggard, *She: A History of Adventure* (London: Longmans, Green, and Co., 1887), p. 151.

as a genre and replace their magic with something seemingly more credible but having the same narratological function, namely the advanced technology of an imagined future. To us the extremity of the plot may be a difficulty which its first readers found attractive, or at least not off-putting. If they were even residually Christian they would feel quite at home with the supernatural and seemingly magical. Nor was the British public in Mitchell's time likely to be perturbed as we may be now by the story's depiction of the African characters as sexual monsters or murderous fiends. Pantomime "aliens" like Shihada Bey were entirely commonplace in English fiction in the colonial period. A double datedness, then, may constitute our chief problem in enjoying *The Calends* today: it was, in its time, not in tune with the modernist aesthetic which, in literary-historical terms, would come to triumph; and in our time the aesthetic on which it depended, that of literary romance, has been deprecated.

A startlingly stereotypical Scotland greets us in "Daybreak", with much "heather on the hills", those hills also abounding in Scotch mist and the enchanting songs of a bonny peasant lassie straight out of Burns. In part the story becomes the first of Mitchell's several attempts to dramatise the miscarriage of their first child suffered by his wife, Rhea, in January 1926, and while this dreadful event undercuts some of the opening's gauche Caledonian kitsch, the reader still has to contend with the thick syrup of Saloney's style as tale-teller: "romance rang her bugles for them again. The great secret was theirs, theirs partnership in the abiding mystery...". Truly laboured play is made on the heroine's name, Dawn, and its associations with morning, light, sun, new beginnings. The couple, Dawn and Roger, are improbably removed to Cairo and take insufficient precautions against a second pregnancy which Dawn has been told would kill her. Into this looming tragedy Saloney continually injects his own strange sense of emotional entanglement, admitting that he was "in love" (sentimentally speaking) with both Dawn and Roger. Wince-inducing dialogue and heavy-handed symbolism suffuse the whole. It is about as close to a not-quite-collapsing disaster as a publishable short story can be. Mitchell is dealing with an experience which involves his own personal grief, something he was not always able to do very successfully in artistic terms in yet later books. He even borrows five letters from his own surname to give to Roger Mantell.

We are now almost a quarter-way into the collection and the quality has decidedly begun to wobble after a decent start. What immediately follows is not entirely stabilising. "The Epic" quickly reveals itself to be a story concerned with the challenge of writing about modern Cairo, which seems a suspiciously navel-gazing activity to be pursuing so early in the volume. An Englishman of Irish descent, "Connan the Poet", dredges up in the city: "'I was Connan the poet. But now I am Connan the lost. I write no poetry, because there is no poetry left in the world.'" The reason there is no longer any possibility of meaningful poetry is the overwhelming and inhuman devastation of the War, which has rendered Connan "a sick man. Mentally. He wrote no poetry. He never read in books. Some thing in life there had been that blinded the windows of his soul." Connan is thus like the legendary wounded Fisher King, impotent and awaiting a healing agent.

Using a writer as a principal character was a growing (now usually considered modernist) trend in the 1920s. Mitchell's first three novels all have a writer as protagonist. In "Daybreak" Roger Mantell, despite being a mediocre journalist, seems to give miraculously instant birth to a successful book at the same time that his wife gives birth to their son. The problem has always been that while, for authors, writing itself may be experienced as a titanic cerebral struggle with language or form or plot, in terms of observable behaviour the writer is doing so little that it is almost impossible to convey with any significant degree of drama. The subjective and usually entirely private trial of writing lacks what T. S. Eliot called an objective correlative, which makes it extremely difficult to present convincingly. Authors are additionally men of words alone, yet often want to be taken as seriously as (and sometimes more seriously than) men of action. Writers like D. H. Lawrence (*Kangaroo*, 1923) and Aldous Huxley (*Point Counter Point*, 1928) ironised the modern writer, satirically emphasising the gap between his grand social or political ambitions and the relative insularity and introspection demanded by his craft. Others, like Virginia Woolf (*Orlando: A Biography*, 1928) and Evelyn Waugh (*Vile Bodies*, 1930) exploit this authorial paradox as a rich source of comedy.

The pre-modernist Saloney rather predictably approaches the issue from the old-fashioned heroic angle, milking the popular illusion that the writer is a diviner or prophet of the kind who can "interpret Cairo's soul". Saloney reads only part of it, but on this slender basis confidently tells us that a revitalised Connan has written "the song of all Cairo, the song of Egypt and the world [...] In the Khalig's colours and voices he had found the tale of all humanity and told it as I had never read it told before". Needless to say, perhaps, not a word of this surpassing literary achievement is reproduced in the story. We are told that it is better than the songs of Shelley, a comparison which probably impresses us now much less than Mitchell intended. But the epic manuscript is, you guessed it, destroyed by its creator, its composition having only exacerbated his madness. Mitchell's story is not poorly written in itself but, again, Saloney's hackneyed romanticism acts like an old blanket cast over it, effectively dampening whatever potential fire it may have. Mitchell's problem, then, is not in manufacturing reasonably good prose or serviceable plots. It is, rather, that the mawkish temperament of Saloney is repeatedly allowed to gloss the stories with reference to outmoded, usually sentimental and populist, conceptions.

Had there turned out to be active volcanoes on the moon, Mitchell's next tale would no doubt now share the praise showered on stories by Wells like "The Land Ironclads" (which in 1903 featured the modern battlefield tank more than a decade before its real-world appearance). Mitchell did indeed personally think that there might be potentially erupting volcanoes on the moon. He says so in *Hanno*. Many others at the time did too, however, so this was not really science fiction (like Wells's novel *The First Men in the Moon*, 1901) but arguably potential science fact. In any case the telescopic search for a puffing lunar volcano is not the nub of the story. Mitchell cleverly integrates an international collaboration in astronomy with the universal debacle of the Great War, showing how the latter, with its narrow partisan national aims, could destroy the scientific quest for knowledge and truth, as well as bonds of friendship. But for Mitchell the grim watershed of the War must be put behind us, and he intimates this by not having the sins of the French and German astronomer fathers visited upon their more enlightened post-War children. The fact that the first observatory in Egypt had been built very close to Mitchell's fictional one adds a verisimilar touch. Saloney's now customary commentary at the end could perhaps have been cut. These curtain calls of his are becoming tedious. Unfortunately, they persist in the stories to come.

"The Life and Death of Elia Constantinides" is at first rather like "He Who Seeks" but cast in a different metal. Instead of Andrei Bal'mont and the Russian Civil War which he flees after the White defeat, we have Elia, a young Greek who deserts his army post after his country's defeat in the Greco-Turkish War. Both re-encounter in Cairo a woman from their past, though in Elia's case she is not someone he is actively seeking. The woman is a prostitute to whom he lost his virginity, and he marries her. A more profound difference is that Elia seems to have suffered periodic hallucinations since before the War, which Mitchell plays with ambiguously as potentially having some supernatural significance, using the idea of "the unquiet dead" already introduced in "The Epic". By this means an air of mystery is effectively created and deliberately left unresolved. Has Elia, himself beset by visions of the unquiet dead, become one himself? Unlike the youngsters in "A Volcano in the Moon", no better future welcomes him now that the fighting is over. Saloney's ritual exercise in moral uplift at the close of the tale does, at least, mitigate the dark tragedy of his young death and, one reflects, if it was one of Mitchell's intentions to explore how people experience catastrophe – how they cope with it, escape it, or are marked indelibly by it – he has to an appreciable degree succeeded in several of these stories.

"Cockcrow" is an attempt at deconstructing a commonplace binary opposition, as "East is West" will do later. In this case one can readily suspect that Ravelston, the medical researcher who oscillates between his need for long periods of private, almost solipsistic study, but also comes just as desperately to desire married love, maps somewhat on to the early Mitchell himself, constantly writing, writing, writing, but at the same time obviously treasuring marriage and parenthood. Pamela, who suddenly becomes Ravelston's wife, is at first bored but then outraged when she discovers (thanks to the monumentally unconfidential and clearly somewhat malicious Dr Adrian) that Ravelston may have married her because he believed she had cancer, a cure for which he is researching. She walks out on him and goes off to Alexandria on an ill-conceived sexual bender. Into this framework Mitchell injects biblical parallels: the tale could easily be called "The Prodigal Wife", for example, and the cockcrow of its title, which brings Pamela back to her senses, evokes Peter's temporary denial of knowledge of Christ after his arrest by the Romans. Objectively speaking the entire story is pure middle-class melodrama, which Mitchell accomplishes with what the more demanding reader may regard as worrying competence. On the other hand, he was to address the difficulties and tensions of marriage many times more in his works, often from the woman's point of view, and we may choose to approach this story as a prototype of these better ventures.

In "Vernal" we are presented with a contrast between yet another puritanical Calvinist father and his modern semi-liberated daughter, a generational difference of a kind one expects to have been accentuated by the social concussions of the War. There is nothing particularly surprising about its plot. By now we have surely got used to the recurring pattern of prohibitive, fixed-minded old folk having their pre-War assumptions and expectations overturned by the actions of bright young things determined to move into a more positive future, as the blooming spring follows bleak winter. Within these oppositions, Mitchell again contrives a melodramatic means of defusing conflict, resulting in a reconciliation and forgiveness rather than an estrangement. These are solid Christian virtues and, now quite well into the book, we may pause to consider just how much religious values (if not belief) seem to pervade it. "For Ten's Sake" is directly inspired by an Old Testament story. In "He Who Seeks" Andrei quests to find Natasha "as once men sent forth to seek the Holy Grail" and in "It is Written" we will witness Godfrey Steyn in search of "a Lost Testament, in the handwriting of our Saviour Himself". In "The Lost Prophetess" a religious cult is established. "The Life and Death of Elia Constantinides" toys with the idea of "the unquiet dead", ghosts or phantoms who persist on earth in some liminal supernatural state. In "The Gift of the River" we will be offered some kind of bodily resurrection or transmigration of the soul. "Cockcrow" replicates the plot-structure of the parable of the Prodigal Son. Even the handful of stories which do not play directly on religious sensibilities often refer conspicuously to passages from the Bible or other religious sources. None of the book's many glances at various creeds and forms of devotion reveal an intent to critique organised religion, but more likely a wish to occlude its pious excesses while preserving its moral positives. What is clear from these facts is that Mitchell, himself steeped in the Bible from an early age, expects his audience to share such a grounding in religious knowledge and experience. One could go further and say that, ideologically, *The Calends of Cairo* is a straightforwardly Christian Socialist text, which is a surprise conclusion if we come to it knowing the reputation Mitchell/Gibbon was later to acquire of being a partisan writer in favour of strong "communistic" political solutions. As the autobiographical elements in his first two novels also indicate, Mitchell was some considerable way off being "revolutionary" in his early fiction. One may struggle even to think him radical.

"East is West" is a story which overburdens itself by trying to do too many things in too short a compass. It is a deliberate attempt to dramatise an anti-racist "message", but uses terminology and categories which most people today would consider irredeemably racist and which (more importantly) do little to disrupt or alter the stark racial prejudices of the characters. A mawkish love-story is also thrown in. Mitchell, self-appointed futurologist since the publication of his essay *Hanno*, also reprises the earlier work's inexplicable pessimism towards the aeroplane and tries to promote the utterly impractical ornithopter over both it and the (yet to be invented) helicopter. This part of the plot seems derived from elements of Wells's novel *Tono-Bungay* (1909), but Mitchell was clearly not in Wells's league when it came to technological predictions, and was seldom to be deterred from committing himself confidently to what we now see as obvious lost causes, some of those choices (like Diffusionism and British Communist politics) being rather more egregious than his failure here to predict the future of aeronautic engineering with accuracy.

"The Gift of the River" also seems to be treading ground already tilled by Wells. Keith Landward's aims with regard to creating "a flexible, synthetic World-Speech" recall Herr Heinrich's similar ambitions in Wells's novel *Mr Britling Sees It Through* (1916). In his wounded grief at the death of his wife Landward is yet another Fisher King figure with suicidal feelings, like Connan in "The Epic". His salvation arrives in the unlikely form of a Greek girl he rescues from drowning in the Nile who speaks only classical Greek and seems to be a reincarnation not only of his wife but also of the Greek mythological figure Kora or Persephone (whose return from the underworld restored fertility to the earth). Saloney, ever superstitious, flees the scene in childish fear, and Landward appears to take the girl as his concubine. It is a slight and inconsequential tale.

The paradox of Mitchell incorporating supernatural elements into some of the stories seems partly dramatised in "It Is Written", in which Gillyflower Arnold, "Reared in a dogma of unbelief as stern and uncompromising as any Calvinist's creed, [...] felt her no-faith crumbling and dissolving even as the world of the ancient materialist has crumbled and dissolved into the unchartable atom-swirl of the modern physicist". It is hard to see how this analogy works, however. The claim that ancient materialists would feel themselves entirely confounded by atomic theory is difficult to uphold. Modern science accepts at large the fundamental philosophical assumptions of materialism. A materialist who comes to entertain belief in an immaterial god would, contrarily, seem to be in the throes of a revulsion against her foundational principles. There is no reason to suppose that the socialistic Mitchell, himself largely a materialist, was seriously grappling with religious or supernatural challenges or having a crisis of "no-faith". I suspect he felt that stories involving some kind of mystery permitted, and may even have been improved by, deployment of the potentially or "actually" supernatural, or that they may simply have had more popular appeal. Such "tales of the uncanny" had provided great market success for contemporary writers like Algernon Blackwood and M. R. James, they fitted well with Jarrolds' crowd-pleasing list, and Mitchell would write more in the same vein until the end of his life. But that he should choose to centre his story on the hackneyed quest for a text written by Christ, and largely ignore the fictional possibilities of the truly contemporary novelty he introduces (Western oil companies beginning to exploit the vast hydrocarbon resources of the Middle East), says a great deal about the orthodoxy of his aesthetic preferences at the time.

In the final story, "The Passage of the Dawn", Saloney encounters another White Russian exile, "the Princess Pelagueya Bourrin", with whom he is in hopeless love, but who is consciously prostituting herself "as the mistress of a millionaire". Her morally depraved cynicism is a threat and an outrage to Saloney's romantic sensibility. She is "a princess who had strayed from a fairy story into the legend of Gomorrah", an allusion which sends us all the way back to the original scenario of "For Ten's Sake". She ends up immured alone in a castle in Abu Zabal like the archetypal imprisoned princess, saved from the dragon of marriage to the millionaire by being conveniently widowed in advance, as it were. Unfortunately Mitchell seems undecided as to whether the story is about her or the millionaire Gault, to whose thinly-adumbrated perspective there is a final unexpected shift. The story seems to evaporate rather than end, Mitchell signing off in a haze of dreamy prose: "Somewhere, beyond the mountain walls, there was wonder and the morning." Accessing this "somewhere" which is "beyond" a seemingly impenetrable barrier was to become, for Mitchell, a fictional trope to which he returned repeatedly. His second novel, *The Thirteenth Disciple*, opens with his *alter ego*, as a child, coming to believe that if he can somehow "batter in the Walls of the World" then "an incredible adventure awaited him". If nothing else, then, *The Calends of Cairo* shows us in embryo what were to be several of Mitchell's abiding themes and preoccupations.

A single short-story sequence did not exhaust Cairo or the Arab world for Mitchell. In 1932 he published a novel, *The Lost Trumpet*, which seems a direct sequel to *The Calends*, being set in Egypt and narrated by Saloney a year after the end of the timeline of the short-story collection, involving many of the same characters. In the front papers of *Three Go Back* it is listed as "THE LOST TRUMPET: Swansong of Colonel Saloney", although it was not to be published for another six months. In the same year he published *Persian Dawns, Egyptian Nights*, which purports to be a series of tales from archive manuscripts in the Monastery of Mevr, written by a bishop of the mid-thirteenth century, stories he called "his Polychronicon". These are told by another refugee ex-teacher from the Kazan Gymnasium, Sergei Lubow, a friend of Saloney's who might as well be Saloney.

A major reason why these three books have all dated badly is that the colonial world they take for granted was entirely to unravel after another war and a few decades of persistent nationalist agitation for independence by the colonised. Consequently, nothing quite like colonial Cairo has existed since the end of the Second World War. Although there was a British military presence in Egypt until as late as 1954, in D. J. Enright's *Academic Year* (1955), a novel based on his experience in Alexandria in the period leading to the 1952 Revolution, one of the recently arrived protagonists has "seen nothing of those halcyon years between the wars when Englishmen in the Middle East enjoyed considerable respect and lived in a certain style". [19] There are still "world cities", to be sure, and any writer attempting to replicate a location like Mitchell's now would probably choose somewhere like Bangkok, or Mumbai, or Rio de Janeiro. The "cosmopolitanism" of these twenty-first century cities, however, is almost entirely an effect of commercial tourism and the global nature of modern capital, not imperial occupation or forced diaspora. There are still many refugees in our time too, of course, but for the last seventy-five years or so they tend to have been trying to escape *to* Europe, not, as Mitchell's are, *from* it.

Egypt in any period would always have the glamour of its ancient history to enhance it, but in the 1920s this age-old attraction had been dramatically magnified by a number of cultural happenings:

[19] D. J. Enright, *Academic Year* (London: Secker and Warburg, 1955), p. 22.

> In December 1922, the world's press announced the discovery of Tutankhamen's tomb and a flurry of excitement soon followed. By spring 1923, women in Paris were wearing Tutankhamen hats. Two film companies, one in Los Angeles and the other in Prague, had announced they were working on a Tutankhamen film. In London's West End, designers modelled their new dresses on discoveries from the tomb, and in America a handbag company had already applied to trademark the name Tut-Ankh-Amen. Egypt was all over the front pages, and Cairo's residents must have felt they were living at the centre of the world. [20]

Egypt had already seemed an indefatigably popular subject. There had been late Victorian and Edwardian "Egyptomania". A lot of that was originally fuelled by the Bible-inspired reverence for Middle-Eastern locations that encouraged Europeans, for example, to refer commonly to Palestine as the "Holy Land", as well as endless fascination for the first historic civilisation on earth. But in the renewed post-War British occupation Egypt was again fashionable in more consumerist ways and all things Egyptian the rave, for a time. Mitchell's publisher, Jarrolds, was in on the trend as early as 1920, when it published *Sunshine on the Nile: A Novel* by May Crommelin, an ageing pulp novelist who had churned out almost forty volumes of fiction since 1874. The Derbyshire writer Edith Maude Hull's novel *The Sheik* (1919) was an unexpected international bestseller and in 1921 was adapted as a feature film which made its star, Rudolph Valentino, a romantic heart-throb for the five years of his short life that remained. [21] *The Son of the Sheik* (based on a 1925 sequel of Hull's) followed in 1926, and was released two weeks after the actor's death, which gave rise to mass demonstrated lamentation among his (mostly female) fans. Hull also published an illustrated travel book, *Camping in the Sahara*, in the same year, and continued to grind out several more desert novels until 1931. While these were not necessarily Egyptian in location, they gave a new lease of life to the genre of "desert romance" ploughed previously by popular Egyptomaniac fictionists such as Robert Hichens, whom Saloney will once mention deprecatingly.

In addition, what was partly set in Egypt, and added a whole new dimension of modern romance to the entire region, was *Revolt in the Desert*

[20] Raphael Cormack, "How Cairo Became a Cosmopolitan Destination in the 1920s", *Literary Hub*, 18 March 2021 (https://lithub.com/how-cairo-became-a-cosmopolitan-destination-in-the-1920s/).

[21] The reprint of *The Sheik* I possess (London: George Newnes, 1923) was the publishers' seventeenth impression in the twenty-one months since its first in July 1921.

(1927), the mass-produced abridgement of the subscribers' edition of *Seven Pillars of Wisdom* (1926), the autobiography of T. E. Lawrence, a much more famous post-war RAF enlistee than Mitchell. Published by the then relatively minor house of Jonathan Cape, Lawrence earned £17,000 from this short-lived popular edition (almost £900,000 in today's money), one sign of what a runaway success it was. Another was that when Lawrence, as planned, withdrew the popular edition from sale later in 1927 there were already 90,000 copies circulating after several rapid reprints. [22] Whatever he thought of Lawrence, we know that Mitchell became aware of him and of the similarities of their concurrent careers. Lawrence had even undergone initial training at RAF Uxbridge in 1922, as did Mitchell in 1923. Such a close-at-hand example of the terrific potential of writing about the Arab world would surely have encouraged confidence in Mitchell in using such a setting. The defining difference was that Lawrence was already a "name" by 1927 and was demonstrably well-connected. Mitchell was neither. There would be no reprint for his book until now.

Most inspiring of all, however, must have been the personal memory of that astonishing year spent in North Africa. One of those Cairo residents, albeit a temporary one, who "must have felt they were living at the centre of the world" in December 1922 was surely James Leslie Mitchell. The largest city he had ever lived in before leaving Britain was industrial Glasgow in the immediate post-War period, and that for only half the duration of his spell in Cairo. To be in the mythical sun-drenched desert of Egypt must have been an extraordinary experience for the twenty-one-year-old lad from the Mearns, and surely influenced his later expressed enthusiasms, particularly on the Egypt-centric theories of the Diffusionists and the importance of exploration, if not detectably his politics. There is no further explanation required for Mitchell's personal motivation for writing repeatedly about contemporary Cairo: his sojourn there was evidently a momentous adventure in his life.

[22] Michael S. Howard, *Jonathan Cape, Publisher* (London: Jonathan Cape, 1971), p. 93. Indeed, Lawrence's relations with Cape began because he persuaded the company to republish an obscure and neglected Arabist title first issued in 1888, C. M. Doughty's *Travels in Arabia Deserta* (2 vols., London: Jonathan Cape, 1921), for which he wrote an introduction. It was a most unpredictable success for the fledgling publisher in its first year of existence. In *Academic Year* Enright typifies new teachers arriving in post-Second World War Egypt "with the *Seven Pillars* in one hand and the *Seven Types* [*of Ambiguity*, by William Empson (1930)] in the other" (p. 16)

The base text is that of the first British edition published in London by Jarrolds in July 1931. It was never reprinted. An American edition was simultaneously published under the title *Cairo Dawns: A Story Cycle with a Proem* in Indianapolis by Bobbs-Merrill, but this edition has little authority. It was Mitchell's first fictional US book publication and he seemed keen to make matters as quick and easy as possible for its publisher. He wrote to the Vice-President of Bobbs-Merrill on 30 May 1931, including the corrected English proofs and adding, "There will be no need for you to send me CAIRO DAWNS proofs for correction. And, of course, you may vary the spelling of words according to American usage." [1] The British first edition is therefore the only one Mitchell saw through the press at all stages.

All the stories had first been published in *The Cornhill Magazine*, twelve under the title "Polychromata", between 1929 and 1930. "For Ten's Sake", not initially part of a series, was the first published (in volume 66, 1929), followed by six stories in vol. 67 (1929) and six in vol. 68 (1930). The order of the stories was different in *The Cornhill* and one, "The Road", was in the book retitled "The Lost Prophetess". The original *Cornhill* texts have all been reprinted in their original order in Valentina Bold (ed.), *Smeddum: A Lewis Grassic Gibbon Anthology* (Edinburgh: Canongate, 2001), although she omits the consecutive Roman numerals which headed each Cairo story in the magazine. Bold reprints "For Ten's Sake" but keeps it separate from the stories originally categorised as "Polychromata", as it was. The present edition rectifies the unusual situation of Mitchell's early (not final) versions of these stories being the only ones in print, and puts them again into a self-contained volume, as the author wished.

The differences in running order between the separate publications can be tabulated thus:

The Cornhill Magazine	***The Calends of Cairo***
For Ten's Sake	For Ten's Sake
He Who Seeks	He Who Seeks

[1] Letter to D. L. Chambers, 31 May 1931, correspondence TS., The Lilly Library, Indiana University (my thanks to William K. Malcolm for pointing this letter out to me).

The Epic	The Lost Prophetess (title changed from "The Road")
The Road	Daybreak
A Volcano in the Moon	The Epic
The Life and Death of Elia Constantinidos	A Volcano in the Moon
Cockcrow	The Life and Death of Elia Constantinides (one letter changed in title)
Gift of the River	Cockcrow
East is West	Vernal
Vernal	East is West
Daybreak	Gift of the River
It is Written	It is Written
The Passage of the Dawn	The Passage of the Dawn

We do not know very much about the order in which the Cairo stories were written. Mitchell secured an agreement with *The Cornhill* in December 1928 for what was then ten stories to be published over two or three years, but at some point in the first half of 1929 this became twelve stories published over the extent of a single year. On 26 May 1929, he tells Alexander and Ellen Gray in a letter that he has written nine of them within the previous six months, adding that he is currently working on the tenth. Two weeks later (13 June 1929) he lets Ellen Gray know he has sent off the eleventh. Exactly a month later (13 July 1929), just as *The Cornhill* published the first of the twelve, he informs the Grays that he has been working on the first draft of the last, "The Life and Death of Elia Constantinidos". [2] All of this tells us that Mitchell was working hard to wrap up the writing of the series by the time it started to appear in public, no doubt because (as is also clear from the letters) he had other projects pressing on his time.

The ordering of the stories is of some moment if we are persuaded by Mitchell's later-expressed view (12 March 1931) that "'Polychromata' isn't a collection of short stories; it's a story-cycle, an episodic novel". [3] However, he was then writing to his prospective American publisher with the aim of getting them to bring it out, so we could suspect him of overselling. It was

[2] The spelling of the surname of the hero of this story was slightly altered in the version published in *The Calends*.

[3] Sources for this and the preceding paragraph are correspondence TSS., National Library of Scotland, except the last quotation, which is from a letter in The Lilly Library, Indiana University. My thanks to William K. Malcolm for drawing these letters to my attention.

certainly not the same as the order in which they were written, because for one thing the last Cairo story completed was the fifth to appear. But how deliberate *The Cornhill*'s running order is (and who dictated it) we do not know. The *Calends* collection offered Mitchell an opportunity to optimise the sequence in retrospect, and one of the changes he made was to re-order the stories (except the first two and last two) as well as burnish the text. The present edition does not record all the many small variants between the *Cornhill* and *Calends* texts, but the few significant revisions are noted. Mitchell essentially tweaked the *Cornhill* texts at the level of occasional word, phrase and punctuation, but neither deleted nor introduced much significant material. The largest excision was his cutting of the last two paragraphs of the *Cornhill* version of "It is Written", which are reproduced in the Notes and Commentary at the end of this volume.

The book did include a little new matter, but hardly any of it by Mitchell. "L'Envoi" is a poem by A. J. Hall (an Australian friend) sent to Mitchell after the publication of the *Cornhill* stories. The title page of the first edition, under the volume title, bore the words:

Introduced by
MR. H. G. WELLS
and
DR. LEONARD HUXLEY

These words have been omitted from the present title page. Their original placement certainly suggests that someone (perhaps Mitchell himself) wished the names to be prominent as they provided "celebrity" endorsement of his work and thus advantaged it commercially. [4] They may be there simply (or also) because the prefatory puffs by Wells and Huxley are not listed on the Contents page. One could logically omit their meagre contributions from this edition as not being the work of James Leslie Mitchell, but it would be odd in the first ever reprint of the book to exclude their warm recommendations, which have regularly been quoted by critics and biographers. They are therefore included (as they were in the first edition) before the "Proem" titleface, and continue to be unlisted on the Contents page.

The dedication, originally placed before the Contents page, has been relocated to appear before the beginning of the text proper.

Mitchell's collection employs single quotation marks for speech and double quotation marks for quotations within quotations. The present

[4] They were even reproduced in the list of other Mitchell publications in the front papers of his next book, *Three Go Back*: "THE CALENDS OF CAIRO (*Introduced by H. G. Wells and Leonard Huxley*)".

edition retains this convention in the main text, but not in the editorial apparatus, where quotation is throughout signalled by double quotation marks (and quotation within quotation by single quotation marks).

The block-capitalised words used to entitle each story have been rendered in small capitals. Titular abbreviations such as "Mr." and "Mrs." and "Dr." are reproduced without the period ("Mr", "Mrs", "Dr"). Mitchell's sometimes old-fashioned punctuation (or occasional lack of it) has been silently modernised when no possible alteration in meaning can result (but such changes are extremely infrequent), as have several elements of the original publisher's house style (such as spaces before exclamation and question marks, lengths of dashes, etc.). Ellipses, used to indicate hesitation or silence or trailing-off, are not consistently deployed in the first edition. Sometimes they appear as a full stop with three similarly spaced periods immediately following it ("...." or ". . . .") which, in this edition, have been regularised (to ". ..."). On other occasions, usually following a closing question or quotation mark, they are marked with three evenly spaced periods (". . ."), here spatially commuted (to "...").

Mitchell is profligate with hyphens, seeming to prefer to hyphenate than not in cases of doubt, sometimes (in the present editor's view) mistakenly. However, this is an issue only for an extremely nit-picking editor and is probably entirely negligible to the average reader. In cases where it may be distracting, I have opted for a pragmatic, context-sensitive solution. Now obsoletely hyphenated words (such as "near-by", "to-night") have been given in their modern forms ("nearby", "tonight") but, because Mitchell's hyphenation is highly idiosyncratic and at times deliberately unusual, such emendation is conservative rather than thoroughgoing, and is applied generally in cases of either such marked obsolescence or unquestionably incorrect usage (e.g. "fellow-scoundrel" has been corrected to "fellow scoundrel"). Where the first edition is inconsistent in this regard, its majority usage has been rendered uniform. I have assumed in this matter that the rôle of an editor is to compromise where appropriate between the reasonable expectations of a modern reader and the author's original choices: pedantically correcting the text on occasions when it contestably misuses a hyphen would serve no purpose when its meaning is not in any doubt. Mitchell himself was not an assiduous proofreader, probably for these very same reasons, and his novel *The Thirteenth Disciple,* it should be noted, contains near the beginning of its third chapter a mordant dismissal of linguistic pedantry ("the relation between grammarians and the decay-bacteria in a corpse have always been perfectly clear").

Obvious spelling or typographical errors have been corrected and an explanatory note attached in all significant cases. It would be presumptuous, for example, to correct the spelling of Mitchell's Cairo locations, because this often varied when the names were transliterated, something that is still true to an extent. The collection itself acknowledges (in "The Passage of the Dawn") that "uncertain orthography" is part of the Cairo experience. Unusual spellings (especially of proper nouns), which may have been valid in contemporary usage but have since changed, have not been amended. Likewise, the use of ligatures (as in words like "gynæcologist") has not been modernised despite the potentially antiquated effect. However, modern orthography is used in the Explanatory Notes and Commentary at the back of the volume. Reference to this supplementary matter is made by superscript numerals interpolated at appropriate points in Mitchell's text.

In 1932 Mitchell published a novel, *The Lost Trumpet*, which seems very much a sequel to *The Calends*, set in Egypt and narrated by Saloney a year after the end of the timeline of the short-story collection. One has to be cautious when cross-referencing *The Calends* to a later, yet to be written work, but where the novel elucidates obscurities in *The Calends* a note is made in the commentary. Incidental differences between the two texts (such as the spelling of Saloney's patronymic in the first as "Kyrilovich" but the other as "Kyrilovitch") are, however, here ignored.

The spacing and layout of indented material in the first edition (for example, verse and letters) have been generally respected within the governing typographical constraints of this edition, but not slavishly reproduced.

THE CALENDS OF CAIRO

TO

MY FATHER AND MOTHER [1]

Mr H. G. WELLS [1] to Mr LESLIE MITCHELL

April 4, 1927

Dear Sir

Very good story. Stick to it! You *can* do this sort of thing and will certainly come through.

Very sincerely yours
H. G. Wells

June 24, 1931

Dear Leslie Mitchell

I never write prefaces, [2] but why not print this and my letter of April 4, '27?

It will add more to my reputation as a prophet – since I had then seen only your first short story – than to yours as a short story writer.

Yours
H. G. Wells

INTRODUCTION

Nearly three years ago there came to the *Cornhill Magazine* [1] the manuscript of a story with a covering letter from the author to the editor he had never met. The manuscript, this letter explained, had undergone one rejection after another from the 'popular' magazines: it had even been refused as 'too good' – too far above the literary standard of the ordinary reader. Finally, it had drawn a private appreciation from Mr H. G. Wells, who recommended the author to try the *Cornhill.*

Mr Wells was right. Its sweep of imagination, its human sympathies, its skill in hinting the finer issues to which dramatic romance could be turned, made instant appeal, and with one or two minor retouchings the story appeared in the *Cornhill* under the title of 'For Ten's Sake'.

This was the beginning. Mr Mitchell, with his vivid knowledge of the East, went on to plan a set of stories which would have the mysterious heart of Cairo for background, and should be linked together as the experiences of a Russian exile living in the city. The result was the series of a dozen tales of many-coloured romance, 'Polychromata', which duly appeared in the *Cornhill* [2] and are now issued as *The Calends* [3] *of Cairo.* In the pages of the magazine the 'Polychromata' tales have always found eager friends: now that they are gathered up into a book, may they find many more!

LEONARD HUXLEY [4]

PROEM

I

It was Easter Day. [1]

Under the feet of the watcher on the Hill of Burial the earth suddenly shook, quivered for a moment as might one in a nightmare, and then slowly subsided.

Mevr, the Hell-Gate of the East, [2] lying asleep in the afternoon heat, scarcely stirred from its siesta; [3] since its foundation in the days of Asoka [4] as a meeting-place of the Central Asian caravans [5] it had known the shocks of minor earthquakes. Like an obscene, sated animal it sprawled under the vacant grey eyes of the watcher. The heat-haze shimmered above it; northwards, its streets straggled towards the dim bulking of the Kablurz Beg; [6] westwards, across the dun tundra, wound the white tract to Persia and far Iraq; eastwards, another caravan route vanished on the horizon towards Baluchistan. [7]

As so many streams they seemed, these roads; streams flowing into the dark cesspool of Mevr and emerging from it – cleansed. Behind, in the City of the Plain, [8] the caravans left their floating scum to fester and reek under the brassy noonday sky, under the sickened stars, under the seemingly endless patience of God. ...

The vacantness vanished from the eyes of the watcher: they blazed with the hatred of the fanatic, the monomaniac. A tall, gaunt figure, he rose from beside the dark mound where he had been crouching and outreached thin, clutching hands.

'How long, O Lord?' [9]

So, for a moment, he stood, threateningly, weird in his shabby black, a prophet of wrath above Mevr. Then the dullness returned to his eyes; his glance grew wandering and fell on the mound at his feet. Suddenly he dropped to his knees; in his throat came a dry sob.

'Oh, Dick, Dick! Mevr might have spared at least you.' Janet it took, me it will take, but you – Oh, my son! ...'

Farther up the Hill of Burial two grave-robbers, Abdul Khaled and Osman the Nameless, had also been squatting on their haunches and looking down on Mevr. The cry of the man below reached their ears and they peered down at his black-coated figure. Then Osman (who was nameless in that, being a Turk, he was known merely by a contraction of Osmanli) [10] spat expressively and contemptuously.

'It is the Englishman, the mad hakim, [11] making prayers by the grave of his son.'

Abdul grunted. He was a soured man, for their day's work had so far disgorged nothing of value – not even a skeleton hand bearing a ring. In'sh allah! [12] the greed of relatives these days was growing to unbelievable bounds, so poorly were kindred disposed of. The mad hakim did not interest him, except professionally.

'The grave of this son of his may contain some trifle of value,' he suggested.

The Nameless One shook his head. 'No unbeliever buries even a brooch with his dead. Did we not but yesterday spend two hours over the resting-place of that accursed Russian pig – may his bones poison the jackals who have since doubtlessly come to scrape them, seeing we did not fill in the pit! – and find nothing?' He rose up wearily, a burly brute, bestial faced, with squinting, red-rimmed little eyes. 'We'll seek a night's lodging at Miriam's. Eh?'

The fat Abdul had uttered a sudden gasp of pain. Now, clutching at his side, he rolled over on the turf. Then he tore something from the dirty djibbeh [13] which enveloped him and flung it a yard or so away. Osman saw hit the ground a small green viper, [14] yellow underneath upturned, broken-backed, writhing.

'Allah! It is the end.' Abdul began to beat the ground with his feet and suddenly composed himself and drew a knife from his belt, for it is better to die by the bite of steel than the slow virus of the green-backed viper. Osman tore away the knife.

'Wait. I will call the hakim.' Forthwith, waving his arms, he shouted down the hill to the far, black-coated figure. In a little the latter stirred, stood upright. Down the windless air was borne Osman's shout.

'Haste, effendi. [15] My brother has been bit by a yellow scorpion!'

For a moment the old man, who had once been Richard Southcote, M.D., [16] stared up at the gesticulating Turk. Then returned to his eyes the same light as had been there when he had risen and threatened Mevr. He laughed, laughed aloud, ringingly, unemotionally, so that Osman dropped his arms and stared, and presently saw the hakim deliberately turn his back and walk down the hill towards Mevr. From the ground Abdul groaned.

'Give me the knife, Nameless.'

The bestial-faced Turk stared down at his fellow scoundrel. His hands began to shake. Then, abruptly, he dropped by Abdul's side and tore away the stained djibbeh. His intention was evident. Abdul shrank away.

'Fool! Not that! It is death!'

The Turk's great hands gripped him. 'Peace! I drink worse poison every day in the Street of Ten!'

With that, he bent his trembling lips towards the little oozing incision on the brown hide of Abdul the grave-robber.

II

As the mad hakim entered Mevr from the Hill of Burial, the foetid city began to stir to life. In a narrow alley beggars squabbled querulously, stealing the chance alms dropped amongst their blind. The old man passed unseeingly amidst the sprawl of diseased, wasted bodies. In front he heard a shouting and commotion and the beat of a little drum. Coming to the great bazaar of the Suq es Iraq [17] he was in the midst of a familiar scene.

A caravan – lines of laden, dusty camels and thirstily vociferous drivers – had newly arrived from Bokhara. [18] The dust arose in clouds, babel of many tongues [19] filled the air. From the near-by streets the vile things which had once been women were already flocking into the Suq. They mingled with the caravan drivers. One, a ragged harpy with a shrill voice, Southcote saw wheedling at a black-bearded camelier, [20] already drunk and sitting, cup of arrack [21] in hand. Suddenly, with an insane ferocity, the ruffian leapt to his feet and smote the woman a blow that cracked her jaw. She fell with a scream of pain, and wild guffaws of merriment broke out. Loudest of all laughed the two Persian gendarmes [22] who patrolled the bazaar. The camelier stared vacuously down at the woman. ... It was, set against its background of heat and dust, a scene that might have been filched from hell.

The old man looked about him with smouldering eyes. Slowly he made his way towards the centre of Mevr. Presently he found himself passing by the entrance to that which stank in the nostrils of even the City of the Plain – the entrance to the vile Street of Ten, a loathsome resort of thieves and murderers, where were practised unnameable vices of which even Mevr talked under breath, where no gendarme had ever dared patrol, where of a morning the knifed and rifled bodies of the night's victims were flung out into the reeking gutters of sunrise, whence, two years before to a day, young Dick Southcote had been brought, a bruised and lifeless and dreadful thing, to his father's house.

As Southcote passed there stood by the entrance to the Street of Ten two whom he – and, indeed, all Mevr – knew by repute. One, pock-marked, [23] lithe, white-clad, was a murderer who killed openly, with bravado, who sold the services of his knife to any who sought them; [24] the other, Selim of Damascus, [25] was a spy of the desert robbers, warning them of unarmed caravans, sharing in the loot of massacred trains.

Yet in Mevr they went scatheless. [26] No gendarme dared lay hands on those whom, it was openly rumoured, the Governor himself had hired upon occasion. Indolently, insolently, they lounged in the hot afternoon sunshine. About them, from the cotes [27] nearby, pigeons wheeled with a blue flirr [28] of wings.

Two horsemen, Europeans both, came trotting past the entrance to the Street of Ten. [29] To the lounging scoundrels they nodded, under the pigeon-cloud ducked. Then in front of them, disappearing up a side street, they caught a glimpse of the bent figure of Southcote.

'The old man has been visiting his son's grave.' It was the short, burly man who spoke. He was the German Consul, not long transferred from Alexandria, [30] but finding Mevr congenial and reminiscent of East African days.

'Then he has been visiting the foulest spot in Mevr.' The thin, debauched-looking Greek in white ducks [31] who was known as 'Mitri', called himself a doctor, and had a reputation so unsavoury that the German raised amused eyebrows at his remark, looked after Southcote with a twisted grin. 'Poor fool! And to think, Herr Consul, [32] that that crazed Englishman had once a European reputation!'

'So?' The German was indifferent. He had pulled out his watch, looked at it, and was now mopping his moist forehead. 'Twixt [33] his horse's ears 'Mitri' was surveying Mevr with the owlishness of one unsoberly reminiscent.

'European. He was "Earthquake" Southcote. In Italy and Syria he spent years in seismological studies, was decorated by the English Society, [34] and was famous. These things I know, for I learned them from his son.'

'Ah yes, the son.' The German, newcomer though he was, had heard something of the Southcote story. 'And how came this Academician and his son to Mevr?'

'Because this place is in the Central Asian earthquake belt. The Doctor Southcote came to study it, and brought his wife and son, who was a boy of eighteen. The wife died of malaria six months after they came. Though a scientist, the old Southcote was a Calvinist [35] with a God waiting round the corner ready to be unpleasant. In such manner he took the death of his wife. Six months after that, when his son was killed, he became a madman and now abides in Mevr he knows not why.'

'You knew him once?'

'Mitri' stared unwinkingly ahead. 'I knew the son. Pfuu! [36] ... Me the old Southcote looked on as a native, and hated me on some Old Testament authority; [37] me he considered an evil influence on his son.'

The German chuckled greasily. 'Mitri' abruptly reined up his pony. They had come to the Midan. [38] The Greek pointed leftwards.

'You will be late for your festa, [39] Herr Consul. And the Governor's desires are his belly's.'

'Auf wiedersehen.' [40]

'Auf wiedersehen.'

'Mitri' slowly rode down the rightward wall of the Midan. An 'evil influence'? He?

Something dreadful came in his face. Then, with a twisted grin, he looked down at his shaking hands – the hands which had strangled the life out of Dick Southcote.

III

Coming towards the tumble-down native house which he and Janet had furnished three years before, the mad hakim encountered Ahmed, the water-seller and scavenger. The latter was slinking along in the gutter in his usual fashion. Though it was late in the day, his bleared eyes were of a habit fixed on the ground, for from the pockets of such numerous drunkards as speckled the early morning gutters of Mevr he gathered the wherewithal to augment his scanty legitimate earnings. At the old Englishman's approach he glanced up swiftly and shiftily. Dull, tortured eyes met dull, evil ones. Upon his thigh Ahmed made with two crossed fingers an obscure sign – the age-old sign wherewith the East wards off the evil eye. [41]

Southcote's face twitched unhumorously. Ahmed was well known to him. He paused in the doorway and looked after the scavenger, broodingly. Impersonated in the foul carrion-grubber was Mevr itself. ...

Entering from the street, he made his way to the room which was study, laboratory, and dispensary in one. The dingy walls showed streaked with a steamy damp, the furniture was ragged and thick with dust, for, beyond seeing to meals, the old Iraqi woman who acted as housekeeper did nothing. Southcote laid aside his hat, sank into a chair by the window, and there, upright and still, sat staring bleakly and unseeingly. Minutes went by. On a ledge of the window which tunnelled the thick wall a golden-eyed lizard flittered to and fro. The house was utterly quiet.

Presently Southcote moved. Under his heel something crunched. He glanced down and saw that the floor was strewn with broken glass. Then, catching a glimpse of a broken photo-frame under the table, he bent, gaspingly, and picked it up. It was a photograph of Dick, shaken from a ledge by the recent tremor.

Beside it, flung to the floor by the same cause, was a small, black-bound book. That Southcote let lie. With thin, unsteady fingers he smoothed the crumpled cardboard of the photograph. From a narrow, slatted window the sunlight streamed in and dappled the pictured face of the boy who lay beneath the mound on the Hill of Burial. Over the youth and freshness and the gladness in the young eyes the mad hakim sat and yearned, as a thousand times he had done. Dick, the strong, the light-hearted, his murdered boy. ...

Two years to a day since the murdered lad had been carried into this very room: two years to a day since that black morning when something inside his brain had seemed to crack as he called down God's vengeance on the City of the Plain. Certain of its coming, certain of the doom that would fall on Mevr, he had ever since waited, his hatred of the foul place growing upon him month by month so that he shunned the native populace and the moving scum of the caravans, refusing help to the hurt even when they came to his door begging it. Never dependent on practice for a livelihood, he avoided even the few whites of Mevr because of that otherness of purpose for which he knew that God had designed him.

Once, when Kuchik Khan [42] was sweeping down from the north with his army raised on Soviet gold, it had seemed to Southcote – unconsciously grown Eastern, un-European, a fanatic at once egotistic and sublimely selfless – that the hour was nigh, that in fire and rapine was God about to cleanse the earth of Mevr as once before He had cleansed the world with the sword of Tamerlane. [43] But Kuchik's army had melted away, and Mevr breathed again, and Southcote, with vacant, staring eyes, had climbed the Hill of Burial and looked to the skies and prayed for even such patience as God's own. ...

But now, sitting with the crumpled photograph in his hand, an aching misery came upon him. He was only the mad hakim, dreaming a dreadful vengeance, living an insane hope. Of Dick was left nothing more than the captured beauty of his pictured face.

Upon that face he had never noted – as any stranger would at once have done – the heavy, sensual mouth, the contraction about the eyes which, spite [44] the youthfulness of the latter, spelt viciousness. To the father they were the eyes of murdered hope, staring unavailingly in a black world that knew not retribution.

It was the first moment of doubt within Southcote's last two years, and, in the instant of it, the ground shook under his feet. Upon the floor the little pieces of glass danced: the walls groaned ominously: a cup fell and smashed.

It was the second tremor within an hour.

IV

Into the eyes of the mad hakim had come an unwonted interest. Now he laid aside the photograph and rose to his feet. From the table he picked up a box of matches, made his way from the still quivering room, turned to the left, descended a flight of stone stairs. On a landing some eight feet below ground-level he stopped by the entrance to a small doorway and lit a candle which stood on a stone ledge.

The door opened easily at his touch. The candle lit up the smaller cellar of the house. In one corner was a chair and table; in the centre of the room an instrument embedded in the floor, held down by iron clamps, and rearing itself up, a cluster of thin glass rods, to a graded aluminium dial and pointer.

The Southcote Seismometer is a scientific toy, a mathematician's dream gone astray in the realisation. In seismological works its possibilities are constantly referred to and its absolute unreliability demonstrated. As an instrument the purpose of which is accurately to gauge and foretell a many hours' distant earthquake it is recognised as a magnificent failure.

Yet there, in front of the old man in that stifling cellar in Mevr, was that seismologist's dream, the Improved Southcote, standing as it had been left on the day of its first installation, exactly two years before.

Candle in hand, Southcote approached it. Every day – single surviving habit of the one-time scientist – he came down into the cellar to clean the mechanism and make readings. Mevr, situated as it was, seldom failed to register some forthcoming or passing tremor. On the twelve gradations of the dial the pointer more often than not hovered between zero and one.

Southcote flecked some dust from off the instrument, and then bent to read it.

The pointer quivered above nine.

V

For a moment, after his first amazed start, the old man was merely the scientist, calm and deft. He tested the apparatus, searching for flaws, altered gauges, diminished the mercury pressure in one of the long glass rods, and then changed back again to normal. Promptly, with the last move, the pointer swung again to nine. Then it began to creep up the dial towards ten. ...

And then, equally suddenly, the scientist died in Richard Southcote. Realisation smote him like a breath of fire. Back to his eyes flashed their uncanny glow, only with it was now triumphant assurance as well.

Mevr was doomed!

In less than an hour, uprising out of the earth, its fate, swift and awful, would leap upon it. Richard Southcote's prayers had been answered, his faith and his patience justified. Far in the bowels of the earth an awful force, more stupendous than that of the San Francisco earthquake, [45] was minute by minute gathering to rise and smite and utterly blot out in torrents of falling masonry and crashing landslides the Hell-Gate of the East.

VI

Quietly the mad hakim left the cellar and went to the room above. There his preparations were simple. Alone of Mevr had he been warned, alone knew of the impending doom. And from the Hill of Burial he would watch, as, ah God! how often had he watched and prayed, that doom overtake it.

He picked up his hat, glanced round the bare, dismal room, and turned, God's witness as he knew himself, to leave the house and Mevr for ever. Then his eye fell on the book which had lain on the floor beside the photograph of his son.

It had been Jenny's Bible. He picked it up, mechanically seeking to reset it in its shattered binding, to smooth its soiled edges. As he did so, with a strange deliberation it opened in his hands.

'Peradventure there be fifty righteous men within the city. Wilt Thou also destroy and not spare the place for the fifty righteous men that are therein?

'... And He said, I will not destroy it for ten's sake.' [46]

Outside, through the drifting heat-waves, came the droning purr that was the voice of Mevr; within his house the mad hakim stood and reread of the mercy promised to another City of the Plain.

'... And He said, I will not destroy it for ten's sake.'

If there should be ten righteous men in Mevr –

Suddenly Southcote's laughter cracked the silence. The Bible, hurled against the wall, showered the floor with flimsy leaves. ...

Underfoot, in Mevr, and for the third time that afternoon, the ground shook.

VII

It was near sunset. Out of the east the massing clouds drove swiftly towards the City of the Plain. A thin wind blew.

Through the deserted Suq es Iraq a mule clattered. Its rider was an old man with smouldering eyes. Squatting in an alleyway were two beggars, and one of them leant out to peer after the rider.

'God! Saw you the mad hakim? His face –'

'I see only the sky,' said the other, uneasily. 'There is death in it.'

Upon the foulness of Mevr, in its brutal pleasures and its jaded vices, began to descend some such feeling. A strange quiet held the city. And overhead, steadily, unwonted storm-clouds massed.

Hastening from the doomed city to the Hill of Burial, the mad hakim looked down the street towards the Southern Gate and saw it thronged with the stalls of the afternoon's chaffering. [47] The way was blocked.

Southcote pulled up his mule. One other way out of the city remained for him to take – through the street unvisited and loathed, the place where his son had been murdered. Was it not fitting that he should pass through there?

At the thought he shuddered and turned his mule. Then he glanced up at the sky. He must hasten.

Right down through the narrow opening he drove his mount, betwixt open cesspools, under the evil lower of overhanging, crumbling balconies. And then, above his head, in Persian in the Arab script, he read an ancient inscription:

THE STREET OF TEN

VIII

What was that? Some dim associations of numbers clashed in his mind. He half-halted the mule, and the beast, clumsily, swung to one side –

'Curse you!'

The mad hakim looked down. Almost under the mule's feet sprawled a naked brown child. Its mouth was open, its eyes pierced upwards a surprised terror. ... Came a stamping of unshod feet in the dust, a lean arm outreached, and the brown mite whisked away. Ahmed the scavenger, weeping salvage in his arms, and cursing with the resourceful obscenity of the East, glared up at Southcote.

Dazedly the old man met his eyes. Within his brain, as at the stroke of a bell, he heard some voice count.

'One!'

The mule plunged on. The street twisted leftwards. On the sidewalk a man and woman moved lurchingly.

An everyday sight in the tainted city; some woman of the streets leading a customer to her house. Yet, passing, it seemed to the mad hakim that somewhere, before, he had seen those two –

An unnameable impulse made him look back. The man was the black-bearded camelier of the Suq es Iraq: the woman, she whom Southcote had seen him fell to the ground. Came the ruffian's shamed voice:

'Courage, little sister. I will not leave you.'

And again, within Southcote, spoke an unknown voice:

'Two!'

With the mad hakim rode some haunting presence. Up to the sky he looked again. The sun had vanished. The overhead wind was a thin scream. A lowering greyness had fallen on Mevr. Far thunder rumbled. From the path of the mule a strange group arose and staggered aside.

It was a man, bent almost double under the inert body of another. Southcote pulled his beast up, heard a voice that was not his own question:

'What ails the man?'

From under the weight of the Turk, Abdul the graverobber looked up at the Englishman with red-rimmed eyes.

'He is my brother. I was stung of a viper. You would not come when he cried your help on the Hill of Burial. He sucked the poison from my wound. Now he dies.'

Haggardly the old doctor stared. Within him, ever since entering the vile stew where his son had been murdered, had arisen an awful doubt. Now it clamoured in his brain. Ahmed, the camelier, these graverobbers –

Crash! went the thunder. For a moment, blindingly, a dagger of fire quivered down the Street of Ten. Southcote's terrified mule bucked and pawed at the air. ...

IX

When he came to himself he seemed to be peering through a red mist. In his back was a terrible pain. He tried to move and lay unmoving.

The red mist cleared. A crowd of faces were peering down at him. The mule had flung him violently against a great corner-stone.

He tried to moisten his lips; failed; made a desperate effort to sit up; lay still. ... And then, yet seeing clearly, hearing distinctly, he understood.

Paralysis. Death.

And upon his tortured brain at the thought, wearily, there came great peace.

X

In Damascus, twenty-three years before, a querulous old man had died, cursing the son who had disgraced his name, and who stood by his bedside, dry-eyed and scornful, to the last. In life the old man had availed little; in death he left a memory that had consequences unguessable.

Through the crowd Selim of Damascus pushed his way and knelt by the side of the mad hakim, and gathered him in his arms. As he strained to lift the limp body, one touched him on the shoulder.

'I will take his feet, brother.'

It was Ali, the murderer-bravo. [48]

'For he is old, Selim.'

Together they lifted him. Homeless themselves, they looked around them doubtfully. Then a woman's voice called nearby.

'In here.'

In the doorway of a house of shame stood a weary-faced woman, beckoning. Overhead the thunder rumbled as Selim and Ali bore the body of Southcote into the dark entrance of the house of Miriam the harlot. She guided them down a corridor into a large room where, on a bed, another woman lay moaning and fever-flushed. The heat of the place was stifling.

At a table a man was pouring a dose from a medicine bottle. He looked up. Miriam nodded.

'I bring another, "Mitri". He was thrown by his mule.'

She motioned to the two men. Southcote they laid on a pile of rags which did duty as another bed. Miriam knelt behind him and raised his head. 'Mitri' came across the room, halted suddenly, stood swaying unsteadily.

'My God! Southcote!'

So, for a minute, 'Mitri' standing as if petrified, Selim and Ali lingering in the doorway, the harlot kneeling, weary-faced. Then, drunkenly, 'Mitri' spoke.

'Do you know who this is, Miriam? – The father of Anah's seducer; the father of the thief who ruined the daughter whom you reared to be other than you are; the father of the man who made your daughter – that.' He pointed to the wasted woman upon the bed, and ceased, and swayed a little upon his feet.

Outside the lightning flashed. Miriam looked up with weary, unchanging eyes.

'I know it is the mad hakim – the father of Dick, whom you killed because always you loved Anah and I prayed you to do it. But our hate helped nothing, friend. Anah dies, remembering only the dead lover whom she tried to save. ... You must help this old man. And God will judge.'

By the side of the Englishman 'Mitri' knelt unsteadily. As he did so the old eyes opened, and slowly from them a tear trickled down the still face.

XI

A living soul in a dead body he had lain, the while blinding revelation came upon him. Dick, the son for whom he had cursed Mevr – Dick, a seducer and thief; Dick, righteously killed by the drunken 'Mitri.' ...

For a little, listening to their voices, that alone had been upon him, and bitter as death was the taste of the knowledge. And then, printed as in letters of fire across his vision, he saw the passage in Jenny's Bible.

'Peradventure there be fifty righteous men within the city. Wilt Thou also destroy and not spare the place for the fifty righteous men that are therein?

'... And He said, I will not destroy it for ten's sake.'

Blindly, blasphemously, he had rejected what was surely a command. Righteousness? Who were the righteous? Who, in the shadow-show of life, might lift him a light whereby to judge and condemn his fellows? Yet he, vengeful and hating, had done so, the while the harlot and the thief, the drunkard and the murderer, reached to unguessed heights of pity and forgiveness, heroism and shamed kindliness. ...

Righteousness? As a silver thread he saw it now, winding through the lusts and cruelties, the filth and crime of every life in Mevr. And of Hope and Faith and Charity [49] was it woven. Before him he saw the scavenger, the two grave-robbers, the camelier, the murderer and the thief, 'Mitri', Miriam, Anah – those in whom, unguessed of him, had lain the seeds of righteousness – passing in the vomiting doom of Mevr, the doom of which he alone had been warned, the doom he was helpless now to avert. ...

Was that God's will? Up at 'Mitri' he stared, and remembered that voice which had counted within himself as he witnessed the unguessed heroisms of the Street of Ten. Surely he heard it speak again. ...

Kneeling beside him, they saw the sweat start out on his forehead, [50] heard him breathe as one in a nightmare, saw the glare in his eyes. Then, with an awful effort, he sat upright, heedless of their attempt to restrain him. His head swam.

For an awful fear had suddenly gripped him. Was his vision false? By some new law other than that which had doomed the Cities of the Plain could righteousness indeed be reckoned?

Aloud, in the stifling room – desperately, with sudden inspiration – he began to count. Ten righteous. ... From Ahmed the scavenger to the murderer of his son. ...

... *If there should be but Ten. ...*

And there were but NINE.

Again, peering round the dusking room, he counted. Then, in the shadows about the doorway, between Ali the murderer and Selim the thief, he saw stand for a moment One whom he had never known, One with bleeding hands and feet and hidden face. [51]

. . . . . .

A quarter of an hour later the bells of warning clanged out over Mevr, and from house to house the watchmen cried the message brought to the Governor from a brothel in the slums. [52] Out into the safety of the plains and the falling dusk of that Easter Day, just as the first tremors of doom shook the City of the Plain, streamed the multitudes of fugitives.

And through the multitudes a murderer and a thief, two of those reckoned in the sum of the righteous Ten, [53] carried Southcote to safety.

THE CALENDS OF CAIRO

I

He Who Seeks

I

Many-coloured? It is one of the names of our little Cairo – Polychromata. She has many names, the Gift of the River, and nowhere do her colours flaunt as here, in the Khalig el Masri. [1] Long the evenings I sat and puzzled till I knew the Khalig and Life for one. Key-colour to the kaleidoscope, master-note in the syncopation – it is Quest. [2]

For what? Full bellies and purses, laughter and love, woman and fame and fantasy. ... All the so-desired apples of that mirage-orchard that flourishes by the Dead Sea. [3] ... Eh? A cynic? God mine, I am only a dragoman! [4]

Happy he who finds not what he seeks – it is the oldest of axioms. But when the desperate seeker himself acknowledges it, he grows a wonder and a legend in the eyes of men. As, indeed, may yet the tale of Andrei Bal'mont and his quest. ...

But of course. And beer – English beer. I think the gods must drink of English beer in Olympus [5] these days, when they have laid aside their bowler hats [6] and the last so-bluff American has made his tip and gone. The little Simon [7] first stocked it here, not by command of the Anglo-Saxon, [8] but at wish of me, Anton Saloney, dragoman, guide, ex-colonel of horse in the army of Deniken, and one-time Professor of English Literature in the Gymnasium of Kazan. [9]

The tale of Andrei? See, I have become a teller of tales – I have invented more so-scandalous royalties than ever the dynastic tables [10] held, I had a madam-tourist in tears this morning when I told of the suicide of Rameses II from the top of Kheops' Pyramid, [11] because of the false love who jilted him – yet this tale of Andrei. ... I have loved and hated it, as must all men, felt the ache of it and the beauty of it. Yet it needs some subtle tale-smith as your own Morris [12] to tell it. Indeed, I think the little Andrei himself was of the Hollow Land, a faery-knight and a faery-saint. [13] ...

Yet perhaps he was a Russian of the Russians, the Slav eternal. Perhaps he was Man himself.

Look, my friend, I once knew and talked with this Andrei, yet already to me he is half a myth, a figure on that painted gauze of legend that covers the face of the East. How shall I make him live in English eyes – he and his tale and his quest?

II

I met him twice in life. The first time was at Perekop, on the bridge of the Crimea, [14] twenty-four hours before the Communists stormed our lines and littered the seas with the wreckage of our armies. He was a captain, holding an outpost on the marshes, and I came on him the last inspection I made. He was alone, holding an outpost, for his men had deserted; he marched on sentry-beat, rifle slung on his shoulders, head bare to the cutting wind, thoughts far in dreams. ... Long I remembered him.

He was a youth, a student, with the pale, dark- framed face of the Little Russian. He had come south to fight the Red Terror, even as thousands beyond Perekop had come south with the Sovyets [15] to fight the White Reaction. He was lighter of heart than I ever knew soldier in the shadow of defeat.

'The world is wide, and there are other dreams,' he said.

I waved him goodbye and went back to my squadron. In twenty-four hours I was riding to the coast and safety on a French destroyer. Of Andrei Bal'mont I saw nothing more, nor ever again expected to see.

Yet he also escaped. Somehow he cleared the rout, and drifted south across the bitter Crimea. Late in the hours of the second day he tramped through the whoom [16] of a snowstorm, and so, half-blinded, yet still with untroubled heart, came to Yalta and the sting of the sleet-wind from the Black Sea. [17]

It was night-time as he made his way through the deserted streets on the outskirts. The snow whirled thickly about him, and not a light could be seen in the harbour, though he heard the beating of the waves. Then he tripped and almost fell over something that lay in his path.

He lighted a match, and looked, and in the momentary radiance of the little flame saw the drift of the snow, saw the white glimmer of a face. Then the match went out. He lighted another, shielding it in his hand against the bitter wind-drive. Then he looked down at the girl who had been asleep in the snow.

She was dark and sweet and fair, even there in that hour of storm and terror. She had a little hollow in her throat, and the light gleamed in it, wonderfully.

'I have been sleeping,' she said, and rubbed her eyes like a child, then smiled up at him so that he loved her.

He bent to help her. 'If you stay here you will die. What is your name?'

'I am Natasha Grodine. I am refugee from the Sovyeti. [18] In the darkness I twisted my ankle and lost my way. But now you have come and I am safe. You are –'

'I am Andrei Bal'mont,' he said, and lifted her in his arms. He could not see her face till her cheek touched his. The snowstorm had cleared, but in the overhead, thin and bitter, high up, screamed veter, the wail-wind of the Russian winter. [19] And suddenly, so-lost and desolate as they were, their lips met and they kissed each other with great gladness. In the night she wound her arms around his neck, and laughed a little, tremulously, pressed against his heart.

And to the little Andrei, bearing her to the seashore, it was as if a light had suddenly sprung and flamed in the darkness. All his years he knew had been but prelude to the moment when Natasha's lips touched his. He stopped and bent and spoke in an urgent amazement.

'I love you.'

'My dear,' she whispered, and kissed him again.

III

And all that night, sheltered in a hut on the quays, he knew of her presence near him in the darkness, and the fragrance of her hair. And because of love and Natasha, life was sweet in his mouth. The kisses of love – sweet they are in the shadow of death! Close-pressed for warmth, they sat and talked of the wonder of this which had come to them. Once Natasha fell asleep, and, hour after hour, unmoving, he sat and held her in his arms. Once she moved and whispered in sleep, and he soothed her, as one might a tired child. Then he rose and looked out, and it was morning.

With that dawn they found a refugee-ship putting out to Stamboul. [20] Andrei carried Natasha aboard and paid their passage with the last of his French money. [21] The ship was crowded, but shelter they made in the lee of a hatchway, and lay wrapped together in Andrei's greatcoat the while the white coasts rose and fell, and flickered and dimmed through the driving sleet. Misted were the eyes of Natasha looking back at the fading shore. Andrei kissed the little hollow in her throat; it had seemed to him that a man might die to kiss that place. But she turned to him and caught his hands, and suddenly was weeping.

'Oh, Andrei, I'm lost – lost and afraid. Russia I've lost and all its days and sunshine and kindliness and laughter. They seemed everlasting. I never thought they could pass and finish. ... My dear, my dear! Say you will always love me, that it won't pass and fade, that you'll never forget!'

And Andrei kissed her hands, and swore that never would he cease to love her, that never would his love grow old and tame, that never would he forget the night and snow wherein he had found her. So he swore to keep time and fate and life itself at bay. ...

Twenty miles out from Yalta, up out of the mists of dawn came a Sovyet gunboat, shelling the refugee-boat and signalling it to stop. Andrei and six others were in the uniform of the White Raiders. For them there would be no mercy.

Then Natasha planned to save them. She flung aside the coat of Andrei, and beckoned to the far side of the refugee-boat as it slowed down. The soldiers must go over the side of the ship, and hide in the water till the search by the Tovarishii [22] was over. When the Red sailors had gone, they could climb aboard again.

Andrei was last to slide down the rope to the buoys. To these the others already clung in the shadow of the ship. Death to remain aboard – death perhaps in the freezing waters. And then, for a moment, it mattered nothing, for in that moment Natasha, as he clung there, bent and kissed him, and her lips were salt with tears. ...

Paddling and freezing in the lee of the refugee-boat, Andrei heard a sudden shouting and confusion. Then one of the others by his side cried out and gestured. The scream of shell-fire woke the sea. From the west, dimly, he saw a great French cruiser steaming out of the sleet-storm to engage the gunboat.

'Look – the ship!' cried one of the men.

Andrei turned his head and also cried out. They had drifted many feet from the refugee-boat, and, as they looked, it forged away with beating screw [23] into the bank of fog that had crept out all morning from the coast. Into the same bank, with guns flashing redly, went the cruiser, half a mile to the left.

For a little they swam and paddled and shouted, deserted, in that suddenly vacant sea, under the sting of the sleet. Then one cried out and sank, and two others drifted away into the fog. Inside that fog the gun-fire had clamoured for a little, then ceased. Andrei and his two soldiers tied themselves upon their buoys, and lashed the buoys together. ... It seemed to Andrei that only a moment had passed when, looking at the two beside him, he saw that they were dead.

Already, in the icy water, his own legs and the lower half of his body had grown numb. Then a strange warmth surged slowly, steadily, up through his frozen body, and when it came to his heart he knew he would be dead. He began to paddle again, desperately. He cried out, and sang, and shouted, to stay the menace creeping upon him from the waters. And then he was suddenly tired, so tired, and sleep more desirable than ever life had been. He ceased to struggle, and the grey waste of beaten water blurred in his eyes. Night.

And then a great light awoke on the sea and beckoned and beckoned. He knew it and rose and struggled again, and cried 'Natasha!'

IV

He was picked up by an oil-carrier and taken to Stamboul. There, in hospital, raving, for two months he lay, and at the end of that time, weak and a pauper, came back again, with the spring come, to the world of men and the memory of Natasha's lips.

But he came not back the same Andrei, I think. He had wandered in mist and dreams for many days. He came out to a world that had dimmed and blurred at the edges. One memory, one hunger of desire alone possessed him. So clear was that memory, clear and unforgotten his oath as he held Natasha's hands. 'Always will I love you. Never shall I forget.'

You see him, dreamer and saint as I think he was, he who had tasted of love and seen that tenderness no man may ever awaken twice in the eyes of a woman. He set out to seek Natasha as once men went forth to seek the Holy Grail. [24] Found – God mine! [25] he would have peace, would kneel at Natasha's feet and lay his head in her hands, and sleep and sleep till the world died. ...

He set out to search in the nameless flotsam-drift heaped on the Golden Horn [26] with the destruction of the last White Raid. He tramped from consulate to consulate, from shipping-office to shipping-office, through a drift and tangle of rumour and legend. For we of the last White Raid were already legendary. Now he would glimpse at some street-crossing men whom he had once known; one time he saw his own brother, an officer of the Imperial Army, selling fruit outside the Mosque Sophia. [27] And to Andrei these men – even his own brother – were but the faintest shadows. Yet half-remembered faces rising up out of the street throngs would set his mind to ache and ache, seeking names and memories and associations. Had they known Natasha?

Sometimes, on gutter ledge or wharf, he would fall asleep – for he was still a sick man – or into long trances when he sat unsleeping, yet unthinking, the mind fainting and fainting within him, crying, 'Cease! Come and sleep!' And from such moments he would rouse with a passion of anger at himself, because of that memory of Natasha's face, her eyes so pitifully misted. ...

But neither of her nor of the refugee-ship in which they had sailed from Yalta could he find any trace. He had never known the name of the ship, nor the name of its captain.

Yet day after day, working here and there for bread, sleeping only when exhaustion came on him, he tramped the quays of the Golden Horn. In those miles of jetties his intent, white face must have become familiar. I think the story of his quest long followed after him in rumour and surmise. Because of that rumour, because of the ache of sympathy which every lost lover may stir, he was met with unbelievable kindness – that amazing kindliness of the kennels. [28] He was helped by the stray and the waif with whom he would never have associated the pity of the Christ. [29]

And one morning he awoke to find his spirit had fought his body, and triumphed, and health was returning to him again.

Out of delirium into monomania? So, perhaps. But I think his face grew the more gentle, and the hunger went from his eyes, and there the dreams came back. Yet was he the passionate pilgrim, with his ache of quest. But all the winds and dawns and colours of life were his again, interpreting that ache even as they accentuated it.

And then, late one evening, when he stood on a quay watching a ship unload, a man cried out at sight of him, and swore in Russian. In the smoke-blur that was Andrei's memory flamed remembrance. The man was the captain of the refugee-ship.

He stared and stood, and grew white, thinking Andrei a ghost. Then he talked. The refugee-ship had left the swimmers and made its escape that it might not be blown out of the waters in the fight between the Sovyet gunboat and the French cruiser. When presently the two warships, still shelling, had passed into the haze on the Crimean coast, the refugee-ship lowered its boats and sought in the fog for the swimmers. But they were nowhere to be found. ...

'Natasha Grodine? I remember her; you carried her aboard at Yalta. After we came to Stamboul I heard she joined the ship of refugees that sailed to Jaffa, to the Russian colony in Palestine.' [30]

V

He was a pauper, as I have said. But a Greek boat of the coasts took him for deckhand, and on that boat he drifted southwards, down the painted coast of the Levant, [31] so magical in summer days, more magical still at night when the masts dipped against the stars and the forecastle tuned its guitars. He learned the ways of a ship and the lives and beliefs of the men who with him worked, and he entered their poor, stupid dreams, and forgave those dreamers of their kind who had driven him from Russia. Food on the ship was bad, and the captain a bully, but when they stagnated in semi-mutiny it was Andrei who made the peace, and brought concord, and lured the ship south, ever in pursuit of his tireless quest.

So, in midsummer, they came to Jaffa, and Andrei bade farewell to the Greeks. They wept at parting with him, and cried farewells for long as he waved from the shore. Then he made his way to the shipping companies and set his enquiries afoot. A day later, when he came back to the quays, the Greek ship had gone.

He found no Russian in the town, but instead street fighting between the so-brave Arabs and the immigrant Jews. For a day, stayed strangely by memory of Natasha, he forewent his quest and helped in the streets, carrying the wounded to safety, walking through rifle-fire unscathed and unafraid.

Then at length, from the Greek consul, [32] he learned that six months before a party of Russians had indeed come to Jaffa. But they had gone up to settle in Jerusalem, [33] to live by the tourist trade.

So Andrei took the road to the north, working his way across the dusty tundras, through the brown mud-villages, up to the green foothills. A week he stayed to help in the harvest of an orange grove, then set out again. And one nightfall, outside a convent of the Irish nuns, [34] where he sat drinking milk and eating bread and goat-cheese, he looked up and saw the black bulking of the Mountains of Moab. [35]

Because he never begged for money, but only food in return for work, he was a pauper as on the day when he left the Golden Horn in the Greek coaster. But now the mountains, in a moment of weakness, awed him. He went down to the railway, waited for another evening to come, climbed aboard a covered truck, and in the morning found himself in Jerusalem, in a land of greenery and sudden rain.

He went up to the city in that rain, with beating hope in his heart that here certainly was his quest to end. Yet where to begin?

Then, as he stood mazed [36] in the streets of English Jerusalem, [37] came that adventure that was yet to tell no tale of his hidden self to Andrei's heart. For he saw a girl go by – a white girl in the brown-skinned throngs. And at sight of her he stood suddenly sick at heart. For it had seemed to him that it was Natasha, his lost love.

Then he awoke, and cried out, and turned, and ran down the street in the direction she had gone. But the crowds had swallowed her.

All that day, in a mad passion of fear and the remorse, he hunted the streets and stews of Jerusalem. ...

He knelt, wearied, yet finding a little peace, in the Church of the Holy Sepulchre, in that little room where legend tells was the gentle Christ laid when brought from the Cross. [38] Then he went out on the steps of the Church and so again came face to face with the girl whom he had thought Natasha.

And it was not Natasha.

She drew aside, then stared at his white face, faltering a query in words which stayed him. For she spoke in Russian, with just such voice as Natasha herself.

'I am not ill,' he answered, 'only I thought you one for whom I search. My name is Andrei Bal'mont, and I was of Deniken's raid. Have you ever heard of a Crimean refugee, a girl Natasha Grodine?'

At that she gave a cry, and caught his hands, and flushed and paled. 'Andrei Bal'mont! But I have heard of you. Oh, I have heard of you. I knew your dear Natasha in Stamboul and loved her. You are the captain who saved her in Yalta, and hid in the sea from the Sovyet gunboat –'

'She is here – in Jerusalem?'

'But no – she went to Alexandria [39] with an uncle she found in Stamboul.

... Andrei Bal'mont – oh, I have heard of you. Natasha remembers. She does not believe you dead. ...'

But she knew nothing of Natasha's address in Alexandria.

'Stay with us here, us Russians. We will help you, though we are so poor. Stay with us and write letters to Alexandria. There is a Colonel Saloney in Alexandria, he made the Refugee Committee, and may know where your Natasha is.'

He bent and kissed her hands. 'I cannot stay a day, little sister. For Natasha remembers and I remember.'

Then she wept a little, I think because of his youth and his saint's face. But he went out through the rain, up the dark alleys, and on the outskirts of Jerusalem turned south again.

VI

And of all that Odyssey that finally led him to Egypt [40] I know only in outline – in the outline and surmise. Westwards and southwards he went, crossing the mountains of Moab on foot that second time, holding south by the jungle swamps of Ludd [41] and so on and on, as the summer waxed, to the fringe of the desert. And, as he went, and the days passed into weeks and so to months, ever clear and shining, a pillar of light by night and a pillar of smoke by day [42] led his quest.

And he learned to know the stars of the beggar's night, and thirst and hunger and the sleep of exhaustion. Sunsets he would watch the Evening Star [43] come out, in morning would see it lead the sunrise up over the sands. He came to look for it as one looks for the face of a friend – the star that crowned his quest and led his feet.

On the wild highroads of Palestine and Transjordania [44] none sought to harm him. He tramped them, a man invisibly shielded and guarded. Near Amman [45] he joined a camel-train, and went south and east, into the desert, to some Arab city of the wastes. From there he struck out north-west again, and, at the long length, five months after leaving Jerusalem, came to Kantara on the Suez. [46] There, for a little, he was stayed, and, as on the Golden Horn, searched from ship to ship for work. Luck favoured him again, for on the third day he was taken on as stoker of a boat going to Alexandria.

He landed at Alexandria in November. No Russian consulate was left, nor Refugees' Committee any longer, so from house to house his searchings began anew. At night he slept in the kennels of the poor, for bread worked at the wharfs an hour each day, unloading coal. At these wharfs he heard by chance of me, 'English' Saloney, the hotel guide, and remembered the name the girl in Jerusalem had mentioned.

Brown and sinewy, desert Arab in speech and appearance, I yet knew him on the instant that evening I found him awaiting me on the hotel steps. I took him to my room, gave him food and clothes, and sat and listened to him and all the story of his quest from far-off Yalta.

'Grodine?'I said, 'I remember the name. And the old Committee records contain the address of every White Russian in Egypt. Your quest is ended, my friend.'

VII

We looked up the books, and there was the entry: 'Lef Ilyavetch Grodine and niece Natasha, 12, Harun-Badrawi, Khalig-el-Masri, Le Caire.' [47] Andrei Bal'mont stared at it as though it had been the writing of Belshazzar's feast, [48] then kissed me, and was suddenly gone from the room. I ran after him.

'But you will need money – I will lend you –'

'Little friend, leave me my last road.'

So he waved and went, and I never saw him again.

VIII

Now has my story been as Andrei himself told it me. But hereafter is only the dream I built on the so-few facts I sought out later that year. [49] One man there was who saw him enter Cairo in the sunset, one who saw him pass over the Bulaq Bridge. [50] And there was Aida ed-Dowlah, the cripple, who squatted in the shadow of a garden wall in the Khalig. ...

But of that tramp from Alexandria to Cairo and its Khalig of many colours – how shall we guess? Certain at last, at last on his final road, he went eastwards. But as he walked the night ways he saw with an ache and an amazement the stars less bright than of yore. And his feet were heavier, and the smell of the wind stung him not at all. ...

It was sunset when he came to Cairo and sought his way to the Khalig-el-Masri, through the throngs of Polychromata. Up there, perhaps, beyond Abbassieh, were the Red Hills crowned in fire, [51] and he stopped and looked at them and looked back across all the days and roads he had traversed. And suddenly his eyes were blind with tears.

Sunset over Cairo. [52] ...

Then, at length, out beyond the Khalig's colour and clamour, he came to the garden wall of a house, and looked, and suddenly stood still. For there in the gloaming lowe [53] of the garden, no dream, but sweet and real, stood Natasha herself, more dear and desirable than in all his memories.

He clenched his hands and choked back the cry that quivered up into his throat. He stood suddenly sick at heart.

Knowing nothing of his nearness, white and dim in the fading light, she stretched out her hands, and he heard the sound of her tears, heard her whisper to the sunset his name. ...

Night and dreams and quest, the dream that was Natasha herself – or a weeping girl in a garden?

He stood heart-wrung, his lips half-opened to call. Then, overhead, faintly, came out the Evening Star.

IX

Half an hour afterwards, out from Cairo over the Bulaq Bridge, to the night and the high road and the sting of the wind, Andrei Bal'mont tramped forth again on his quest. [54]

II

The Lost Prophetess [1]

I

Some religious procession, I think. Ah no, the Warren strikers. [2] ... And look – God mine, here in Cairo! – *a women's contingent!*

The first I have ever seen. Surely Jane Hatoun marches there, surely somewhere in that brown drift is her face and voice uplifted! Surely at least she turns in dream, dreaming she hears the ring of feet on that Road she prophesied these thirty years ago!

Some friend of mine? Jane Hatoun? She was memory blowing down the night before ever the good *sovyeti* replaced in Kazan Gymnasium – if replaced him they have – the Professor of English Literature who fled to join the Whites. [3] A legend of the bazaars, a tale of the *harm* and *soq*, [4] embroidered and miracle-adorned, that Woman's Deliverer who was once Jane Hatoun and walked your English fields. ...

But the legend that stirred me to an aching wonder that night I heard it in a room beyond Khan Khalil [5] – stirred me so that I wrote to England for the upturning of records, so that even to Angora [6] I wrote. ... What irony of fate that with me alone, alien in race and sex, should rest the full tale of the Prophet of Sharikhan! [7] Powder and dust, and yet – and yet – I may never hear a discussion or read a book on the women's regeneration [8] but I hear Jane Hatoun's voice come ringing across the years.

II

This from your records English and those of the Egyptian official: in [9] 1878 one Lutf Hatoun, a student, was expelled from El-Azhar [10] for the heretical beliefs and liberalism. He escaped but narrowly with his life. Yet he was rich, an orphan, had no ties, and reached to Alexandria in safety.

From there he sailed to France, and so to England, to gather yet more of the foreign liberalism. Three months after this arrival in London he married an English girl; before the lapse of the eighteen months he and his wife were dead, killed in the great train accident. [11]

They left but one child, a daughter.

Such the ragged record of official fact upon which I, with my letter from Angora, may weave the imaginings. She was brought up, this child Jane Hatoun, by the aunt artistic and advanced. There was much of talk and poetry and misty idealism all through her early years. She was given the education and freedom beyond that decade even in England.

The aunt, an artist, was member of some society of the painters that may have been your Pre-Raphaelite Brotherhood; [12] she was friend of Ruskin and Morris [13] and the gentle rebels of those days. The New Age [14] was nigh when all men would be free and kindly and happy, and all women not only the equals of men, but the goddesses to inspire. ... Except in the brown lands of the Nile, which had haunted Jane Hatoun from childhood – her father's country, where was still the untinged darkness, where women were the cattle-slaves and dolls, where the light Pre-Raphaelite had never shone.

In the breathless resolve that grew stronger and stronger with her adolescence, Jane Hatoun determined herself as the missionary to carry the gospel unique to Egypt. In England were many to guide the coming age, but she – she would go to Egypt, where were none. ...

In 1899 the aunt died. Six months later Jane Hatoun, aged twenty-one, with the little luggage and the great faith and the incomplete knowledge of Arabic, sailed for Alexandria, which her father had left in flight twenty-two years before.

III

'She was tall and slender, yet with full bosom and eyes like a deer,' was one to write of her. The type forgotten – of heroic mould, large of limb, young and eager and unawakened. She had little evidence of the Egyptian blood, but colourful hair and the white skin whereneath would rise the quick blood. And of her is there one phrase written that is curiously illuminating. 'She had beautiful hands – kind hands. They were kinder than the mercy of God, her hands.'

And for background our Polychromata – brown and seething and sullen and vivid, aged and unwearied, veiled of face and soul.

She came alone, but with letters of introduction to notabilities, native and European, and with the youthfulness and enthusiasm set about her intention express of seeking out the intelligent women of Cairo and holding with them the meetings and discussions.

From the women of the *harm* soon drifted strange accounts of those talks. For she urged them to learn the reading and writing, to demand the freedom and the shedding of the *pushi*, [15] to organise the Women's League of Al-Islam. [16]

It sounds a teaching harmless and pitiful enough – Freedom and the Alphabet. [17] But to that Cairo it was a gospel of blasphemy, and there grew the mutter of anger against this English girl. It might have become an official protest, have resulted in the closed door and expulsion from Egypt. But for the happening mysterious.

Jane Hatoun disappeared. In a night she disappeared. Followed the questionings and the searchings by native police, but they were the searchings unavailing. She had been wont to walk the bazaars and hovel-lanes unguarded and unattended. ... It was the quest regrettably hopeless.

IV

Sixty years of age, politician, schemer, a Muslim of the *Haj*, and, had he had his way, a Muslim of the *Jihad.* [18] Such Ali Mabkhut esh-Shihada, Bey, [19] high in favour with the Khedive, [20] but uncertain friend of the English.

He was the strange hybrid, an Egyptian-Japanese. His mother, of one of the few Muslim families in Japan, had been brought to Egypt in 1840 to implement some primitive Pan-Islamic plotting of Holy War.

Old and with the shrivelled face and the beast eyes, a man like a hyena, he lived in the barrack-palace of Sharikhan, upon the Nile. When Jane Hatoun first came to Cairo he was in the Yemen, making the marriage in the rich Yahya clan, [21] and from there he at length returned with his new bride to those rooms in Sharikhan that had known so many women, where I think the very air was choked with the murdered soul-stuff of women. ...

A week thereafter he heard of the English girl, but saw her not, and his *harîm* remained undisturbed, as was he himself. Until the one day when, coming from the visit to a friend in the Muski, [22] they pointed to her passing in the street.

You understand, she was friendless and counselless in Cairo, and with confidence and enthusiasm unbounded. Presently was she receiving the invitations to visit a house on Nile-bank, the small house where lived two women Egyptian, widows, eager for the new knowledge. She was delighted, and made the many calls, and at length, one night after the long talk, was induced to sleep there. A servant promised to take a note to the hotel, telling the guest's whereabouts. ...

In the night that guest awoke with stifling breath and the feet and hands bound in cloths. Across her face were also bound the cloths. Underneath was the motion of a boat on water, and overhead the dip and sway of a lateen sail. [23] She was upon the Nile.

She sought to struggle, but a great hand stayed her, and she lay wide-eyed in the unquiet darkness. Then the boat stopped, and she was carried up a dark flight of water-steps till the lap of the Nile was lost. Through the many corridors with the unpainted walls she was borne, then into a room that with lights blazed, that hung sick with the smell of musk, that was strewn with the gorgeous rugs in the barbarian clamour of colours.

He who carried her was a giant negro, but she had no eyes for him. On the divan sat one who smiled at her, who smiled the tigerish smile from withered, evil face the while her face and feet and hands were untied, who smiled while she stood blanched and horrified, who smiled even while her screams were echoing down those corridors of night.

V

For the week she was a creature demented, raving and weeping in that guarded room to which the Bey went daily. And then from terror and agony came merciful release. [24] The screamings ceased to be heard in the nearby *harîm*. Instead, came other sounds – sounds which smote the whispering groups to amulet-clutching silence. [25] They were peal upon peal of laughter, laughter which rose and fell and never ceased, the laughter of the mad.

The Bey's visits ceased with abruptness and next day Zuria, the new wife from Yemen who for a season had been supplanted, overheard the conversation between Shihada and the head eunuch, [26] Aida-ed-Dowlah – a negro who had for the beast-master of Sharikhan the strange love and unclean devotion. The mad woman was to be gagged and flung into the Nile in a sack, as one drowns a dog.

But the day following came the change in Jane Hatoun. No longer was the wild laughter, but only the crooning and the muttered talk, and when Zuria, with the secret, vicious plan at heart, went and begged the life of the mad girl as a new toy, Shihada did not refuse. She who had been Jane Hatoun was taken from the painted room, given the corner of a couch in the *harîm,* and set to the menial tasks.

VI

Drudge and slave and butt of the *harîm* she became, as fear of her childlike insanity faded. Two of the women indeed befriended her, and these – so strange our hearts! – Ayesha the Abyssinian and Namlah the Copt [27] – the two who had posed as the widows in the little house on Nile-bank. Ayesha was dark and secret and of her friendliness made little show, but Namlah, when she could, tended the mad girl with the scared pity that presently waxed into a strange adoring love.

But the most followed in the blind hate of Zuria – of her who could not forget that she had been robbed of her lord a month after marriage. Freed though she was from sight or touch of the Bey – he had the orthodox horror of the mad – Jane Hatoun's life was the unceasing persecution, the deliberate torment. There were the orders not understood but mercilessly punished, the setting of heart-breaking tasks, the blows and jeers – all the slow, evil cruelty of the idle and sex-obsessed.

At the first, in the visits from other Cairene *harm*, it had been the custom to hide the mad Englishwoman away. But with the passing of time even that ceased, for there was none who dared betray the secrets of Sharikhan. And the chatter and coffee drinking would interrupt the while of the white slave of Zuria was made the exhibition and mock.

'I saved her for our amusement – from the death of a drowned dog I saved her,' Zuria would repeat the many times, and not until one afternoon in late October, when the room was crowded and Jane Hatoun crouched at the feet of Shihada Bey's chief wife, did the miracle happen.

They saw the slave suddenly rise and confront Zuria. Suddenly, and for the first time, she spoke in the clear and ringing Arabic.

'From such death will none save you, O evil woman. ... Be silent, fool who has vexed my hours. Silence – and look!'

She flung her arm towards the deserted end of the room, where hung the heavy velvet curtain above the doorway. Aghast, silenced, they turned and stared.

And it seemed to them as they looked that upon that curtain was flung a sudden picture. [28] Ever the darker grew the room and the picture ever the brighter, and when it stood clear and yet shaking and fading in the wind movement of the curtain, there arose a moan of terror.

For the picture showed the water-steps of the palace at night, and a woman, naked and bound, being uplifted and flung into the water by the giant negro, Aida. Behind was flicker of a lantern upon the dark Nile, and lighting the face of the woman whom death awaited.

And the face was the face of Zuria.

She screamed, falling forward on her hands, and at that the picture ceased and vanished. Above the grovelling thing at her feet stood Jane Hatoun, with the light unearthly in her eyes and hands outstretched to the terrified women.

'Look and believe, women of Egypt! By this sign shall you know me, the Prophetess of God!'

VII

Shihada Bey was not in Cairo. He had gone on the secret political mission to Turkey, leaving Aida-ed-Dowlah in charge of Sharikhan. And, while all unknowing he plotted in Stamboul, from his zenana, [29] on the Nile, there spread through women's Cairo the story amazing of the Prophetess of God.

No mere thaumaturgist, [30] but the first woman Prophet of God, one who superseded Christ and Mohammed, [31] one who came to deliver the women of the world. ... Nightly to her came the revelations and each dawn she would chant account of them to the rapt and shivering audiences of the zenana. Not one of her audience could read or write, and no record but the fragmentary verbal survives. [32]

'And the day shall come when our bodies shall be no more houses of shame but temples of the living God.' [33]

'And Woman shall build a City, and its name shall be Freedom; and Man shall come against that City with a Torch, and its name shall be Lust; then woe to that City if it trust in walls, for it shall not endure...'

Yet she preached no war on men, but rather the flaming creed that was to purge love of cruelty and abomination for those who set their feet on the way, *El Darb*, [34] the Road of abstinence and sacrifice and selflessness. ...

El Darb – it haunted her teachings. Somewhere, attainable by a mystic Road, was an amazing, essayable happiness, life free and eager, life in the sunlight beyond the prisons of fear and cruelty. ... The Buddhist Eightfold path, the Aryan Way, and yet also a Road to be built and laid to the City of God. [35]

And it was woman whom she called to the paving of this Road, woman not as the lover or mother of men but as that dispossessed half of humanity which has never asserted the individual existence. She called her to an Expedition, a nameless Venture, out in the open air and the starlight, she preached her a God scorned and denied of men, she preached her a soul and a splendid endeavour. ...

Aida-ed-Dowlah and his eunuchs, freed from their master's presence, kept but careless watch. They were seldom seen, and from them was the Prophetess guarded and shielded, so that of these happenings – other than the increased number of visitors – they knew nothing. First of disciples, first to come forward from the ranks of those who merely looked and listened and feared, [36] were Namlah and Ayesha. But there was the convert amazing almost as soon. Zuria, whose death the Prophetess's first curtain-picture had foreshown, became the Paul of the wild, new faith! [37]

From that one may guess that there were things other than the ascetic Road in the teachings – the colourful, incoherent imaginings of the Eastern mystic, the startling, incomprehensible revelations, the phrases of magic and prophecy. ... No mere thaumaturgist, miracles were yet of the daily occurrence – the miracle-pictures of the *harîm*-curtain, the laying-on of hands [38] – all those strange powers that lie with the spiritually over-stirred.

Such our nature, perhaps through the wild prophecies and miracles it was that her fame spread amidst the Muslim women and even into the quarters of the Greeks. [39] She was not once betrayed, and presently the story ceased to be a story, became the secret cult and the kindled fire, awaiting to blow out in flames of faith upon the winds of the world. ...

And then over Cairo that November, out of the lairs of the Black Warrens and the Khalig Canal, spread the cholera [40] plague.

VIII

When returning one night in secret from his political mission, and bringing the secret guest, Shihada Bey entered the palace of Sharikhan and found a quarter of his servants dead, including two women of the *harîm*. Of those who still lived, half were smitten with the plague of the fouled waters and Cairo no place for a wise man to tarry.

Tarry he did not, but fled to Alexandria. With the dawn he was gone, but his secret guest remained still in hiding, for entry into Egypt was forbidden

Dirhem Ragheb.

Ah, you have heard of him – Ragheb Pasha, the Ghazi's friend [41] and confidant. Enemy of the Faith, the mullahs [42] have called him, him who has fought to destroy the creed of his fathers, with all its tenets of black bestiality and sex-enslavement. But this was some thirty years ago, and though member of that society that was later to become the Young Turk, [43] he was not yet the ascetic and fanatic, but a young man with the courtesy and the ready smile, the humour and impatience of restraint and convention. He had no illusions regarding the Bey; they were but temporary political allies.

He had a palace wing almost to himself, and passed the days in reading and smoking, till on the fourth afternoon of his coming he looked out on the great central court, the *hôsh* [44] of Sharikhan, and saw that which made him drop his book in wonder.

Pacing the *hôsh* was a woman, a girl of the English surely, or his eyes lied, a girl tall and stately, with the eyes unearthly and a little smile upon her lips. And after her, a pace behind, two native women.

They were Zuria and Namlah, who had brought the Prophetess to walk in the open air after the hours of nursing and prayer in the palace. And as he gazed Ragheb saw the very beautiful happening – the English girl stop till the two native women were beside her, and put her arms about their shoulders, and point to the sunset. So, in that grouping they stood for a minute, so still and crowned with fire that he followed their gaze.

Seen through the opening of the *hôsh,* magically paved in rippling gold upon the Nile, lay a road that stretched from their feet to the sun.

IX

'I loved her from the first moment I saw her pass below me,' he was to write, and I have thought of him and that very sweet and ancient song in your language. 'I would have burned down Sharikhan for her,' he says, the grey-headed confidant of Kemal. [45] ...

But he did not burn Sharikhan. Instead, he waylaid her next evening she walked, and that time alone. She stopped and stared at him with the mysterious eyes, unafraid and unrealising. He stood bare-headed in front of her, and fumbled in his English.

'My lady, who are you?'

She put her hand to her forehead, still standing so and staring at him. She stammered the confused words, and then suddenly her face was suffused with blood, and she gave a low, wailing cry and would have fallen but for his arms. So holding her he was aware how fragile she was, but at his touch she struggled like the mad thing and sank to her knees.

He stood over her in the pity and the doubt, and something of apprehension also, for he knew not that the eunuchs of the palace were but recovering from cholera, and none but women likely to interrupt them. And suddenly, he says, unknowing her story, he was blindly angry.

'By God, the Bey! You are no Muslim woman. He stole you, abducted you?'

She raised a frightened face from which the light unearthly had gone. It was the face of a child, remembering horror.

'Stay with me,' she whispered. 'Stay with me. You are my friend?'

X

The madness that had veiled from her the past had shivered away in an instant. Came back horror and remembrance and understanding. ... And then sight of the kind and compassionate eyes of the one human being who seemed not alien.

That night she passed through nightmare hours. One of the women was dying, and she found herself kneeling with the whole of the *harîm,* praying an insane ritual prayer through which revolved and returned some jargon of a Road, some means to salvation which she had preached in her madness. And when the woman, her eyes fixed in adoration on the Prophetess, gave the last gasp, Jane Hatoun found herself bending over the corpse and making upon it the mystic sign she had taught. ...

Almost that night her reason reeled again, in the smell and reek and the chanting, and there came on her a shuddering horror and disgust of the *harîm* women who seemed to be her especial disciples – the eager Zuria and the faithful Namlah.

But alone, early in the dawn, she managed to steal away from them to the room where hung the great curtain, and attempted unavailingly to summon upon it the images. Morning was breaking outside, and she unlatched the never-opened windows and watched the light come upon the Nile.

That day she had again a secret meeting with Ragheb. 'I swore I would take her away as she begged – to France, to England. Nor did I make any conditions. Oh, sometime, beyond the seas – for I was to abandon politics and country for her, my English lady – perhaps then she would come to me.'

He made the arrangements for a boat to come from Bulaq and take them away next sunset. All over Cairo the cholera plague was receding, and there was no difficulty.

But of the new conditions in Cairo another was aware, for that night there arrived at Sharikhan the messenger with news that Shihada Bey was returning in twenty-four hours.

XI

All that momentous next day were the swift rainshowers upon the Nile, and – thing unprecedented in Cairo – a haze that almost blotted out the opposite bank. And within Sharikhan, in the *harîm* of Shihada, Jane Hatoun sat and listened to the dying Ayesha.

Sometimes she wandered in delirium, sometimes came out of dreams and recognised the Prophetess, and made the little struggles to remembrance, the pitiful confessions.

'The Road, the Road, O *khâtûn*! [46] So little I have done, I have been weak. And the Way is steep and hard, the shining Way of Women. I have hardly trod it. Will God understand?'

Over and over again. And it seemed that not the miracles and chantings, but vision of some wondrous Way of Life had lighted her dark, starved soul. ... Kneeling there, repulsion forgot, Jane Hatoun listened with a breaking heart.

And against the window the wonder of Cairene rain!... Rain that fell on the long fields and the pleasant lanes and the lamplit streets of the kindly towns, rain of the lost England to which Ragheb would take her. ...

'I found her at sunset waiting on the water-steps, as we had planned. She was transformed to wonder, with flushed cheeks and breathless laughter. She hardly seemed to see me, but pointed across the Nile.

'I looked. It was our boat.'

XII

They started and fell apart, and Ragheb turned with pistol gleaming in his hand. But from the shadows came no eunuch, but only the Coptic slave-woman – the hysterical woman who stared and then fell on her knees and caught the skirt of Jane Hatoun.

'Oh, leave us not, us who are your children, us to whom you have brought the Faith – leave us not, O *khâtûn!*'

Ragheb caught the stem of the boat, and steadied it, and turned with outstretched hand. But Namlah clung to the Prophetess with the courage of desperation. 'Ayesha is dying and calls for you, she who is passing from the Road. She calls your blessing –'

'I thrust her aside. "Quick, into the boat. We can be at Bulaq before darkness. And then the road to the sea!"

'But from my English lady came the strange, strangled sob, and she looked at me wildly, and drew back with strange words.

'"Go you, go you. Haste, for the Bey comes, and already Aida-ed-Dowlah has seen you speak with me."

'I stared at her and did not understand. The shadows grew deep upon the waters. And then my English lady raised the slave-woman and stood with her arms around her, and looked at me with tormented eyes. And these are the words she said, as I remember them:

'"Oh, I cannot come!" And suddenly she wept, and spoke my name, which she had never done. "So easy to escape – my heart is breaking to come with you! Love and you – there was never woman who heard such call but went. Oh, I am only the mad Prophetess still, I think, and these women have followed and believed in me, and how may I desert them?"

'I pleaded with her, but she did not seem to hear. The boatmen, frightened at nearness to Sharikhan, kept calling from the water-steps. And then I saw come again on my English lady's face the unearthly light.

'"Forget me, Dirhem, [47] I have never been. Yet beyond the Road I would have loved – more than life I would have loved you!"

'And then for the quick moment she kissed me, I who had never known of her love, and so was gone.

'I never saw her again.'

XIII

What happened with the return of Shihada is the dim and tangled tale, the swift confused falling of last sands heard in darkness. Perhaps he looked upon Jane Hatoun again, and the beast-desires stirred in him. Perhaps he had heard from Aida-ed-Dowlah of the meetings with Dirhem Ragheb and the flight of the latter. At the least, there occurred in that *harîm* room a scene unprecedented. Zuria, in defence of the Prophetess, struck with her knife at Shihada, and while the Bey grappled with her Jane Hatoun picked that knife from the floor and drove it through his hyena-heart. ...

They stripped and bound the two women, the eunuchs, and carried them down to the water-steps, Aida-ed-Dowlah, who had loved Shihada, transformed to a raving madman with no thought of the morrow and its explanations. Behind them they clanged to the great door above the water-steps and thereon beat the demented women [48] the while murder was done in the rain and darkness.

But through that door they [49] heard Jane Hatoun crying courage to Zuria, crying that the sunset Road was theirs. And then they heard her singing by the waters, in the alien tongue and the unknown words. Struggling and splash, a single sharp cry, wild and agonised. And then the singing ceased for ever.

XIV

But in the women's legends of Cairo Jane Hatoun perished not that night at the hands of the eunuchs. She escaped upon the water and the darkness, and some day – surely from that Avalon where Arthur dreams, and sleeps the Danish king [50] – she will come again and preach the faith that is to deliver the women of the world. ...

And who may say that she will not?

III

Daybreak

I

The little cluster of bell-flowers – From Scotland? But it has travelled far! I may smell it? ... God mine, it is heather!

It cloaks your mountains in purple this time of year, does it not? Never have I seen it before; but I have smelt this smell. I have smelt it blowing on a wind from those mountains I have never trod, a breath of that autumn I have never known. ...

Eh? In imagination? But no, in reality – here in our Cairo, almost the year ago today.

II

And the tale begins, if I must tell it, not here at all. It begins in the far Scotland that sent you the heather, with Roger Mantell [1] on the autumn walking tour up through your Urals. [2]

He was the young journalist in London, this Roger, and very poor, as is proper for the journalist. Something of your own height and appearance he had, with that brownness of hair and eyes that indistinguishes [3] the Englishman, and a certain far-awayness of outlook that made of him the not too-good journalist. History was his passion, and he had taken the walking-tour to plan the writing of a book. This book was to refute the foolish Spengler [4] – him who believes all history goes in cycles, like the mad dog chasing its tail.

And one night-time, very late, passing through a village amongst those hills, he heard a girl singing a peasant song – so sweet and strange and beautiful in the dark that he halted and listened. And the song was this:

> 'Oh, the memory and the ache
>   They have stown the heart fra me,
> And there's heather on the hills
>   In my ain countree.' [5]

All next day, though many miles away, he found memory of singer and song haunting him. So pressing was it that he turned about and went back to lay this ghostly thing. Outside the village school he heard the voice again.

Then, in growing amazement at himself, he rented a room at the village inn, in three days obtained introduction to his singer, and within the week, though his history had not progressed even in the draft beyond so-hairy

Eoanthropus, [6] was planning nothing of greater import than to steal the singer from her hills. [7]

Her father had been the village schoolmaster and she was teacher of the school. And because he had been a poet this dead father of hers had called her Dawn. To watch her stand against the sunrise, as many a morning she did when they tramped the hills together and the mists were rising, caught the amazement ever again in the throat of Roger. Slight and slim and dark and quick, this singer of the hills, with clear eyes, grey and grave, but with the little twinkle-lights deep down in them. She had a pale, clear skin with the faint blood-flush. She detested the poor Spengler [8] and could run like a deer.

Indeed, though one who had lived in the hills all her life, she was of the most modern – one of that woman's miracle-generation that knows nothing of the reserves and hesitations and tantalisations. She had the body of a gracious boy and the mind of an eager Greek.

If Roger first loved her for her voice, I think she loved him at first sight, protectingly, because of that far-awayness of his look. Under painted skies, children in a world transformed, they walked that autumn. Roger had been the unawakened tourist, but Dawn took him out into mornings of wonder when, in the silence, he would hear the sun come audibly [9] up from the east, hear the earth stir and move as from its sleep. Or into fervid noons, to lie on a mountain-side and listen to the drowsy under-song of bees rising and falling on the never-coming wind. And the brown night would creep over this land of Dawn's as one very ancient who went home from toil. ...

It seemed to him that she had deeper kinship with those things than he would ever fathom. 'I don't believe you are human at all,' he said to her once. 'You're out of the hills and the sunrise.' [10]

She laughed at him, and then was grave, in that fashion that somehow had power to wring his heart absurdly. 'I never remember my mother. She died when I was born. And my father was always lost in his books. I carried all my desperate wrongs and fears to the hills.' She sat with cheek in hand and looked across the sun-hazed valleys. 'I think they love me, those hills, almost as much as I love them.'

'How can they help it?' said Roger, her lover. [11]

III

In the little time they were deciding when they would marry and how many children they would have, and whether it would be better to wait until Roger made the thousand a year or only eight hundred. [12] Not till there was security and certainty were they to mate. ... At the least, that was Roger's planning, and Dawn, this so-amazing Greek boy who was more than boy, sat and looked at him and her hills, I think perhaps with the twinkle-tapers lighting her grey eyes. [13]

For he had come in the first months of the autumn. Day by day it deepened around them. Purple grew the mountains and under the long heats of day climbed to heaven in a shimmering blaze. Out of the earth rose all the songs of fruition and ending, and that second week there was a moon that came and never seemed to set. They could not keep their beds, these two, but stole out to meet each other in the white radiant wonder.

Till one night – this but the guess-work of mine – they kissed each other and in their kiss was already a wild regret. The hours are on wings, on wings! beat the shadows that were night-birds. Now, now! beat their own hearts. ... Perhaps Dawn held him at arm's [14] length, and laughed at him with a little breathlessness. 'But, Roger! ... A thousand a year!'

And then, whatever his answer, in some such hour of the earth-magic they came to their decision.

One night, under a moon that trembled on the wane, but waited for them still, they climbed together up into the hills and the radiance, and not a bird that called in the shadows but was their friend, and there was none of the need to say good night.

IV

But no moons endure for ever, and presently Dawn was with Roger in a little flat in London and those days on the hills dimmed till they were of a dream.

I have never seen your London or known its life, but it seems they went to live there in the season of the fogs which rise from a blind little river [15] amidst the streets. They began their life in a half-twilight, with the million under-murmurs of other life a still roar about them. In the morning Roger was gone to the office of his gazette; [16] often he did not return until midnight. For many weeks they would see each other only at night-time, each wearied and a little tired. ...

And in the little was the amazement, I think, and silent tears shed in the darkness that love could ever tarnish so. For they came to look on each other searchingly, even on the wild occasion angrily – Dawn to see her dreamer of the hills visionary and unpractical, immersed in his book and the refutations of cyclic catastrophe, irritable over the refractory [17] phrase or the inadequate reference. And to Roger it sometimes seemed that he was tied, by all unreasonable bonds, to a boy quickly bored and swift to anger, one whose eyes could light with other than mirth, one whose laughter could ring cruel and very clear. ...

But these are things inevitable? They are not the less heart-breaking. Sometime, both knew, they would come to the adjustments and live with lesser friction. They would, in their English phrase, 'settle down'. But the ache in the dark of love, a thing so shining, to look forward to the settle-down!

Yet was that never to be, for a day came when they looked at each other in unbelief and the settle-down fled out into the blinded streets and romance rang her bugles for them again. The great secret was theirs, theirs partnership in the abiding mystery. ...

But who am I to speak of it or understand? We of the unmarried are emotionally unborn, even though, wistfully, we catch a glimpse of understanding. This child of theirs was to be – oh, that hero that every child may be! – a captain of the hosts of the morning, [18] Dawn and Roger in one, doer and dreamer, one who was to confound all erring Germans and bear the torch of vision yet another league up the Defile through which march the hosts that have climbed from the beast. [19]

And they named him, and dreamt of him and hoped for him; and the months fell away, into spring warming London, into summer, till there came the day when Dawn must pass through her hours of agony and Roger doubt his vision of history. For there arose the complications and the bringing of a surgeon. ...

In the end was the child born dead, and for the little it seemed that Dawn herself would die. [20]

V

But she lived, returning to life wan and a stranger from a desolate land. She must bear no more children, nor must she stay the winter in England, the doctors said.

Roger – a Roger grown practical at last – took her north to the brief summer-autumn of her hills. So soon as he could leave her he went back to London again. In a week he was sending her the news that he had found a gazette willing to send him abroad for a year, to Egypt, to act as the correspondent and write a series-impression of Cairo and the Nile-country. [21]

VI

So they came to our Polychromata, those two. [22] On the voyage Dawn grew again the Greek boy, and her laughter came back, and the little twinkle that changed and yet abided in her grey eyes. They came from the ship at Alexandria and found a *pension* at Kubbah. From there they set to search for a house.

At the length, up on Nile-bank to the north of Gezireh Island, they came one afternoon on that at sight of which Dawn cried 'Oh Roger!' in the tone that stirred in him always a memoried cry from a day of agony. They stopped and looked at the desired possession and laughed eagerly, and kissed like the children they were.

For that was the supreme wonder of their days – their love that had flamed anew. As never before it flamed. But the burning is the wrong simile. It burgeoned and blossomed, strange and sweet, not the love of the first early days nor yet the compassionate passion of the dark London time. It was something that made of their first wild desire a childish greed, of the settle-down necessity a humour and a fantasy. ...

They surveyed the empty house by Nile-bank and went back to Kubbah [23] in the apprehension that it would be gone by morning. But the next day they found the agent, rented 'La maison Saniosu', [24] and engaged two Egyptian servants. It jutted out upon the Nile, the house, old and of crumbling stone, mantled with a brown creeper that reached down its tendrils to the water. It was two stories in height and had a high-walled garden also skirted by the Nile.

They had taken it furnished, so after a few necessary purchases in the bazaars, and in the intervals of Roger writing the so masterly series-impressions, they had but to debate a new name for it.

Above the door was its name carved – Maison Saniosu.

'Let's call it Sans-Sous [25] and be done,' said Roger. And this, because they were very young and very poor and very happy, was a great jest, and almost on that name they decided.

But one morning – a morning early in October – happened that which solved the so urgent matter. In their room Dawn was the first to awake. Upon the window was the urgent tapping of a twig and she looked out on the wonder of a Nile daybreak. Presently she awakened Roger and they sat side by side watching in the sky the silver that changed to amber and so to copper and then into the blind flush of azure.

They had been awakened by the first of the seasonal morning winds which bring the end of the khamsin time, [26] but that they did not know until later. Only that unexpected wind had brought to Dawn an inspiration.

'I know – name for our house! Was there ever such suitable name!'

Roger stared at her. 'What?'

'Why, Daybreak.'

He teased her. 'But that is your own name. It is Dawn.' Then he laughed, and there were words in your English Bible that he remembered, very wonderful and beautiful words:

'"*Until the day break and the shadows flee away –*"' [27]

VII

I met them first in mid-November, in front of the Sphinx, [28] when Dawn was posing it and her Roger and an Egyptian dragoman for the photograph. I also had come to photograph it for a client I had.

Roger apologised for his Philistine [29] wife who insisted that he and the dragoman should stand beside the Riddle of the Sands. [30] I made her the bow.

'I think she is wise,' I said, 'for this is no Riddle; only a foolish vanity in stone. If I might I would have madame in my photograph with the Sphinx.'

I have that photograph still, with the little madame, slight and sweet and brave, standing beside that owlish carving of the foolish dead. Then I helped them catch the donkeys which had strayed and we went to Mena House [31] and drank the much-needed tea, for the donkey-catching had been a task of the mirth and great speed.

From the first I think their liking was for me as mine for them. Presently, when we had ceased to laugh at memory of a donkey which had raced Roger for almost a mile, they were telling me of the house called Daybreak and that sudden wind from the Nile that now tapped their window each morning.

'It is a *green* wind,' said the little madame, and paused in the doubt of my understanding.

'I know,' I said. 'It is of the Delta [32] crops and harvesting. Yet few know it for a green wind.'

'I am a peasant myself,' she said. 'Is that why?'

I looked at her and wove the fantasy. 'You are of the most ancient race, I think. Of the brunet [33] race that held the Mediterranean lands long before there was Celt or Saxon or Slav. [34] They are not of the history-books: they passed north and south into bleaker lands before history opened. But perhaps there was one of them, some far-father of yours, who once tilled the Delta lands and woke to that green wind. Perhaps it is a memory that has come to you across ten thousand years.' [35]

'That is a wonderful thought,' said Dawn, and looked at her Roger.

'I will steal it for an article,' said Roger, and there was the laughter amongst us.

VIII

In the little I was a frequent visitor at the house called Daybreak. I talked of the Nile and Cairo and gave to Roger good copy for his London gazette. Soon to both of them I was the close friend, and knew this tale of theirs I have told you, even as they knew mine. When I told Roger of those Four Years which ended for me in the storming of Perekop by the Sovyet heroes – heroes they were, though my enemies – I remember the long silence that fell.

'That is life,' he said. 'And it seems blind chance and aimlessness. ... But there's something behind it greater than a dark malignancy. Though that malignancy is real enough. Perhaps in ancient Egypt they saw it, the Dark Shadow, and built the Sphinx and Pyramids to ward it off.'

'And this other thing,' I said. 'What is it?'

'Oh, something equally nameless and untheological. It has led us up through the dark Defile of history, has turned in many guises to help again and again the stragglers and the lost in their hour of utmost despair. It will lead us to the sunrise yet.'

'That Daybreak the poor Spenglers have never visioned,' I jested at him, though I loved his faith. We heard the singing of Dawn inside the house. 'And the little madame is its prophet.' [36]

He laughed and was a poet. 'She was made in secret when the Dark Gods slept!'

Never since Kazan had I known such friendship as those nights when the little madame and I would sit and talk under our Cairene moon, with the bulking of Bulaq beyond the garden wall and the far wail of native song in our ears. Sometimes was Roger with us, but often indoors, working on the so-great book that was not in the contract with his London gazette – the book that was to bring him reputation and money. I brought my violin to that garden, and Dawn would sing for me peasants' songs that left me homesick for my Volga lands [37] – though they were songs of that Scotland I have never seen. Once she sang that verse which had halted Roger in the hills, and I have forgotten it never:

'Oh, the memory and the ache
    They have stown the heart fra me,
And there's heather on the hills
    In my ain countree.'

But of course I loved her. From the first moment I think I loved her. And with Roger also I was in love. They were to me the surety of my dreams. I loved them as one loves those dream-children, keen and beautiful, who will people our happy world a thousand years after we are dead.

IX

And then, in February, there came the horror into their lives.

At the first I did not understand their silences and strangeness. I said to myself that I was the too-frequent visitor – what need had these lovers of such alien as myself? For a little there was bitterness with me, and I stayed away from the house called Daybreak, going there not at all until the passing of two weeks. When next I went it was to endure their reproach and in the eyes of the little madame a hurt puzzlement.

'You have tired of us? Why have you stayed away?'

I kissed her hand. 'But I had thought you tired of me,' I said, and blundered over words which I desired not to say. 'There seemed a difference the last time I came. ...'

Then was the silence, though Roger broke it with a sudden laugh and talk of indifferent matter. His eyes were the eyes of a sick animal. And when presently we were alone he went to the window, and looked blindly out on the sunlight and the Nile, then turned and told me.

And then, God mine! I also knew the sudden sickness of mind, and had no word to say because of the horror of the thing.

For another child was coming, and, as they had been told, Dawn could never live through such a thing again.

X

I proposed the committee of doctors which may deal with such cases, but Dawn, modern of moderns though she was, would have none of it. For she could talk of these things, being my friend and of her miracle-generation.

'I think – oh, I don't know, but it would be cheating.'

'But this is the absurd fatalism,' [38] I pleaded, as Roger also had pleaded. The little twinkle set its lights in her grave eyes.

'Anton, my dear, was it absurd fatalism that led you to fight a hopeless fight in your White army? ... And have you lost – even yet?'

That was in the garden of Daybreak, in the late March, and we were silent as she leant on the wall and looked down on the hastening waters. She had a sudden idle thought.

'Oh, that morning wind from the Delta – it does not blow now.'

'Eh?' I said. 'The wind? It will not come again for many months.'

XI

I procured for them Dr Adrian, the English, [39] who is my friend, Dawn liked him, for he is the droll, but to Roger he talked with a grave face, for he had from London the particulars of the case when the other child had died. The little madame must know no unhappiness or worry. Also, she must leave Cairo.

For the summer months drew on. They blazed their strong heat that summer as never before, I think. Yet Dawn, even when Roger at this would have written to his London gazette and made resignation, refused. They would stay on at Daybreak. On the little madame was the Cairene spell – that spell which makes of a chance house and garden in this strange city more homely than home.

But never so long a summer. ... A tent was set in the garden, and through those long days of white warmth we watched Dawn with the stealthiness of criminals who fear their gaze may be detected. So she told us, laughing, but with wistfulness. I doubt if Roger comforted her; it was she who gave the comfort. For him it was to start out of even the happiest moment into the blank silence when terror walked his brain and looked from his eyes. And from that would he be awakened with her arms about him, and her teasing tenderness. ... Then I would stride away, with the sick fear upon me also.

God mine, it was pitiful, heart-breaking.

But I set out to be the droll, even as did Adrian – he who has said that no gynæcologist can be anything but gynæcolatrist [40] – in his visits to the house called Daybreak. We sought to weave the conspiracy, we three – the conspiracy to keep afar the malignant shadow of which Roger had talked. Presently the Egyptian servants also understood and were in that conspiracy. With the ending of the khamsin time [41] I organised many of the late afternoon excursions – to the Barrage, to Heliopolis, [42] to the desert, borrowing a car from Adrian to take them to those places.

One afternoon in late September I took them to Abu Zabal. [43] For mile on mile we went into that brown country, where stand in sleep the whitewashed villages under their smoke pencillings, and there is no other colour at all, but only the white and black. We had tea as a picnic, making it under the lee of a ruined dyke in the sunset. It was such sunset as seemed to fire the world.

'It is the Ragnarok,' [44] I said, and Dawn poured sand on Roger, who was lazy and lay flatwise, to make him sit up and look at it.

'I've seen a Grampians sunset [45] like that,' he said.

The little madame caught her breath. She began to speak in a whisper.

'It's autumn there now. Oh, my hills, my dear hills! Can't you see them and smell them, Roger, climbing purple into the sunset? And hear the curlews [46] crying down the glen?'

We said nothing, and then we saw that she was weeping – desolately, with uncovered face, she who had been so brave. ...

And the time drew ever nearer like a black wall of sand.

XII

There came a night when Roger Mantell and I tramped that garden through hours that seemed never-ending. The cruel aloofness of the yellow stars and the whispering Nile! And it seemed to me then, as I think to Roger himself, that the dream of his history was false, that alone and unfriended man wandered amidst the cold immensities of space and time. ... Beside and above us, against the southwards sky, were the lights of the house called Daybreak.

To and fro, hour on hour, I walked Roger, and talked to him of the stars. I remember I stood pointing out to him Alpha in Centaur [47] when Lesdiguières, [48] the French colleague of Adrian, called him from the garden-door.

For Adrian was not there. That night of all nights he was in Alexandria, and, though we had sent the telegram for him, would not be back until morning. Lesdiguières, good and careful, but of the old school and the old fashion – it seemed but a moment when I next heard him calling me. But it must have been longer, for in the east were the ghost-limnings [49] of the day.

'The child – born alive, yes. A boy, [50] and of the complications none. But the girl' – and I knew he meant the little madame – 'is exhausted. She will not see the day, I think. She is calling for you.'

I shall not tell you, my friend, of that so-close room – the windows Lesdiguières had closed against the night miasmas [51] – nor the smells of the antiseptics, nor the stout French nurse who was presently gone out of the room with the doctor. I knelt and kissed the hand of the little madame – so tired, a child herself, lying there, Roger's arm under her head. She was sinking very quickly, dying of exhaustion. But as I rose to go she whispered 'Stay.'

I looked at Roger, but for me he had no eyes. I turned to the closed window and saw in the sky a pallor that waned and flushed and spread. And there came in my mind then, into that silence a bitter memory – the words Roger had quoted the day they named their house.

'*Until the day break and the shadows flee away* –'

Suddenly there was the rustling sound and I looked round. The little madame had sat urgently up in the arms of her lover, her eyes shining.

'Roger, Roger, look – the hills!'

And then upon the window I heard a little tapping. I wheeled to it and saw the urgent twig beating upon the pane. It was the first of the Delta winds. Of sudden impulse I undid the catch and flung the window open to the Nile daybreak. ...

And then I heard from Roger the little cry of wonder.

For suddenly, borne on that first Nile wind, out of the dawn the room was flooded with a nameless scent, and it seemed to me a moment I stood in a great valley, and up the grey slopes climbed the dawn, and as it climbed those hill-slopes mantled a misting purple. ...

A moment the thing was, in a strange, sweet silence, and then gone. I turned and looked at Roger's white face.

'My God!' he whispered. 'Did you smell it? *It was heather!*'

We looked at the little madame lying silent in his arms. I thought her dead, and then, while we stared, we saw she was asleep.

XIII

And she lived, coming out of that health-giving sleep with no memory of the morning happenings. In the spring Roger took her and his son away from Cairo and Egypt, back to her hills, for he was by then the great man because of his book. And me she kissed farewell – me, the dragoman! – and there was a mist in her clear eyes. ...

But Adrian when he came that morning: 'You saved her life,' he said to me, while we three stood in the garden and the little Dawn slept in the room above the Nile. 'It was the Delta morning wind that did it – the change in the temperature, you know. That fool Lesdiguières must have half-suffocated her.'

Yet until prevail the years that make all things dim will it seem to Roger and me that once, in an hour of desperate need, we were granted glimpse of the kindlier, nameless thing that verily shines and abides behind all the blind ways and destinies of Nature.

IV

THE EPIC [1]

I

But you are of the moderns, my friend, and therefore primitive. In the squatting-places of the dawnmen [2] also was the telling the story. They honoured the stylist long before there was the written style. Art was of art, not of life. But to me the tale without theme, the poem without purpose – it is salt without meat. The theme is the man. ... God mine, as Connan proved!

Here, under the night-sky, above the Khalig, where once Connan sat and planned to snare the immortals – who may believe that all the tales are told? Our Cairo – she pens such plot and theme through every hour as makes of all recorded tale a ghostly script, a story writ in water.

Mother of aliens, [3] alien to us all! Yet what city is like to her? In the scents and smells of her, her days and nights, colours and chance voices there are that wring the heart. Unreasonably. Unforgettably. Her very street-names cry in our ears like bugles: Ismailia, El Musky, El Manakh, Maghrabi, Shiekh Rihan. [4] They ring beyond their meaning. ...

Surely no language like the English in which to tell the Cairene tale! Only this wayward, featureless, fatherless tongue may sing our Polychromata. Not even the Arabic, I think, comes near to English for him who seeks to interpret Cairo's soul. [5]

As Connan sought to do.

II

He came to Cairo, this Englishman – though I think he had perhaps the Irish blood [6] – John Connan, early one July, when there were but few tourists and the khamsin blew every morning as a furnace back-blows upon a stoker. [7] I met him outside the Hotel Continental [8] and he engaged me as his guide because I did not call him Mister nor say that I would take him to the place of the genuine antiques.

He was a wit. 'Russian? Good God! Do any survive outside Dostoievsky?' [9] And he regarded me with amazement and sadness, then selected one driver of arabiyeh [10] from the smellsome [11] horde that surrounded us.

'We will go to the Pyramids,' he said. I assumed surprise.

'Do they exist outside the little Hichens?' [12]

Thereafter we became the more friendly, though he did not cease to yawn. He was a man whose soul and mind yawned; me he reminded of those bull-men of Assyria [13] whose faces are curved and cruel, yet stamped with an awful weariness in their stone. Then I remembered the frontispiece of a little book.

'You are Connan the poet,' I said. 'I read your poems in Kazan.' [14]

He closed his eyes and mimicked this book-English of mine – for I have never made to learn your speech argots [15] – still wearily.

'I was Connan the poet. But now I am Connan the lost. I write no poetry, because there is no poetry left in the world. I know, for I have heard men screaming on wire entanglements, and known a woman who sold her body and taunted the buyer.'

'These things have been,' I said. 'Always they have been. They are old as the world is old.'

'I also am old,' he said, 'and every minute I listen to moralists – especially moralists out of Dostoievsky – I age an hour.'

He followed me amidst the Pyramids, Kheops, Khefren, and Menkaura, [16] yawning. Only the Sphinx amused him. He said of it disrespectful things in that fashion I cannot imitate, with the humorous no-humour of the Englishman or American, comparing its face to that of a notable pugilist. [17] The next fortnight I took him exploring the Cairene bazaars.

And slowly in that fortnight, in the hours we tramped the Khan Khalil or the Suq el Fahlamin [18] – where the little artists of Europe pursue the local colour and the wood-workers of Egypt pursue their art – I came to know that his indifference was no pose. He was a sick man. Mentally. He wrote no poetry. He never read in books. Some thing in life there had been that blinded the windows of his soul. Perhaps that woman who had taunted the buyer.

Once he had been a poet of note in your English world. But that time was long past. He had written nothing for many years.

You must see him, a bull of a man, this Connan – great, with the black-blue hair and the blue eyes and ruddy face. His was no bodily sickness. Never I learned the story of the wanderings that had brought him to Cairo or that thing which had shocked the assurance from his heart. Perhaps the woman I imagined was not all to blame: such the idea that grew on me. Yet I liked him. ...

The English 'like!' So English a word, the word of a-little-cold-love!

He had been the ruthless individualist, with a little courage and a little splendour, one who could sing of passion but not of pity. And he had found no pity. He might have been a genius but that he was a brute.

III

And then, towards the end of that fortnight, came the change upon him. He yawned not so much. He walked and looked with a stirred interest, a dawning wonder. All unknown to me, some Cairene colour there had been, piercing his darkness, and he had awakened. In a little while I saw in him grow, dimly yet, a purpose and desire.

For evening after evening he turned, though we were far in El Katal or El Fostat, [19] and led back to this place where I had once brought him – here to this table in front of the café of Simon Papadrapoulnakophitos. [20]

Then I understood that the Sharia Khalig [21] had gripped him also, though I knew not to what ends, and I told him the history of it – this street young in Cairo, this street where once was a canal and one may still see the tide-markings of the waters. Young though it be, it is somehow Cairo itself, and immemorably ancient, as though the city had awaited this street since the first of its years. If you sit long enough in the Khalig all Cairo will sometime pass by – boyar [22] and beggar, brown man and black, and the men of the shades of white, and all the women of the history of the world, the vile and the fair and the pitiful. And you will hear the drifts of all speech and all passion, all hope and all desire if you sit and listen in the Street of All Egypt, [23] that is older in soul than the Ramesids [24] and so young that it rides the electric tram-car. [25] ...

Perhaps I told him these things, perhaps I told him more. He listened, but the last night of the fortnight it was he who talked. And he invented a little child-game, as I thought it. We would sit and scrutinise the Khalig's throngs, looking for the face that symbolised the Khalig's – the soul of Cairo herself passing by.

'If we sit long enough we may – who knows? – look on Cairo herself. Eh, colonel? And we'll know her at once. A face will rise from the crowd-drifts and haunt us, and be gone in a minute, and we'll know we've looked on the Khalig. And all our lives we'll remember that face.'

I took up the jest and played with it, for I also have been a poet. 'Why a woman? And what will she look like?'

'Could the Khalig or Cairo be anything else but a woman? Oh, she'll look a princess and a dream, fair and wild and dark and splendid, robed and crowned, with jewelled feet and jewelled hands. Age-old and very young, evil and dear and desirable, she'll go by. ... With the pride of all her days [26] and all her blood and all the colours of Moqattam.' [27]

But there had come on me the irritation. This bullman unwearied I found I liked less. The Nietzsche, the fascist, [28] the bolshevik – how may any one of them ever reach to the heart of a maid or a sunset? 'Perhaps like the Christ she will pass, poor and despised, with hidden face, without splendour or sin, this Cairo's soul you dream.'

And I can still hear the roar of his bass-laughter.

IV

For a week or so I did not see him at all. He knew his Cairo by then, and could heed to himself. But I had to live and seek out other employers.

Just then came another my way, and for some days I forgot Connan. He was a so-rich Egyptian millionaire, my new client, and had made much money putting the cattle into tins in Argentina. [29] Now he had returned and built a great house in Heliopolis, and me he chartered to compile his family tree. At the end of three days I had proved his descent from Akhnaton, Cleopatra, and de Lesseps, [30] but he was still unsatisfied. But also he paid well, so I took no ease, but spent another three days creating and allying his ancestors to Moses, Mohammed, and the Mamelukes. [31] When I had run out of ancestors I remembered Solga Yon, the Tartar who burned the monks in Kiev. [32] He was my own ancestor, but I take no pride in him. So I brought him on a raid into Egypt and married him into the millionaire's family, thereby ridding my family history of unpleasantness and adding fresh valour to the blood that had tinned the good bullocks of Argentina.

This work kept me away from the Khalig, and to the café of the little Simon I came not. But the evening I returned again, there, where you now sit, great and black against the sunset, like an Assyrian bull-god, was Connan. He was very drunk.

'I will have beer,' I said, 'English beer.'

He shook his head, calling me Fedor, for it was still his jest that I came out of Dostoievsky. 'A man who will drink beer in the Khalig will crack monkey nuts on Mount Olympus.' [33]

'It is a kindlier drink than Greek brandy. I would drink but little of the good Simon's cellar, my friend.'

'I am very certainly drunk, Fedor. But it's a celebration.' He ordered beer for me. 'For I am no longer homeless. I am a citizen of Cairo, and the rat-like Simon boards me by the month, brandy and all.'

He had rented a bare room in the Khalig and bought himself a table and chair and an Indian string-bed. [34] Simon Papadrapoulnakophitos sent him his meals, and he spent his days in sleep and his nights in wandering the streets.

'Down in the Gozi quarter, [35] my room, and above where the metal-smiths chink their tools in early dawn. High up it is, Colonel, and you can hear the rustle of Cairo awake and watch the morning come down the streets like – oh, like Wilde's girl with silver-sandalled feet. [36] And the wind comes from the early Nile, across the Cairene roofs. ... Must come and see me there. Sometime. Moralise to your heart's content, and I'll show you the ugliest nigger that ever salaamed outside a Beardsley grotesque. [37]

'A decadent place, the Gozi.

'Rented the room from an old Jew who takes the precaution of being an absentee landlord. The house has canal tidemarks on it still, is five stories high, and rocks in the traffic. Like a tomb inside – a greasy tomb full of the unease of the unquiet dead [38] – what a phrase! A warren where pallid things live like worms cut off from the sunlight. [39] When I am not listening to the

Khalig itself, I lie abed listening to the house up there in my garret – as God probably lies and listens to the attenuated whisperings of terrestrial life. ... When you come, look out for the stairs, Colonel. They're of stone and have no banisters, and they sweat in the night-time.'

'How long are you to stay there?' I asked.

'Eh? Till I die or Simon's cellars empty.' He brooded for a little and was not drunk. The Khalig cried below us. I heard his voice come in the half-whisper. '... Or I turn poet again.'

So, only for a moment, then he moved his glass of brandy, and laughed his bass-laugh, and was the ruddy animal.

'What a street! Even its ugliness is as nowhere else. Should see the new femme de chambre [40] in the Gozi house. She came three days ago – brings up my food from Simon's waiter and cleans out the room. A Sudanese I think she is, and as hideous as a harpy. [41] Kinky and clumsy, with a plague-pitted face; [42] a body and soul both embryonic. ... Ugly as sin, though willing enough. Hangs round unnecessarily, as though she had something to say and had forgotten the way to say it.'

'A slave, perhaps,' I said. 'There are still slaves.'

'Are there?' He had forgotten me again. So intent did he sit that I turned to look at that which drew his eyes. But it was only the Khalig. Then he spoke again in a whisper.

'Oh, it'll come to me yet. Some day it'll come to me, and I'll write it all – stuff that'll blind and drown the Georgian poetasters.' [43]

'Eh?' I said. 'What stuff?'

'God, man, haven't you eyes? The Khalig – the Epic of the Khalig!' [44]

V

Next night, though I came here to the usual table, there was no Connan. Nor the night after that, nor the next. Perhaps he had gone from Cairo, grown wearied, I thought, or wandered in some other part of our Many-Coloured. I asked of him from the little Simon. He still sent meals to the Gozi quarter, but himself had seen nothing of the Lord.

By this he did not refer to divine revelation, but to Connan, whom he believed a noble, being English, and it being a proper thing for Englishmen to be lords. Just as we of Russia who are neither bolsheviki nor boyars are incomprehensible to English minds.

But the fourth evening the waiter told me a woman awaited me with a message. I went down to the Khalig and the woman who waited came out of shadow and gave me an envelope. Then I saw her face and knew she must be the Sudanese slave.

I turned my eyes quickly from that poor, hideous face, so alien and unlovely. She stood silent, looking at the Khalig, the while I broke open the envelope. It held an unsigned note.

'Come with the messenger, colonel. I have something to show you.'

'This is from the Khawaja [45] Connan?' I asked, not looking upon the face I knew was turned towards me. But she said nothing, and I raised my eyes to her. She was making motions with her fingers. As she did so, set in that so-grotesque mask of a face I saw her eyes, deep and brown and sad, infinitely patient and beautiful eyes. I made foolish noises before I understood.

She was dumb.

VI

The Sudanese left me to climb alone, and in the darkness I found that the stairs did verily sweat, as Connan had made avow. The stairs were without the rail, and far down, as in a well, was the lamp of the street doorway. I spread my fingers against the wall and so climbed to the ultimate attic, where was Connan's room.

I knocked and went in, and Connan, sitting in his chair, wheeled round. For a moment I thought him again drunk. He sat with hair like feathers, and his ruddy face as one sleepless. He read my thoughts and laughed aloud, and at that his laughter echoed down and down into the silence of the house. Not until I heard the echo had I ever noted how cruel was that laugh of his.

'Drunk as a mujik, [46] Fedor. But not with brandy. There was never yet man drunk what I've been drinking.'

He waved his hand to the room, and then I saw. It was littered with the scrawled sheets of paper. On the table in front of Connan was a disordered pile and on the string-bed another. He thrust a bundle upon me.

'Sit down, man, sit down and read. Not all of it – it would take you hours. Only that. Read it.'

I sat on the bed with the pile of pages on my knee, and for the little while the so-dim light of the oil-lamp and the English script vexed me; also it was a chance page, and much had gone before. But almost at once a line leapt to my eyes and rang in my brain. In a minute I had forgotten Connan and his room, and was far on the wings of Connan's genius.

For I had lied. He was a genius, and I knew that this century might never see his like. Once I was the Professor of English Literature, and I have read much in the language, but nothing to compare with those sheets that lived and sang in Connan's garret of the Gozi.

For it was the song of the Khalig he had written, the song of all Cairo, the song of Egypt and the world and the days unnumbered since first the brown Stone Men [47] drifted their dusk hordes across the Nile. In the Khalig's colours and voices he had found the tale of all humanity and told it as I had never read it told before – not even in the songs of your Shelley. [48] Of the dædal [49] wars and love and death and the birth was his tale; sunset and morning and the travail of heat and the lash; the battle-song ringing across the waiting lines at dawn; the bridal song and the birthnight agony, and all the quests and fulfilments of men. All the voices that Cairo has ever known cried from his pages – the emir's [50] voice and the voice of kings and the love-song of the slave outside his wattle hut. [51] ... God mine! I can but remember it now as one remembers the faint chords of music once heard and lost. ...

And I sat and read on and on, till presently, out of the Khalig's colour and clamour I heard arise a new note, faint at first, but clearer growing till it dominated. And I understood with sudden flash of memory of Connan's child-game at Simon's café. What I had read was but background and scene, and this was the Epic of Cairo's soul – of her who was life and more than life, Purpose and Desire and Achievement. Out of the dreams and changing fantasies she came, veiled and singing, lonely and alien, she who was love divine itself – and yet had known no lover. ...

I knew of a great silence. I had finished the last page. I looked at Connan, great, a bull-god in the black shadows from the little lamp. But in the dimness his eyes were bright-shining.

'Well?'

'You are a genius, friend Connan,' I said, and could think of no more.

'Genius? I have achieved the impossible, colonel.' His voice rang with arrogance. 'I've done what every Cairene poet has dreamt of since the days of Harun [52] – found the Soul of the Khalig, as I swore I'd do. One by one I draw the veils from her face.' His cruel laughter boomed again. 'To her first bridal [53] I bring the Spirit of the Khalig.'

I cannot explain it, but a strange shiver passed through me then. I made ready to go. 'If you do not rest and sleep you will have the breakdown.'

But he did not hear me. He had pulled more paper towards him and had begun to write, and when I said good night I might have been to him but one of the murmurs that ever haunted that room.

Then I passed down through the dank darkness, and so into the midnight Khalig, with the music of Connan's lines still ringing in my head. Out in the night-quietened way it was cool and sweet, and I stopped and looked up at the stars. ...

And suddenly a great desolation came on me, under those bright stars. For I could not doubt the truth of Connan's vision. Life – beauty and splendour, blood and strife and colour – and nothing more. Pity and faith and hope – the foolish whispers drowned in the roar of the Khalig. ...

I remember standing with that foolish, wistful ache at heart, looking up at the light-glow from Connan's room.

VII

From dawn the next day I was followed and haunted by a premonition – the foolish thought uprising urgent and crying: This happens, this is Fear. It wheeled through my brain as I worked in a room of the millionaire's house at Heliopolis. Somehow its concern was Connan. All day it haunted me, and in the evening when I returned to change, before taking the millionaire and his family on a moonlight excursion to Gizeh and the tombs of their ancestors, I made a determination. I would go down the Khalig and call at the Gozi house.

But opposite the little Simon's I was seen and a letter brought to me. It had been awaiting me since midday.

I looked at Connan's writing. 'For God's sake come to me. I am afraid.'

That shock that follows a premonition justified was mine. In ten minutes I was in the Gozi, had climbed the stair, and knocked on Connan's door.

He bade me come in, but in the dark doorway I stood hesitant, I remember, till he lit a match, and so the lamp, and we looked at each other. ... And I looked upon the face of a man who had seen terror.

His black-blue hair above the temples was patterned in crisp-grey. I stared at that hair of his, and it seemed to me that the markings were in shape like the impress of fingers. Then I looked round the room. The papers were gone, but in a corner – there was no fireplace – were heaped great piles of charred pages.

'Yes, that's the Epic, that's the song of Cairo's own soul that the world will never hear.'

I turned back to him. He laughed dreadfully and covered his face with his hands. So doing, his fingers covered the greyed lines on his hair, and I stood frozen with understanding.

'God mine, but why?'

'Why? If I hadn't burned it, man, hadn't sent for you, I'd have gone mad. Do you hear?' He stood up and his voice rose to the scream. 'Mad. Look at me. ... God, say it – say I'm not mad I ...'

And then, in a burst of remembered fear and horror, he told me of the happenings of the night and morning. He had written all through the night, leading the Epic triumphant to its triumphant conclusion, but with the coming of dawn he had stopped exhausted. The lightening of the east 54
roused him a little. He went to the window, and opened it, and leaned out into the air. The false dawn had passed from the sky, and it seemed to him quieter than the first morning of creation. Down below, far off in the quarter, he heard the tinkling tools of some Gozi smith. Something else also he heard, but thought it a delusion, and still leant there, leaning with closed eyes.

He had thought he heard a footstep. The delusion persisted. He opened his eyes and turned round. ...

'My God, don't look at me like that, colonel! She was real, I tell you. She stood not three feet away from me, her arms outstretched – *The Spirit of the Khalig, the woman I had created!*'

He covered his face again, then jumped up and raved at my silence.

'She was real, I tell you, real. Veiled and unearthly, but real. [55] I think I cried out, for I knew I was mad. And then, my God, she was in my arms, her arms around my neck, and we kissed each other, and there was such magic and wonder in the kiss as my Epic had never known. ... A ghost, a dream, a symbol – she kissed my lips, colonel! – and called me the one lover for whom she had waited throughout the ages.'

I tried to laugh at him, but the laughter choked in my throat. He was staring blindly in front of him, and suddenly he broke into a whispered chant.

'*Oh my beloved! you for whom I have sought so long! So weary and never-ending they've seemed, the years in their suns and shadows. ... Tonight, at midnight, I come to our bridal.*'

'I think I fainted then. When I awoke the Khalig was stirring below, and I was alone in the room.'

VIII

So, in that early dawn, he had taken the Epic of the Khalig, the thing of beauty which he had created, and burned it. Page by page he had burned it, then spent the rest of the day fighting wave after wave of madness which rose up out of his heart to engulf him.

But the exhaustion he had held off crept on him now. He had sat down on the bed, and, while I talked, his head began to nod in weariness.

I talked on, and he lay back with closed eyes. Of anything and everything I talked, except poetry and the Khalig. I talked of autumn and stars and his English fields, and smell of ploughed lands, and kindly peasant song. Of all the quiet secure things I talked, and in a little I looked at him and saw he was asleep.

I spoke on, dropping my voice to the whisper, then stopped, and tiptoed over to him, and listened to his breathing. Nature had come to his help and he was safe from dream and delusion. ... I remember his face turned from the light, and of how I thought it, in despite its cruelty and wan strength, the face of a child, pitiful and uncomprehending. ...

I closed the door of his room and crept down the stairs of that unquiet house. The darkness moved as if alive. There was no lamp and I had to feel for each step. In the entrance doorway, in the radiance of the street, I stopped and listened, hesitating, then shrugged at the foolishness which had come upon me also.

For it had seemed to me that I heard, far in the depths of the house, the sound of a woman weeping, desolately, as one in despair.

IX

The stuff of dreams that we are! How might I have known – I who do not know even yet?

For next morning Connan was discovered dead in his room. Somewhere near midnight he had shot himself through the heart with the second chamber of his revolver.

In the doorway, also shot through the heart, lay the Sudanese slave. ...

Accident? Coincidence? *God mine, she was clad in the bridal robes of a Cairo maiden!*

V

A Volcano in the Moon

I

That glow above the Khalig? It is the moon-rise. And the so-sudden hush? Always is there this hush at moon-rise. I think our Polychromata turns nightly and looks with startled eyes at that mysteriousness growing to being above the Khalig walls.

A lovers' night and a lovers' moon! But no moon in the world like our Cairo's. ... Tonight they'll be questing the skies from Palais de Kubbah, [1] but perhaps with me alone, who once watched human faith and hope and hate battle amidst those crater-mountains three hundred thousand miles away – battle in the cause splendid beyond their own guessing in days when the Great Shadow [2] still lay black across the world – perhaps with me alone, the spectator, remains the memory vivid still.

Our Cairene moon – she has had the lovers other than those who kiss beneath her light! Not least of them Gellion and Freligrath [3] – Gellion who died of the broken heart because of her, Freligrath who in his last hour must have sat at his study window and peered at that glow in the wonder and the doubt. ...

II

It was in dim days before the War that Thibaut Gellion, coming to Cairo, took to the study of the moon.

He was astronomer with the small private means, the Gellion, a Frenchman of Frenchmen. To Egypt he came because of the health of Mme [4] Gellion and because the clear skies would suit the adventurings of his nights. In the little while the great telescope brought from the Ardennes [5] threatened the stars from an observatory built on the roof of a house in Palais de Kubbah, and in the less while, absorbed, Gellion had forgotten madame. He forgot her often. For she said of the stars that doubtlessly they were leaves in a book of which *le bon Dieu* [6] was author ... but the first page gave her to yawn. Unlike her was Flore, their daughter, who, knowing not God outmoded, had a childish passion for the skies.

He had but few friends in the astronomical world, the little Gellion. Cantankerous, he was the born heretic, the champion of the lost cause and the wild surmise. Yet strict and impartial. His enthusiasm for his heresy of the moment was but equalled by his severity in the sifting of evidence that appeared to support that heresy. As result, he never substantiated the single belief of importance, nor had ever the illusion of so doing – until the year before his death.

After three months of the moon-study in Cairo – in France he had been a Martian, a champion of the good canals [7] – he entered into correspondence with the Bavarian herr professor, August Freligrath, and with him, though for all Germans he had the loathing, became fast friends. Herr Freligrath was among the greatest of selenographers [8] and had long been supporter of the heretical belief that volcanic life was not extinct upon the moon. ...

I am the layman, and all the learned journals of Europe wherein they fight these battles are to me the journals closed. But of Freligrath's belief Thibaut Gellion in Cairo became the supporter enthusiastic. Both had conviction of the play of gases from the volcano in Schroter's Valley [9] (low down there, to the right, above the moon North Pole), but their evidence and photographic records went unaccepted. ... There was not enough evidence, nor was it strong enough, and like Gellion, Freligrath was of himself the severest critic.

In the winter of 1913 the Bavarian professor – he was a widower – came to Cairo with his son, Friedrich, a boy of fifteen. Gellion and his guest passed their days and nights in the Kubbah observatory, and the kindly Mme Gellion, who had even less respect for national animosities than she had for stars, took to her heart the boy Friedrich. He said of the star-study that it did not interest him, being hurtful to the back of the neck, and these two were the pagans disrespectful in a house of sky-worshippers.

He was the boy quick and certain and planful. Upon sight of Flore [10] and the Nile he loved both, and never forgot either. Flore was a year younger. Dispossessed of the observatory, she took Friedrich adventures through the bazaars, into the forbidden Black Warrens, to the far Caliphs' Tombs, to the Ghizeh stones. [11] They were young and light-hearted enough, yet the children of scientists both.

'When I'm grown up,' said Flore, who was a dusky child of the southland French, with the tanned cheeks and steady eyes even then, 'I'll be as Mme Curie. [12] But an astronomer. In America, at Mount Wilson observatory. [13] And discover many stars.' She had an afterthought. 'Then I'll marry Herr Friedrich, and he can do my calculations because he's so good at maths.'

They sat by the Nile, far from Kubbah, while she said this. It was the March day on the seaward-making waters, with Bulaq Bridge in the distance and the world at their feet. Athwart the sunshine spattered and drifted the occasional rain-shower. Long was Friedrich to remember Flore sitting there. But he struggled with the honesty he also possessed.

'You'll be an astronomer, but I – I'll be an engineer.' His second love, the Nile, drew him. 'I'll come to Cairo and build aqueducts and dams to drain and flush the streets each morning. And make an end of dirt and disease and cholera in those horrible Black Warrens.'

She drew a little away from him, being very woman in spite of her youth and her stars. And if you think of their love as childish you understand them not at all. 'But how can we live at Mount Wilson, then?'

He was miserable, but honest still, and you see him, the tow-headed [14] German boy with the puzzled blue eyes, looking from Flore to the Nile. He made halting confession. 'I do not know.'

There was a silence wherein his world cracked, then a movement, and a tanned cheek against his. 'Perhaps Kubbah will do for my telescope.' She sighed a little, abandoning Mount Wilson. 'And I'll love to come and look at your dams.'

'And I at your stars,' he said, and kissed her. A shadow fell on them and the sunshine was suddenly obscured. Flore jumped to her feet.

'We'll have to run. Look at the water glimmering under Bulaq Bridge. There's a storm coming down the Nile.'

III

Six months later, when the War broke out, [15] the Freligraths were again back in Bavaria. [16] The Gellions were at Alexandria, having moved there for the hot weather, and on the first ship that would take him Thibaut Gellion, patriot, was hasting across the troubled Mediterranean of those days to the help of his France. On the day he sailed Flore's mind was troubled with a terrible imagining.

'My father, if you met Herr Freligrath or – or Friedrich – what would you do?'

'Shoot the animal,' he said, and did not smile.

So dim those days – God mine, we may hardly believe them! Least of all that insanity of hate and vituperation which cloaked Europe like the miasma. None of us escaped its poison. Not even science, experimental science, most selfless and international of things, was free. All over the world in the scientific journals rose the wild accusation and the foolish challenge. ... In that lunatic world a German could write an article, in the responsible science gazette, accusing the English of mathematical inability or the deliberate falsifying of their biological experiments – and be believed! Of such cases were many, and of their class were the war-writings of Thibaut Gellion.

He found himself in France too old for soldiering. [17] While he pestered the ministries for employment he furnished the French gazettes with articles on the dishonesty and stupidity of the German astronomers. At the last he even published an attack on Herr Freligrath as the liar and cheat.

No frontier is barrier to hate, and in Bavaria that article was read by August Freligrath, friend and colleague of Liebknecht, [18] one of the two public men of Germany who had tried to keep the peace.

IV

At length in December of 1918, Thibaut Gellion, hospital worker, returned to Cairo to find his wife dead and Flore, up-grown and strange, still holding the house in Kubbah with the aid of her nurse, Mathilde.

Almost a physical wreck came back the little Gellion, and but slowly could his mind turn to the skies and the forgotten stars. He sat amazed and furious in the Kubbah house over the terms of peace and the re-admittance of the German animals to the councils of civilisation.

But he might not long resist the lure of his observatory. Flore, who in the years of his absence had made of herself the competent selenographer, became again his assistant. She found her father one strangely altered. There were long periods when he was the student, quick and sceptical, but those broken by the dark spells when mind and soul seemed to forsake his body. It was as though some shadow wavered across his days – the shadow to her incomprehensible. Unanticipated, mysterious, it would fall and darken even his happiest hour.

Spite all her pity and all her horror, Flore had looked on the War with clear eyes. It was a stupidity; and now it was over, and one might hope and dream again. A week after the return of her father she wrote a letter to Friedrich Freligrath, sending him greetings and remembrances. I think her heart went with that letter, that shy, wistful calling of the boy's name across the gulf of four nightmare years.

The letter was never answered.

V

On some infrequent portions of the dark side of the moon is not always the darkness. In the drunken tilt and libration [19] of the satellite as it swings around our world come the occasions when one at the powerful telescope may glimpse uncharted lands ere these swing back again into the darkness for long periods.

In survey of that shadow-land Thibaut Gellion sought to find his old self – as Flore sought forgetfulness of the wound to her young, proud heart. Hour by hour, in the full-moon glow, they would chart and photograph and sketch.

Then presently the happening unexpected – the night when her father, with amazement in his voice, called Flore to the telescope, and in the little observatory of Kubbah were the strained hours of watching and the hasty erection of camera apparatus. Next night was the same, the while the telescope eye hung above a minute edge of the lunar disc, where the dazzling whiteness of day on the moon fell sheerly off into utter darkness and a snow of stars. On that edge of disc was a crater-mountain, uncharted and little observed. It tilted sunwards, and also almost full to the earth, and far within its towering walls was a drifting smudge like the smoke from a cigarette.

They were looking across the lifeless wastes at the first active volcano indisputable upon the moon.

VI

So Gellion was convinced, for, unlike the volcanoes he had once suspected in Schroter's Valley, it was evidently a crater in the eruption violent and continuous. Yet to the proof of its existence in the astronomical world were the difficulties most desperate. There was no measuring its depths of crater-wall in the position he had seen it, and not for an uncertain period of months would that tract of the lunar land be again observable. Lying inside that borderland where were to be considered conditions and contingencies such as might well dishearten even the super-mathematician, the crater could be but seldom viewed from the earth, and even then at different angles and power because of the approach and recession of the moon-floor. In the most moon observations it would be altogether beyond telescopic range. ...

Yet – to prove its existence and prophesy its reappearance would be to crown his life-work.

I can but glimpse the task enormous of the little Gellion. Later was I to make of the matter a study that I might understand a little. But that is still a little.

Yet, after the stupendous toil of a month, he completed the task of compiling a chart of periodicity – the times when the volcano inside the crater might be seen at its full and no other explanation of the smudge-phenomenon be possible.

In that month of intensive calculation and rejection occurred still the hours when the shadow mysterious fell upon him and he was approachable by none but Flore. But such moods grew the rarer with the nearing of success, and he finished his thesis with the conclusion that once in every three months the volcan-glow [20] of the lunar crater would be clear to earthly eyes.

VII

The day after that first momentous observation I had had with Flore an encounter in the bazaars. It was in Ramadan, [21] and we were both the strayed and foolish spectators of a procession Muslim. For the little it seemed that El Azhar [22] was to cut our throats for reasons religious, but Flore, white-clad and slim like a boy, and unafraid, stood smiling and whistling the little tune, and I spoke in Arabic with the big voice. So they allowed us to pass and we made acquaintance.

'I have to thank you, M. le Colonel.' [23]

I made protest. 'But it was you who saved us. The Muslim – they believe a whistling woman to be possessed of a devil.'

She had the entrancing laughter of the grave-eyed. 'So I would have been if they had touched me.'

So I became the occasional visitor at Kubbah, was once – greatest of favours – allowed to look through the telescope, and was many times lectured by the little Gellion on the subject of star-charts and German iniquity.

Flore had but few friends in Cairo – she had been too busied with her stars – and I took her to the amusement and relaxation she would have denied herself. Then, for a little, she would forget moon and craters and her father's moods and that unanswered letter, and be merely a girl, with the laughter and the teasing and the enchantment.

She had the love for music and dancing and the pretty clothes, and to me, the romantic, there seemed but one way in which these could ever unite and mingle with her passion for the stars. Once, in the half-jest, as we sat in the scraping of violins in a house above the Nile, I asked her when that would be.

Is there anything quite so tragic as the bitter laughter of youth? She turned away, that I might not see her eyes.

'Oh – when the Nile runs back through Bulaq Bridge!' [24] she said.

VIII

He was the Frenchman, Gellion. On the eve of publication of his discovery, which, if verified, would change the face and nature of the science selenography, he delayed that publication, remembering his one-time colleague, Freligrath of Bavaria. Forgetful of all that had passed, he despatched his calculations to Bavaria and invited verification of the phenomenon before it was made known to the European societies. The time for the second full observation of the crater was now near.

But August Freligrath, who had gone through a war and two revolutions, who had once rescued his son with a signed pardon the while that son, young and a rebel, stood facing a firing-squad, [25] was a changed man also. He had been shocked and embittered by the Four Years and their aftermath, and there lingered with him memory of that article which Gellion had written in the far days of 1915.

Yet he was honest. When the letter came from Cairo he was already a sick man dying as result of privations suffered in political prisons. But he began the study close and intent of that section of moon-surface where Gellion believed he had made the epochal discovery. On the night of the full observation he sat long hours at his telescope in spite the remonstrances of Friedrich.

And within Gellion's crater were only the black and steady shadows of no light. ...

All next day August Freligrath sat at his desk, writing as in the fever. A week later, in the German astronomical journal, appeared under his signature the savagely-satirical account of the Gellion claim and his own disproval of it.

'The romantic French amateur, like the poor, is always with us. To suggest – as undoubtedly M. Gellion himself would do were he investigating the claims of a "Bosche" [26] – that he is either liar or cheat is possibly to exaggerate. Rather is it a case of mistaken devotion. With so strong a gift for self-deception and undisciplined enthusiasm, astrology, not astronomy, would seem to call M. Gellion.'

IX

That journal came to the Gellions already dismayed and uncomprehending. They also had looked in a crater-well of blackness and on no smudge of gases from the volcano they believed existed.

To Flore's father, in spite his pugnacity, the article of Freligrath's was as death-blow. He shrank from it, very small and pitiful and suddenly aggressive not at all. I went to see him, ill in bed, and he lay with closed eyes and moving lips. Within the week he was dead.

He was buried next day, for it was summer, and of stifling heat. I came back to the little house in Palais de Kubbah, to one who did not weep but stood with clenched fists and stormy eyes.

'Oh God, those Bosches, those German swine! Father was right always, and I wrong. ... Oh, Anton, my friend, I am so lost. ...'

And she wept a little then, so proud and angry and desolate, and of comfort I had none. Instead, my friend, I stood shamed in front of her – shamed that I was a man and with all men responsible for those twin deserts we make and call by the names of war and peace. ...

I walked home from Palais de Kubbah that evening. Near Zeitoun [27] the moon came up, and I stopped and stared at it and lighted my pipe, with about me on the white road the shadows like dancing ghosts. And there came on me with force of vivid revelation a fantastic thought –

The adventure-soul in man [28] – the sum of its selfless achievements was as that volcano in the moon, the flaring light, the beacon in the wastes. And perhaps, like that volcano, it also was doomed to cease and pass, was already flickering to extinguishment before vanishing for ever in some final night of war and hate.

X

Unexpectedly the new development. I went one night to Palais de

Kubbah and found a cold, pale Flore with eyes of a stranger. She had the story for me. Friedrich Freligrath was in Cairo. He had called at the Gellion house and been refused admittance. Then he had written a letter and enclosed with it a sheet of paper in another hand.

In hesitant French, set out in the ornate German script, the letter. 'I tried to see you, but the good Mathilde would not even know me. My dear, it is surely a mistake. I had no part in the disagreements of my father and M. Gellion.

'A month ago the Egyptian Government set a European competitive examination for a constructional engineer. Spite my deplorable youthfulness, I have been selected to build those aqueducts I promised and which you said you would love to see. May I come and look at your stars? ...'

His father had been found dead at his study window three weeks before, and the sheet of paper enclosed held the beginnings of a letter found amongst Herr Freligrath's papers. It had probably been the last thing written by the Bavarian astronomer.

I spelt out the German. It was a note addressed to Thibaut Gellion. ... They had both, perhaps, been too hasty. There was a mistake in the calculations; they had not allowed for. ...

They had not allowed for death, for there the letter ended.

XI

Secretly I noted the address of young Freligrath. He lived in Abbassieh, and next evening I went to see him and to him explain myself. He sat and stared at me, then laughed and passed his fingers through the upstanding, tow-coloured hair he had retained from boyhood. He was a personable young man, planful and eager still, but with the surface flippancy of his generation.

'So I am the son of a murderer, eh? And the little Flore a chauvinist? What a world! Have a drink?'

We spoke in the French for a while, for I have little German. Then we made a discovery. He was the enthusiast of the language English, as I am. Some far-uncle of his it was, he told me, who translated your Tennyson [29] into the so-exquisite German.

Thereafter we spoke English and were presently the interested acquaintances. I took him with me to see our Polychromata by night, and here, in the Khalig, in the seat where you now sit, introduced him to the little Simon and his so-surprising English beer. And then I heard details that filled out the troubled Gellion-Freligrath story.

'That letter you speak of – I never saw it. Bavaria was too busied with bayonets those days to pay much heed to its mails.'

I told him that in the next moon was another night of the full observation, and that this time Flore Gellion was confident of proving the volcano's existence. He shook his head.

'Her father's calculations are correct enough – so far as they go. Either his premises were wrong, or he forgot some integral fact. I know. Mathematics is my hobby also, and I spent the voyage from Europe in checking my father's copy of the Gellion periodicity-chart. It is absolutely correct. She'll see no volcano.'

'But the uncompleted letter of Herr Freligrath?'

He shrugged. 'I do not know, and what he believed we will never know. In his later years he worked and thought like a man half-blinded in a shadow, my father – the mountain-shadow of the War.' [30]

XII

With but the short space of time for the task Flore, whatever startled ache of memory Friedrich's arrival in Cairo had awakened, flung herself into the checking of the Gellion calculations. To speak of my meeting with Freligrath I could find no opportunity.

But I learned that nowhere in the calculations of her father was a mistake to be found. They must have been built on the false assumptions basically. Yet that was impossible, else how could she have shared the telescopic illusion?

The matter of the uncompleted letter of August Freligrath worried her, though she pretended to scorn it. What had they not allowed for, the German and her father?

Once she and Friedrich met, in the Sharia Kamel, [31] coming face to face and knowing each other at once. I heard of the chance meeting from Friedrich, for of it Flore made no mention.

'She looked me through and then passed on.' He laughed; laughter was his cloak. But presently he was angry. 'Yet she is Flore Gellion and I Friedrich Freligrath spite our fathers and all the years of blood and hate. What have we to do with those weary animosities? I tell you there was a half-moment, before she cut me, when I could have taken her and kissed her, and she kissed me. I saw it in her eyes. ... And then the Shadow.'

He forgot his laughter-cloak, this pleasant young man, and I saw the Spartacist [32] of Bavaria. 'Curse their mean and dirty little nationalisms, their petty spites and their petty patriotisms! Curse the infernal moon and all its volcanoes! What have we to do with their lunatic astronomical past, dead Gellion and dead Freligrath?'

'Some day, being dead, the future may demand that of your past,' I said. But he paid no heed. Instead, stood staring at the sky in the kind of desperation.

Overhead, like a portent, hung the sickle moon.

XIII

From moon-rise on the calculated night Flore Gellion sat long hours in the observatory, looking up under her eye-shades through the light-flooded glass of the giant lens. She sat in a little saddle below the telescope, and in the observatory was a dead silence but for the ticking of the clockwork which synchronised the movements of the telescope with the minute motion of the lunar disc. I sat and looked at her, or wandered to the uncurtained portion of the glass roof and stared up, foolishly, at the full moon. Sometimes Flore brought the great camera into play and I helped with the changing of slides. At moon-set I went down and brought up the coffee Mathilde had made. Flore had come from the telescope. She sat at a little table, her hands covering her eyes.

'Only tired, Anton.' There was the break in her voice. 'And my eyes.'

'And the volcano?'

'Look and see. Quick, for the disc is beginning to fade.'

Our Cairene moon – she sails the sky a mystery and wonder to the naked eye. No less the mystery of her strange lands which start to the being under the telescope. In a little was the blur gone from my eyes and that unearthly landscape lay below me, etched in ink, under its pitiless day.

Upstanding full in the centre of the lens, its outer sides clothed in the dazzle of sunshine, I looked for the first time upon the fateful Gellion crater.

XIV

Here, where I had promised to meet him, Friedrich was awaiting me the following night, and I made no greetings but answered the question in his eyes.

'There is no volcano. Flore herself could see no trace of activity, and the photographs show none.'

There came on his face pity and something of dismay. But I think it was no selfish dismay. 'I had hoped after all. ... I spent the better part of last night, rechecking the chart and trying to find some omission. If only I were an astronomer! ... Did you look?'

'I looked. Tundra and rock and blazing daylight and the mountain-shadows. Shadows like the spattered drops of night. It is a world of shadow.'

There was silence, and then suddenly his quick breathing. I looked up and found him staring at me. 'My God, of course it is!'

'It is? –'

But he was on his feet. 'The seasonal orbit-roll! [33] Why didn't they think – but they were blinded in shadows themselves!... Or did my father guess it before he died? Eh? *The shadow, man, the mountain-shadow!'*

And he was gone.

XV

I spent the next three days with a tourist-party down in Helwan-les-Bains, [34] and came back to Cairo in the evening and the tiredness. It was late and I was about to undress, when I was told of the messenger newly come for me

I went down and found it the good Mathilde, grumbling and indignant.

'You are to come with me, mon [35] colonel. So mademoiselle will have it.'

I made reflection that youth knows not of tiredness. 'She is ill?'

The old Frenchwoman was very indignant. 'Sick of the mind, I think,' and sat opposite me in the taxi which had brought her, saying nothing more.

She showed me up into that moon-showered observatory, with its clocks and instruments, and I knew the telescope in action by the ceaseless tick. But the saddle-seat was unoccupied. There were no lights, nothing but the play of shadows, yet in those shadows the murmur of voices that puzzled me.

Then the electric light came on, and Flore was in front of me, and from the seat behind her rose someone else. She stood as if to conceal this other from my gaze, but I took her shoulders and put her aside, and looked.

It was Friedrich Freligrath.

And then, while I stared from the one to the other, they were as embarrassed children till Flore's arm was in mine. She pulled me to the telescope seat and sat me in it.

'Look, colonel.'

It was the same lunar landscape, the same crater into which I had looked. But in the crater-mouth, in place of the inked shadow, was a fainter blackness, and presently, as I looked, I caught my breath at that wonderful sight and knew something of awe and fear.

For the shadow moved and changed, and suddenly lightened and lightened till it was almost a glow, there, in the wild lands a quarter of a million miles away. I swung round to look at these two behind me, and then back again to peer across the gulfs at that amazing flicker of the gas-clouds.

And then Friedrich's hand was on my shoulder, and he was explaining.

'It was the shadow of the crater-walls M. Gellion did not take into account. He found it impossible to measure the depths of those walls, and then must have forgotten them as a factor – the gradual encroaching of their shadow, in a circular tilt, upon the crater itself. But for that omission the chart of periodicity is correct. The night you and Flore watched, that volcano was moving there, but it lay in the shadow of its own crater-walls. With the passing of the lunar year the acceleration of the shadow is swifter than the tilt of the moon-floor. ... Oh, I'm an astronomer, colonel! I've been absorbing lunar lore through the pores of my skin during the last seventy hours!'

'And now – ?' I asked, and then stopped, for I knew.

'Friedrich had inspiration when he heard you talk of the shadows. He went home, estimated a depth of crater-wall, allowed for the shadow, and amended my father's calculations. ... Oh, the pity of it that they should never know! Last time Herr Freligrath and my father held their observations – if they had delayed two days they would have seen the volcano. This time it was not observable until four days after the originally-calculated date.' She was silent, then laughed a little, but with tears in her eyes and her hands outstretched to the German enemy, putting the question to which she should have known the answer. 'My dear, you've surpassed us all! How did you do it – you whom astronomy always so bored?'

XVI

I walked home again that night, for it was too late to find a vehicle and my tiredness was gone. Flore and Friedrich came part of the way with me, talking of the Gellion-Freligrath discovery which they were to publish. At parting they laughed and kissed me, being both impulsive children of the Frankish [36] blood, and whether they ever went home that night to further scandalise the good Mathilde or else walked the roads singing and planning the storming of the stars, I do not know. But I remember that as I heard their young voices crying au revoir [37] down the white moonlight, there came to me a whimsical memory. Surely the Nile was running back through Bulaq Bridge this night!

Then I forgot those lovers rediscovered; they faded from my mind, cyphers and symbols in a story yet untold, an adventure uncompleted. For I found myself on that stretch of Zeitoun road where, but a short month before, I had stood in silence under the moon, alone with my vision of human futility.

And then I knew that I had dreamed. While the truth remains a passion even in the darkened and wounded mind of a Gellion or Freligrath, while passion itself flowers forth in a Friedrich a bloom that is other than desire, there is no night that may ever blind the flame that lights the wastes. [38]

There are only the shadows that pass.

VI

The Life and Death of Elia Constantinides [1]

I

Pull in the deck-chair here, my friend. So. Now we can sit and watch our Nile slip past, and pity the poor Cairenes this sultry noon. ... Eh, a book even this holiday jaunt to Barrage! A light one, I trust – a mystery of pursuit and villain-exposure? Many such I myself read, hoping that in one at last will the villain triumph. ...

Campanella! [2] God mine, it is thirty years since I read him, since I too walked the City of the Sun. In Russia; surely in the dawn of time! Campanella. ... Perhaps they were his streets that Elia glimpsed; perhaps in those pages long forgotten lies interpretation for another dreamer who saw the Ghosts of Sunland.

Ghosts? The unquiet dead who mow and moan across the astral planes? Not such were they who haunted Elia from that first vision on the Asian hill to the last dark hour of all. Not such are they with whom – who knows? – perhaps this hour, the exile gone home, he walks the City of the Sun!

II

And his tale: three [3] years younger than our century, Elia, born in Samos, of the dark Ionian stock [4] that has watched the nations pass and repass to the Asian shore, the processions phantasmagoric, since the days of Homer. [5] He was an unwanted child, the child indeed unexpected and inexplicable. His mother, a strange, irritating woman who all her life had loved solitude, who would even linger in the night-fields to find that wonder of silence, made no explanations at his birth, for she was dead. So also, for the little, it seemed that Elia would not live.

But live he did, and was normal but for the one ailment that vexed his early years and the Island doctors. This was some complication of the blood pressure, resulting at the irregular intervals in the violent and erratic functioning of his heart. Here, when in Cairo many years later, my friend Dr Adrian [6] tested that heart, and was by it the much and morbidly intrigued. ...

From no such intriguement did Constantinides *papakes* [7] suffer. The brute farmer, desperately delving a livelihood from his land, with already the adequate family, and soured by the loss of his wife, Elia remained to him the unwanted and mysterious interloper. With such the atmosphere in that little farm of the Samian slopes, where from dawn to dusk was the unending toil, it was miracle that interloper survived childhood.

At the age of five or six he was working on the vinelands or tending the goats on the hills. At night he slept in a small room shared by his three brothers. The bed held but three – a jeering three, and the little Elia's couch was a heap of sacking. By dawn he would be out of doors again, trudging errands to the village or driving the flock out to the hill-pastures.

And in that environment he grew into a boyhood the living refutation of all philosophies determinist. He had been born with some unquenchable well of friendliness and wonder – these the gifts that all his life he was to give the world – in his heart. From the other Elia I was to know I can build the mind-picture of that Samian boy of six – slight, and pale, with the shock of the matted dark hair, the broad brow and girl's mouth, the stare of friendly eyes. Not once, I think, in the desperate wrongs and bullyings of those early years, did he apprehend cruelty as conscious cruelty; always puzzlement, never resentment, followed the tears of pain in those eyes of his. ... Once, in the moment of discernment, his father cursed him for those his 'fey' [8] eyes.

And then came the first of those happenings that were to interweave throughout his life like the threads of gold in a cloak of frieze. He was seven years of age, had spent the day in the vine-plots, and was tramping home in the sunset. It had been the day of desperate toil and heat, and his boy's head and body were alike the throbbing ache. But something in that sunset he was so long to remember caught even then his stare of attention. 'It was so quiet I thought it waited for me,' he was to tell.

So, for a moment, then, the thing unknown since early childhood, came a sudden sick giddiness. He fell to his knees and lay against a bank, gasping, the blood throbbing in his ears. In his pain he gripped his head with his hands, raised that head a little, and then, seeing, gave a cry of wonder that he yet heard but as a whisper.

For, below his feet, from that hill that looked out to the mainland and was called the Asian hill, was a Samos and sea other than he had ever known. Where the village had sprawled a moment before swept up to sparkling points a great building of glittering walls, and far in the haze of the sunset in Asia the light struck fire from another such shining structure. Where had straggled the rows of vine-poles were marshalled now against the fervent sky line on line of giant trees, unknown. And upon the wind the smell of those trees came to him, and the smell was as of flowers.

He sat and stared. He was not afraid, only wondering, and then, for the swift moment of the utter conviction that shone and passed upon his soul, he knew that he had seen those trees before, had lain beneath them some other sunset and watched the great birds go wheeling into the gloaming of the Asian coast. ...

There was not a sound but suddenly he became aware that he was not alone. He turned his head and beside him saw standing, very still and intent and grave against the unearthly silence and the horizontal limnings of the sunset, a naked boy.

So close was he that Elia could see the flex of muscles in his neck as he moved his head. That head was crowned with flowers, and, taller than Elia, he stood with one hand resting manfully on an unclad hip and the other shading his eyes. There was about him a still friendliness, a companionship, miraculous when allied to that strange beauty of sun-painted skin and crowned valour of head. So, dimly apprehending, the little Elia gazed at him, the moment of coloured and wonderful silence.

And then, I think for the first and last time in his life, he knew fear. All the dark tales of the Islands and the Asian shores, the debased imaginings and superstitions, clamoured suddenly in his boy-mind. It was a devil who stood beside him, a *phantasma*, [9] a ghost. He crossed himself, tried to cry out, tried to stand up.

And at that the naked lad wheeled round on him with lowered head and sheen of body, and in the so-doing became a mist, a nothingness, leaving a scared and remorseful Greek boy who sat a long hour to stare at the brown-roofed village and later find his way home through a palpitating darkness.

III

Nor, strangely, did memory of that fantastic vision die. It crept with Elia up through the years. Alone in the darkness, he would lie awake and think of it. Out in the fields, in the moments of supreme weariness, bright as ever in remembrance it would return to him. And once or twice, in moments of vivid happiness and laughter – for even were these in that resented childhood of his – it would seem to him that in a moment he would look again on Sunland, that see it indeed he did, dimly, through the shaken boughs of scented trees. ...

These are his words, and I try to follow, watching that Greek lad grow up amidst his vines and goats and the sunsets vision-bringing of the Asian hill. In the little time, as it seemed, his brothers were men, broad of shoulder, quarrelsome still, capable of the much wine-drinking and the sniggering tale. Elia remained the drudge, silenter than when a child, yet quiet, I think, with a quietness that invited no fresh imposition of drudgery. From those eyes that his father held 'fey' something of the wonder had perhaps faded and had come the puzzlement. For all through the years and that silence of his, the friendliness in him stilled but unchanged, grew the questioning: Why?

Drunkenness, blows, cruelty; the seeking of shelter and stifling sleep when the night was a velvet miracle; shame of nakedness; filth of body when the sea cried its loveliness through each dawn; fear of solitude; patriotism and hate; unwanted fatherhood; worship of an incomprehensible and unlovely God; toil and toil from dawn to dusk that toil and toil might be repeated. ... The list unending. These things – why were they?

And here the difference. Not as you and I and the hundreds other in the young revolt did he question these things or their like. No hatred and rebellion moved him. Only the aching wonder, the fantastic disbelief. ... Life was not so, could not be so. It was some trick, some play of shadows, some foolish dream from which he and the world would presently awake.

And northwards and eastwards throughout those cumulating years clamoured the great, unmeaning guns of the European War. Under their clamour two of his brothers vanished to Athens and the army. [10] The third betook himself off to the other side of the island as a fisherman. Was left Elia alone on the little farm with the dour, greying man who drank the more now and seldom spoke a word to the son he hated.

Came an autumn with the guns a dying clamour and Elia seventeen years of age. Constantinides *papakes* had developed rheumatism and might not move, and in the week of the great Island fair it was Elia who loaded the year's produce into the clumsy waggon and with that waggon journeyed miles away, to the seaboard town of Vathy. [11] He had been there but once before, and that at the age of eight, and in the evening of the first day of the fair he wandered the streets like a traveller astounded from the planet Mars. ...

She beckoned to him from a doorway in a side-street, and he stopped and stared at her, at her youth, the eyes unabashed, the painted lips. [12] He knew nothing of women, had hardly ever seen a girl of his own age. The most innocent, perhaps, of any in that city, he looked at her, and then, at sight of that smile, I think his dark boy's face lighted and lighted with the friendliness that was his. He went towards her and she took his hands and suddenly he found himself trembling on the verge of speech and wonder unquestioning.

IV

In the dawn he awoke, in the very first of the light, and the silence that wrapped all Vathy seemed a threatening thing in that foetid room. There was splash of early sun through the grimed window that overlooked the sea. Slowly, unbelievingly, he turned his eyes from the room to one who slept beside him. ...

In sick remembrance he crept out of bed, somehow crossed the room, seized the window-catch and flung it open. The sea-air smote his face like a blow. With that current of wind came sudden giddiness, the gripping at his heart. He gasped, stood swaying and blinking; gripped the window-ledge. ...

The unclean room with its peeling walls and gaudy eikon [13] had vanished. Out from a great embrasure that was not a window but a wide sweep of loggia [14] battled in stone he looked upon the sunrise and the sea. Behind arched a great room with painted ceiling and the flutter of white draperies around a bed that swung in the morning air. And beside him, unheeding his nearness, standing together in the morning swordfall of sunlight, was the boy of the Asian hill and one other.

The boy of the Asian hill – but a boy no longer. Straight and golden and splendid in the morning of manhood he stood, the sea-breeze in his hair, his arm about his companion. And then, as Elia watched, the unknown companion turned half-round in that embrace, glancing up with drowsy eyes into the face of him who held her. And at sight of her and that look on her face, at that white radiance of unshielded loveliness and drowsy tenderness, a moan quivered from the lips of Elia. He sank to his knees: the picture wavered and blurred before his eyes. Yet, for a stayed moment, was one detail vivid – he who had been the boy of the Asian hill swinging round till he stood plain-seen. ...

And then Elia laid his face in his hands and wept, there, in the foetid room of the harlot, with the sea-air blowing upon him.

For it was his own face he had looked upon.

V

He went home from Vathy, a boy still living the memory of a dream. But the shadows came swift across it. Within a fortnight of his return the conscript officers came down from Smyrna [15] upon the village, read the long and puzzling proclamation and marched away Elia and a score of others for training to fight the Turks.

All over Greece that year swept the wave of jingo patriotism. Greece was to grow an empire – again! to hold again in its length and breadth the ancient coast which the dreamy Ionians had colonised. In the great camp on Chios [16] it was an exultant and singing conscript army of which Elia found himself part – Elia with the friendly, questioning eyes and puzzled brow.

For there were things of that life that wrung his soul with the pain of their beauty: reveille [17] shrilling down each clean, sweet morning, the song and laughter and the beat of many feet upon the march, the stark, dark hours of sentry-go. These things that lived though past and dead, shining things. But there were others.

I think they waked in him his first anger – the guns, the bayonets, all the clownish apparatus of mass-murder. Insanities impossible, yet insanities insistent, the hideous nightmare shadows that darkened sunlight from march and camp. They could not be, they were but the horrific imaginings. And yet –

But neither disentanglement of impressions nor rebellion was he ever to achieve on Chios. For within six weeks he and the thousands of other conscripts, long lines of the half-trained columns with shining new English guns, [18] had landed at Smyrna and were marching up through Asia Minor to that battle-line that beckoned and thundered in the east beyond Manissa. [19]

And as they marched ever nearer, and the rattling of great windows quivered in that remote sky, Elia was to tell me how the singing presently died. Then the happening strange enough. For he found that it was he himself who restarted the singing, and the others who followed his voice. A strange white happiness [20] came on him in the midst of that aching horror of surmise that held all the column.

'You see,' he was to tell me, 'I knew it could not be real. Life could not be as mad as that. There was something other than death and mutilation to which we were marching. There was something splendid behind those hills.'

And then came down the rains.

Through miles of warm downpour they marched. But they were never to reach the expected battle-line. For that afternoon Kemal Pasha smote the flimsy Greek lines [21] as with a great fist, and the columns of reinforcements found themselves like bewildered ships breasting the westward-pouring [22] tides of rout. They halted and flung up hasty entrenchments throughout the night, and in the dawn the Anatolians [23] attacked.

He was never to remember that night or its happenings. Not even of shadow-land was it. But later he was to be told of it, and the reason of the decoration pinned on his tunic. For they told him that he sang throughout each wave of attack, fought with mad fury, took over a sector of line when all the officers were dead or deserted, and held that sector with a few hundred amazed and stimulated men till they were in danger of being surrounded. And a madness came on his men as well. For they too sang throughout those beating hours of attack and counter-attack, and singing, led by Elia, marched off through the dusk of next day, an undefeated rearguard.

The Greek army poured towards the sea and Smyrna, and fighting and retreating behind came Elia and his company. Communications were lost, and but for the hasty confirmation of Elia as their commander they had no instructions. Late the second afternoon, the Turks close behind, they marched into Smyrna – Smyrna expectant of massacre and looting, with streets blocked by terrified crowds pressing down to the ships and safety. Here and there a fugitive stopped to scream taunts and execrations at the staggering, blood-weary company that Elia led.

And then, in that black hour, weak for loss of sleep, swaying forward under pressure of a will that was not his own, there happened again to the Samian boy – he was little more – that thing which he had twice known since childhood – the gripping sensation about his heart, the beating of blood in his ears. He reeled but did not fall; instead, found himself marching on, his feet passing and repassing without his volition. The blood-pressure eased from his ears and now there shrilled and shrilled in them music stirring as a trumpet heard at night.

No Smyrna street he trod. Instead, was the glassy way, half-shadowed in sunset, half the strange blaze of light. The way thronged and cheering it was, and down the opening lane of that throng – men and women, flower-crowned and cheering, golden and kind and glorious – he was marching. Behind, amidst that voiced exultation, came on his company – explorers from the outer wastes of the universe, an expedition returned from the deeds that men would sing for ever. And beside Elia marched one whom he knew, one whom he had seen as boy and youth, one who turned calm, searching eyes to left and right.

Then, a glimpsed moment, Elia saw for whom he searched. She stood a little apart, sweet and fair, serene on her lips the little smile. And there happened in that visioned wonder the wonderful thing. For across the ways, not on the glorious being who marched beside Elia, *but on him, himself,* fell her eyes, and in their depths he saw leap swift pity and compassion. ...

The picture of a moment, all this. His little company saw Elia's hand go to his eyes, saw him half halt and turn back. He was in Smyrna, in the raining darkness. Behind, on some hill, raved the nearing guns of the Anatolians.

VI

They took him to Athens, and the story of his fight in the rear of the retreating army – a story of heroism in those dark weeks of shame and black defeat – thrilled through all Greece. He was decorated, confirmed *archegos* [24] in the army, discreetly and hastily taught to read and write – and given the training of new gangs of recruits from the Peloponnesus. [25]

These things happened to him without his consent and barely with his understanding. He found himself in a new life that included the possession of a manservant and the obligation to drink much wine and seek amorous adventure. With smiling, puzzled friendliness he took those gifts in his hands and looked at them. ... To train men to kill each other for no need or reason, to drink when he did not thirst, to seek love of women as alternate narcotic and stimulant. ... It was the idle fantasy, and from it the young and popular Captain Constantinides turned with an impatient sigh to the upbuilding of that strange, dreaming faith evolved in a night in Smyrna.

Somewhere, somewhere if he searched, awaited him his *moira,* [26] his fortune; somewhere was explanation to shadow and sun-dream. Somewhere, in the world of reality, friend and lover, awaited *kore loukophotos,* [27] the maid of the dusk. ...

With that staggering simplicity that was of his soul-stuff he did the simple and obvious thing. He deserted – though he never paused to think of it as desertion. He dismissed his servants, laid aside his uniform, and clad himself in some other clothes he had bought. Then he went down to the Piræus, [28] walked aboard a ship, and asked for work. By some chance the ship, about to sail, lacked its full complement of crew, and he was engaged at once.

He knew nothing of the ship's destination. Friendly, obedient, with that still, dark face and the stare of questioning eyes, he set about learning the tasks of a common sailor. It was the unseaworthy cargo-boat he had boarded, and as it lurched southwards across the Mediterranean an unwonted contentment came on him. His search had begun.

He left the boat at Alexandria in the same unconsidered indifference in which he had boarded it. He came into Egypt, alien, unafraid, unthinking, still that wondering peasant boy of the Asian hill. In the railway station he bought a ticket, found a train leaving for Cairo, climbed into it, and by the end of the journey looked out and saw the Pyramids marching up against the reddened desert of evening.

VII

All that night he wandered Cairo, turning south at Bab el Hadid, down Clot Bey, [29] and so, going eastward, till he came to the Khalig. Through the hours, till after one o'clock in the morning, he stood under an archway and watched the throngs go by. Some night of festa it had been, and faces innumerable lifted and sank continuously from darkness into the glare of the lamps – faces he searched in a wondering wistfulness. Then, crossing a deserted Khalig, he set out again on his nameless search. Down through dark lanes towards the Suk el Nahassin [30] he must have wandered in those still hours, under lighted balconies and shuttered windows, later in the ghostly radiance of flowering stars, seen far up, as from the bottom of a canyon. [31] Drifts of singing and drowsy voices came to him, belated travellers, the fewer and fewer with the wearing of the night, slipped passed him in that silvered darkness. Once he stood a long while and listened to the baying of dogs in one of the khans [32] – an eerie crying of desolation that made him shiver, though he knew not why. And once he heard a lost child weeping, and sought it through a maze of alleys, till he lost himself and emerged a long time afterwards to see the stars paling over Citadel. [33]

In the silence of our Cairene false dawn he turned back towards the Khalig. Long lines of donkeys were passing through it to the early marts. An occasional native, wrapped and hooded, for the morning was chill, hastened by. Elia sat down under the archway, waiting for the day. High up above his head waved already the tentative banners of the sunlight, but the Khalig itself was still in shadow.

Perhaps he slept then, for he started to knowledge of the warmth of day and the sound of approaching footsteps. He raised his head and looked out, the sun blinding his eyes a moment. Then he leapt to his feet.

For the footsteps were those of that girl who had looked her pity at him across the faery streets of Sunland Smyrna.

She, and no other. Down the Khalig she came, the sun a radiance about her head, unveiled, ungarbed, herself the morning, dreams in her eyes. Lightly she came, unconscious [34] that look of his that was a prayer. And then in a moment he had cleared the archway shadow and stood in front of her. The Khalig flickered to his gaze, he closed his eyes, reached out and seized her hands. ...

There was a startled ejaculation, a tugging, a whimper of fear. He opened his eyes – and looked down on the frightened face of the harlot of Vathy.

VIII

He had found his fortune. Only then, I think, did he see for an instant, and for the first time, his dreams and puzzlements as but the idle stupidities – awoke to the world that men called sanity and looked about him – the impossible, fantastic world that made of his love a woman of the streets.

They were married within a week at the Greek Consulate – the frightened, haggard-faced woman and the Samian boy with the dark, puzzled eyes which she too thought 'fey'.

'But you do not understand,' she had protested tearfully. 'I am – I am –'

Dazed, aching of heart, he had yet kissed her, with wonder for her tears and the face marred by things unspeakable. 'You are Kalo [35] whom I love,' he said, with a sick amazement at his own words.

Late that night, when they sat alone together, she said a wonderful thing that yet seemed to stab him to the heart.

'I saw you once again after that morning in Vathy. In Smyrna, before I came to Egypt. It was the night the Turks took the city.' [36]

He turned towards her, a lost child, weariness in his face. 'Oh, I am tired.'

And then, at sight of the pity and compassion dawn in her eyes, he stared a moment and knelt weeping beside her.

IX

With their little store of money they rented a flat of three rooms in a narrow alleyway off the Khalig. Then Elia set to the desperate search for work. He laboured as a road-sweeper, as a water-carrier, finally for a little while as an extra waiter at the café of Simon.

So it was he came into my life the brief while, in the brief moments in the night-lighted Khalig to stand beside me and tell me, because of the bond of friendliness and trust that a chance word had forged, this story of his fairy hauntings.

Lost, fantastically tragic, perhaps I could have helped him, perhaps friended him. But to me, who stand aside and listen and look, he was then only a voice, a tale, another colour in our city many-coloured. Intrigued, insincere, I remember that when he had finished I evolved, for my own amusement, and in the glow self-commendatory, an explanation airy and poetic.

'Perhaps they are of the real world, those your Sun-Ghosts' – *Phantasmata toi helioi* [37] he had called them – 'and you and I and the little Kalo but the vain imaginings, the dark, sad dreams of the People of the Sun. ...'

And then I stopped. For he had turned his eyes on me and behind their puzzled friendliness I had seen that which shamed me, the glib romantic, to silence.

X

So I knew him, and he was gone, finding at length the more permanent work in a Greek printer's. Long hours of work they were, from which each night he would return to Kalo Constantinides and the little flat. And what doubts of himself and his own persistent disbelief, what stilled puzzlements each day brought to his eyes – how shall we know?

Yet that his impossible simplicity suffered no change. He rescued from the street and the tormenting of a gang of urchins a half-crazed negro who had once been a cook. Him he installed as servant in the tiny flat, and was repaid by Salih ibn Muslih [38] with the adoration and the jealous worship – the jealousy that extended even to Kalo.

But Kalo was happy. Always to her I think Elia remained the wonderful, inexplicable lover, so that even when he brought home the crazy negro she protested with but the half-heart and indifference. Life, life that had been the long nightmare since she fled from starvation to the painted houses of Vathy, of Smyrna, of Cairo – it blossomed now its scented hours, a flower transplanted.

And Elia? Even when he held her in his arms did the look of puzzlement go from his eyes? He who knew neither fear nor regret – did her fear of the old negro seem to him a thing unreal? Her little human frailties of temper and desire – were these to him that shadowing of the sun?

I do not know, only look back across the years and see them there, in those little rooms in that little street, amongst the neighbours Syrian and Greek, inquisitive and friendly; Kalo by the open window, her hand to her eyes, awaiting her Samian boy come up the street each evening. ...

That the picture, and for background the twisted body and crazed mutterings of the negro, ibn Muslih.

XI

Then the happening horrific, of which were never the full details known. Late afternoon a woman who lived in the flat below that of Elia and Kalo thought she heard come from overhead a scream, the sound of scuffling. She listened, but heard no more, and thought herself deluded. Then an odd apprehension touched her. She climbed up to the other flat and knocked at the door. Thereat was again the stirring, the sound of struggle, and then scream on scream that was suddenly stayed by the sound of a blow. ...

There were men in the building; they ran and brought gendarmes, and a great crowd collected. They battered in the door of the Constantinides flat, and there, amidst the litter of the struggle, stood in horror till one went forward and covered that pitiful thing whose singing they had heard a few hours before.

At that moment a shout arose from the street. 'From the back window! He escapes from the back window!'

The negro, stained knife in hand, had been seen descending the fire-escape. He made a crazed gesture of defiance and fled up an alleyway of warehouses, the mob at his heels.

Then, even while those who had broken into the Constantinides flat stood there in helplessness, they heard a voice raised in surprise, and turned about. In the doorway, with friendly, questioning eyes, stood Elia.

They parted and made way for him, and, wondering, he went forward. ...

XII

The crowd ran ibn Muslih to earth in a bottle-necked cul-de-sac. At that neck, worked up into a dervish [39] rage, he stood and defied them, knife in hand.

Someone flung a stone and the negro reeled under a shower of missiles which followed that first one. Three gendarmes ran back for their carbines. [40] And then the crowd was flung to left and right, and another madman, Elia Constantinides, with the white face and blazing eyes, fronted ibn Muslih.

Bleeding, defiant, the negro looked up. Over him swept the swift change. At sight of Elia he gave a low wail and covered his face with his hands. The knife slithered to the ground. Elia crouched like a beast to spring, and the mob waited with panting breath.

Then the happening inexplicable. Elia was seen to reel, to grip his head as one in pain, and then walk forward towards ibn Muslih with outstretched hands. Behind him they yelled his danger, and at that shout he wheeled round.

'It is only ibn Muslih. My friend, ibn Muslih. ...'

For a moment amazement held the mob. Then a growl of horror and anger rose. Someone shouted a foul taunt, a fouler accusation. A stone hurtled through the air and glanced from Elia's forehead. But he heeded it not. Fronting them, there had come on his face a light unearthly. He flung out a sudden arm and words incomprehensible as that last cry on the Hill of Crucifixion [41] rang in the ears of their stayed anger.

'Why, it is we – we who are the People of the Sun! Those others – look, look, they are but shadows!'

A panting gendarme, newly on the scene, an Egyptian recruit who knew nothing of the circumstances except that here was a desperado at bay, knelt down, steadied his carbine on his knee, and fired. ... He gave a grunt of satisfaction.

The mad light went from the eyes of the Greek desperado. He coughed, looked round with puzzled gaze, pressed his hand to his chest, and then crumpled and fell at the feet of the glaring ibn Muslih.

XIII

And that is the tale of Elia Constantinides, whose name to this day is an abomination and a hateful thing in the quarters of the Khalig.

But I – I heard of it and wept. What last fantastic vision did he see when he faced ibn Muslih? How transformed, in what strange picture-images did that last scene rise? And who are they – what dreams of life attainable, splendid, unshadowed – those who all his life haunted him?

We question and wonder and forget, like men in sleep. For not Elia alone, but all men they haunt. Under many names and through many faiths they pass, immortal, undying, the shining ghosts we glimpse and remember in wonder and weeping, as the faces of dead children are remembered.

VII

Cockcrow

I

Eh? That? Only the crowing of a Lemnos [1] rooster! From the fowl-run behind this café it comes – the fowl-run of the little Simon.

You had not suspected in him the tastes bucolic? [2] In our Cairene evenings I think he wanders out there and dreams of a farm in Lemnos – he who would die of the broken heart if he forsook the Khalig's colours and call! ...

The challenge absurd in the sunlight – but in the dawn – how of the haunting it is! Haunting, I think, with memories not our own, the stored race-remembrances innumerable since first the jungle-fowl was tamed and that challenge of the morning heard in an Indian hut. What agonies and waitings has it not ended, what vigils and prayers! That drowsy clamour – surely it is in all memories, vivid and unforgettable, for at least the one night that would never pass, for at least the one stretch of dark, still hours!

That morning the many years ago, my friend – think how it must have shrilled above the hills of Jerusalem!

II

If you walk the Shari' Abbassieh [3] today you will see the house of Lucius Ravelston stand shuttered and dusty in the sunshine, with its little garden deserted. Last we heard of him, our Ravelston, he was in Hadramaut, [4] on expedition in search of the sand-cities of the Shiah. [5] In days when that garden knew him he would stride to and fro with the hasting guest [6] by his side, discussing the languages international and the inhabitability of the moon and the character of Marco Polo; [7] of these things he would discuss with the naive fervour that another devotes to scandal or politics. ...

The guest would pant beside him for a little, then give up with a laugh, and sit to watch his host, pipe-smoking, trample the flower-beds in the heat of exposition.

More nearly the seven than the six feet in height, a giant, with the rapt stare of grey eyes under knit brows and the strange brown hair like silk. He had an athlete's body that Phidias would have loved, though of Hellas the good Aristotle would perhaps have baulked at his mind. [8]

Indeed, this would have been but reciprocal, for the good Aristotle he regarded with the utmost detestation. Giant and genius, he was yet something of a child, and men dead and dust three thousand years he could love or detest with as much fervour as though they wrote in the journals contemporary.

'A snippety suburban [9] mind – the mind of a fossil-collecting curate.'

'But I have heard of him as the Father of the Sciences,' I would say, and so bring upon myself recital of Aristotelian fatuities, the while the drowsy cluckings would cease in the native fowl-run beyond the garden, and the good sun, talked from the sky, went down behind the Red Hills. [10] ...

He was the crusader essential, hating all neat, un-originative [11] minds which look on life with the cold, conservative calm. Not yet forty years of age, he had been a surgeon in the Great War, the leader of a Polar Expedition, the assistant of Knut Hammssen in that Odyssey through the Gobi Desert. [12] From such exploits heroic he had settled down in Cairo to study the scourge of cancer. In laboratory and study they fight the last crusades.

Research-worker, student, he yet waged the wars unending in journal and congress and popular press. Enemies in battalions he loved, though there were occasions when he would forget the date of a battle, going into lengthy abstractions as a mystic into a trance. These were escapes to the super-normal when some thought would suddenly fructify in his mind and he would wipe the dust of tragedy and comedy and friendship from his hands, and retreat to the barred room and the microscope and the notes and the lamplit table for days or weeks on end. ...

My friend, Dr Adrian the gynæcologist, also knew him and loved him.

'An anachronism, fifty years behind the times, Ravelston. In the Huxley-Haeckel tradition. [13] Last of the warrior-savants. Science has more triumphs and heroes than ever, but Ravelston's the last of her champions to go out into the arena and defy embattled Stupidity. Pity. They lent colour to life, the giants.'

'They brought fire from heaven, [14] if I remember,' I said. 'But I do not think he is the last. There will always be giants.'

Coming from the house called Daybreak, [15] we were passing through Abbassieh late in the night, and now stood looking up at the flare of light from the room of Ravelston. Adrian laughed.

'The Titan, eh? There was also a vulture in the story, wasn't there? We must warn Lucius!'

III

That autumn the giant went to England, to London, to see to the publication of a book – not the such book as you might write, my friend, needing no supervision, but the production marvellous and intricate, with the diagrams and changing print and the chemic [16] symbols much strewn to confusion and despair of printer. Adrian and I made the occasional call at the Abbassieh house and saw to its ordering. It was a pleasant place, and we spent hours of ease in the great library, or drank the good Ravelston's wine under the lime-trees in the garden.

Behind he had left, in the rough, the great work on which he had been engaged since coming to Cairo. Though only in first draft, Adrian had promised to read this treatise and contribute to it a preface. He would groan aloud over caligraphy [17] and contractions, yet read on in fascination. Once or twice he interviewed clients of the giant, and of one of those interviews told me. The man was a Greek, who had suffered from the internal pain diagnosed by his own doctor as a cancer tumour. Under treatment of Ravelston he had been made well and whole again in a month.

'A month! Unless it was a mere fluke, colonel, Ravelston's in the process of perfecting a treatment for cancer that'll wipe it from the face of the earth. ... Beyond the dreams of Lister.' [18]

We would smoke and meditate, and discuss the absent Ravelston. Of his private life we knew nothing.

'He has no private life, no private ambition. He's a Republican of your Plato, colonel, a Samurai out of Wells. [19] ... Marry? He'd forget a woman in a fortnight – unless she developed *sarcomata*!' [20]

Ravelston telegraphed the date of his return, and I found Cairo's leading gynæcologist, [21] with sleeves rolled up, and the scurry of native servants, flapping the negligent duster around the library. '"Prepare the house," eh? Must be bringing a shipload of zoological specimens.'

It was the afternoon when the boat-train was due from Alexandria. 'It is his jest,' I said. 'Or perhaps he brings a tourist friend.'

'God forbid,' said Adrian, and then we heard a taxicab come in the sharia below and the sound of a key in the door. Then Ravelston's voice upraised.

'Adrian! Saloney! ... Hell, what a dust!'

We went out and waved to him from the landing. He stood in the doorway, in the winter sunshine, and beyond in the street, seemed a fight in progress between the native porters and the mountains of trunks. These things, and then –

Simultaneously we saw her. She stood not in the belt of sunshine, but in the mote-sprayed darkness within the door. I made the bow ineffective and Adrian the fumblement for the collar of his shirt.

'Pamela – Dr Adrian and Colonel Anton Saloney. You people, this is my wife.'

IV

She called him never by his first name, but sometimes 'Ravelston' and sometimes 'Stealthy Terror' [22] – the first because it was fashionable so to address a husband, the second because of some secret jest they shared together. She ransacked the Abbassieh house from top to bottom, and had shaken from it such showers of dust as seemed to warrant the eviction of the Sahara itself. The roof of one wing was cut away and installed with special glass that interrupts not the violet ray, [23] and for this novelty she was the excited child, as indeed was Ravelston himself.

'He has sun-bathing on the brain,' said Adrian. 'God knows why – unless it's to admire the pretty Pamela. ... Done without it all his life and now he pretends it's essential to health, whereas it's merely a craze and a fashion.'

'You do not like Mrs Ravelston?'

'I don't,' he said, with curtness. 'He was a Samurai, and now – Good Lord, look what he's becoming!'

And indeed I also, with amazement and pity, watched the transformation of the giant from research worker and world enthusiast into lover and follower. He planned and rode the excursions with her, the while library and laboratory remained locked and neglected, took her to innumerable balls and festas, humoured her in whims and desires most wayward and foolish. She declared a passion for the language Russian, and determination to learn it, and I was hired to teach such accent as Ravelston himself possessed not.

She was the pupil impossible – would lie deep in her chair and yawn, or look from the window and comment on the passers-by, or remark on my appearance or her own with startling frankness.

'Why don't you trim that nice brown beard of yours, colonel? ... All right, then, Sorry. [24] Where were we? *"Smeyat'cia, posmeyat'cia* [25] – to laugh." ... But how can they? Laughing in Russian must require a surgical operation. Stealthy Terror would laugh well in Russian.' Would drop the book and clasp her hands about her knees. 'Why have you never married, colonel?'

She would smile sleepily because of the sun-bathing, and stretch like a cat, with the winking of golden eyes.

Beautiful? But no. She had the nose too short and the upper lip too long. Yet the charm that is beyond proportions and measurements – the careless, insolent mouth that was somehow like the mouth of Ravelston himself, and eyes very deeply lashed and wonderful, and the sheen of hair, cut like a boy's, and very dark and fine. Beside Ravelston, she looked on occasion like his son.

She tired very quickly of the Russian, and the lessons in it ceased. She tired of the sun-bathing, and I think the first quarrel with Ravelston was over that tiring. Thereafter she carried it out infrequently, as a boring duty. ... 'She would tire of the glories of heaven and yawn in the faces of the Archangels,' [26] Adrian would growl.

Light, irresponsible, blindly selfish, insolently cold and insolently passionate, she seemed no more fit mate for Ravelston than a woman of the Warrens. She was daughter of his publisher, and early on his visit to London they had made acquaintance. Ravelston I believed she had married as the new 'thrill', the new and unprecedented experience – because of his stature and his reputation and that otherness of his – the otherness that now, alas, seemed to have vanished. She had an endless craving for change, for thrill and glitter and running laughter, for the dance and the perfumes, the admiration and the adoration. Anything that savoured of study or the weariness of toil was a horrible thing. All that was enemy of the good time and the careless hour was 'horrible'.

And yet – I could not dislike her. Perhaps because of beauty of gesture and attitude, and the ring of her boy-laughter and that bright scorn she had of things; perhaps because once or twice in her I glimpsed a dark fierceness that might have been her soul, imprisoned and lost, beneath the shifting play of moods that was her life.

V

One morning, near five o'clock, coming from an all-night dance at the Mess Artillery, [27] they overtook Adrian and myself, and gave us a lift to the house in Abbassieh. We sat the four of us hunched together in the little car, and the dawn was in the sky into which we raced. Pamela looked tired, and as we turned into the garden-way of the house I saw that she was asleep. The garden was dim and scented, and through it the giant carried her indoors.

And then, suddenly, a cockerel in the native fowl-run next door flapped and crowed with piercing loudness. Pamela awoke with a cry of terror, struggled in Ravelston's arms so that he halted, and then stared from the one to the other of us in slow realisation. But in her eyes was still terror.

We laughed at her, and then stood awkward and embarrassed, for she laid her head against Ravelston's shoulder and wept with an intensity in her amazing. Adrian and I would have gone, but that the giant motioned to us to follow. In the downstairs room he switched on the lights, and set Pamela in a chair, and knelt by her. She stared into his face with the colour slowly coming back to her own.

And it was then, in that moment of the overstrung, that she told us.

She had been a child of twelve in the last years of the War, in the London suburb, in some area unfortunate traversed again and again by the German air-raiders. [28] Often was the screaming of sirens and the falling of bombs, and her child-nerves played on by the inexplicable terrors, her sleep shattered in sudden hurryings to and fro. ...

And then came a morning that she might not forget. There was the usual alarm and she and her brother, a child of three, were hurried out to hide in a garden-shed, the safest refuge. The nurse left them there a moment the while she ran back for clothes, and in that moment, looking out, Pamela saw the night flash and flash again. She cried out to the nurse, and then in terror ran after her in the direction of the house. Half-way across the garden she heard her brother call her name, and turned, confused and remembering. In that moment came catastrophe. She was flung to the ground by the explosion which wiped out the shed, and the darkness rained splinters of stone and wood around her. She picked herself up, bruised and bleeding, and through the squalling scolding from a nearby chicken-run heard a cock which crowed unceasingly, unendingly, above the clamour. ...

'Ravelston, I heard him scream – I know I did – and I can't ever forget ... and that crowing. Oh, I was a coward, a coward! I killed him. He had that lost boy-stare you have when you sit and think. ... Oh, beastly coward!'

He laughed at her, the giant. 'You could have done nothing. You're brave even to remember it. Tired now. Carry you to bed?'

Adrian and I, forgotten, went out into the morning without the promised refreshments. The laboratory and all the other windows but for one, far up, shone dark as dead eyes.

'What do you think of her now – and this story?' I said.

'Hysteria. [29] Explains a little and doesn't help a jot.' We passed out of the range of that lighted window. 'Poor Ravelston! Titan and Pandora [30] – complete with vulture!'

'Eh?' I said, and would have made remarks regarding the mythology confused, but that he went on:

'Um. You didn't know, of course. There's cancer in her family – *carcinomata*. [31] Hereditary. She doesn't know it herself, but Ravelston did when he married her.'

VI

Here, it seemed to me – I who cannot help finding story and plot in every life I look on – were elements enough of drama. Ravelston, with that secret upon him, with his unsurpassed knowledge of the stages of the cancer-march, turning in desperation from the rigour and slowness of patient research to the sun-bathing and each other of the swift, glib cures; Pamela, insolent, selfish, young, looking forward to years of pleasure and amusement – all that she craved – all unconscious that the most frightful and agonising of diseases lay like a beast awaiting her. ...

But Nature has little stage-sense. She can make of apparent tragedy the thing ludicrous and meaningless, of comedy the thing horrifying. So at the house in Abbassieh. One morning Pamela complained of unwellness, and the symptoms described to Ravelston. With fear upon him, he made the no-examination himself, but sent for Adrian. The X-ray apparatus was brought from the Citadel Hospital, [32] the many photographs taken, and Adrian made a searching examination. Then he went away with the apparatus and in the evening returned to them.

'Mrs Ravelston has a magnificent constitution. There is nothing more wrong with her than a passing ailment.'

‘Eh?’ said Ravelston, and leapt from his chair. Then abruptly he was gone from the room. Adrian was left alone with Pamela, cigarette-smoking, undisturbed, but sitting considering him, chin in hand.

‘What was Ravelston fussing about, doctor? What did he and you expect?’

He had never liked her, and it seemed to him then that the truth might sober her. In a moment he was telling her of the suspicions and the facts, and in that moment regretting it.

‘... Expected I’d develop cancer? Nice. Married me knowing it? – Thought I’d be a convenient subject-study, I suppose? I’ll remember that.’

Adrian stared at her in amazed anger. She nodded to him the insolent dismissal. ‘That’s all, doctor. You can send in your bill.’

VII

More and more rapidly with the passing of the weeks, the lives of these two began to split apart. Ravelston, relieved, exultant, rid of that immediate personal fear, turned again to laboratory and desk. He grew again to the habit of shutting himself up for hours and days at a stretch, immersed in the matters that to Pamela were the incomprehensible unpleasantnesses.

Conscious of his defection from the round of inane pleasure and sight-seeing, he would on occasion burst from laboratory or study to the rooms of Pamela, caress her – and then vanish again in a banging of doors, leaving, I think, one who sat breathless and with singing heart. But so only for a moment.

If Adrian might not, I at least would comprehend something of the startled anger and resentment that followed his revelation. A freak. ... A ‘study.’ ... Even with the cooling of first anger – anger that to her generation is the thing crude and clownish – she forgot not at all. Indeed, the changed behaviour of Ravelston was constant reminder. She had expected, I imagine, that Ravelston would always comport himself as in the days of the honeymoon, with his work relegated to the secondary place. She had expected that Prometheus would continue to bring fire from heaven, but only – in the phrase of Adrian, who disliked her so – ‘to provide her with a damn little foot-warmer’.

Instead, there were now the moments, in the chance meetings and at meal-times, when he stared at her as though she were a stranger. The ‘freak’ had ceased to be freakish, the ‘subject’ had refused to be satisfactorily cancerous, in disobedience to the expectations of heredity. ... She had ceased to interest.

So, knowing that she lied, she must have told herself on occasion, and so, in the mixture of boredom and pique, and with that urgency to grasp from life all that it might offer in sensation, she turned to the gaudy glitter of the

European season, [33] to the dancings and the gatherings, the gossipings and philanderings, [34] the motor excursions and the flowering acquaintanceships; finally, to the growing amusement and interest in Andreeius de Bruyn.

VIII

I encountered them one afternoon outside the Continental Hotel, where I awaited the client. I had been dragoman to him a month before and from his car he nodded to me the mocking salutation.

'Afternoon, St Peter!' [35]

This was his crude jest because of the incident during that month that would smell none the sweeter for the telling. There had been keys in the incident, and I had saved him from the slit throat, and a Muslim woman from the attentions of one who imagined he was honouring a 'native'. It was the incident he had done better to forget.

Before I might reply, she who sat by his side turned her head, and recognised me, and laughed.

'Hello, colonel! *Kak vi pazhivaiete?* Oh, and – *pocmesyaietc'ie*!' [36]

To her and the Russian horrible I smiled then, as she commanded. Perhaps there had been other than an expression pleased on my face at sight of her with de Bruyn. She whispered something to him, and they laughed at me, and the car shot away. ... De Bruyn!

He was the young American with the much money and less perception of responsibility to life than possesses a mayfly. Villains have gone from life as they have from literature, and perhaps de Bruyn was no more evil than was Ravelston, his antitype. Like Pamela, it was merely that the gross selfishness that is in all of us, the thing instinctive, had never known repression or transmutation. Wants and desires were things to be purchased or cajoled, never to be forgone. In Cairo he had already organised the orgies and excursions and fantastic entertainments innumerable. In his handsome face he had eyes which they said could hold and fascinate any woman. ... To me they were the bright, shifting eyes of one morally unborn.

That excursion of theirs I witnessed had not been the first. Alike her insolence and selfishness, and perhaps also her fearlessness, fascinated de Bruyn. He laid the cold-blooded siege, without concealment of desire or intention, as is the fashion of the philanderer modern. From Pamela Ravelston was at first the amusement, and then the something else that was still a mocking thing, that mocked even when at last she found herself in his arms. ... Love or hate, Lucius or Andreeius – what did it matter, so long as boredom was cheated?

As casually as that, and yet quite irrevocably, she must have come to her decision and sat down and wrote the letter which she sent to Ravelston from the Ghezireh ball.

IX

Early in that morning of her writing, I was walking home, all of the meditative way from the Kubbah observatory. [37] In Abbassieh I saw a light in the room of Ravelston, and there came on me a sudden resolve. I would acquaint him with the de Bruyn matter, for in those chill hours it loomed to me as serious.

I went round to the back of the house, through the garden, and pressed the bell that sounded in his room alone. Hardly had I ceased but there was the noise of footsteps, and Ravelston, gigantic, towered in the doorway dimness.

'Saloney!' He gave a strange laugh. 'I thought – but never mind what I thought. Come in.' He banged the door behind me and gripped my arm. 'Come up here. I've something to show you.'

He led me up the stairs of the back, and then, on the landing that led to his study, had a new resolve. 'Not here. Further up, first.'

On that other landing he opened a door and switched on lights and stared round the room. Then laughed again.

'Look, Saloney! She was here yesterday. Everything here is hers. There's not a thing but's known her touch. Eh? And she's slept in that bed; I've heard her singing up here, going to bed at midnight. ... Remember the way she had of singing – with that little hoarseness? And of sitting with clasped knees? Eh?'

He bent down and very gently and deliberately picked up a chair. And then he went suddenly berserk-mad. He hurled the chair at the great dressing-glass and brought it smashing to the floor, and then set about deliberately wrecking the room. I stood in helplessness and watched, and when he had finished the place looked, strewn with torn and trampled draperies, like a murdered girl. Once I tried to stay him.

'But why – ?'

'Come away, colonel. Out of it! Unclean, this place. Come down below and have a drink.'

Below he poured out the whisky and tossed me a letter. While I read it he walked up and down, his hands twitching. In face and voice was that flare of mirth that is the anger of his kind.

'Good letter, eh? "Not being either a dragoman or a doctor, I'm tired of Abbassieh; not being either a cancerous freak or a beastly disease you're evidently tired of me." Who told her about the cancer? Never mind. ... A little adultery for amusement, eh? Who's this de Bruyn?'

I told him. 'A lover? A dirty little lover and her days and nights spent planning dirty little caressings and kissings ... while I've been working. I've been made fool and cuckold because I could not play – the lap-dog! She expected me to give up for her the world, my work, the things that are me. ... For a little loving and mating!'

And suddenly he stopped in front of me and laughed – the laugh of genuine amusement and relief.

'Lord, why didn't I see? I've been blind as a mole! Oh, not only to this dirty little intrigue. To fact. Loving and mating, begetting and desiring – those, or the life without flambeaux [38] or kindliness, of work unending, with nothing but the surety that some day the swamps will be cleared away. ...'

He was walking to and fro again, but no longer in anger. Rather was it the exultation.

'I know. See it only now. My work's been going to pieces. One can't have both; one must choose. Warmth and light and caresses and the safe places – or loneliness and that vision ...'

His eyes were shining now. It was the Ravelston of the garden-talks, lost and forgotten those many months, and I thrilled to meeting him again. I stood up and seized his hand.

'You are right. You will press on to the greater work alone.'

He laughed in ringing confidence, and then dropped my hand and wheeled to the window like lightning. Upon the garden lay the dawn. Again shrilled out that sound that had startled us, and at its repetition he swung round upon me again, gigantic, with horror on his face.

'My God, if she's scared – alone – with that fool! ... What rubbish you've been talking, Saloney! Rubbish! There wasn't a soul to the world till I found Pam! The future's trust to me. [39] And I neglected and forgot her. ... Lost her now, I who could have kept her mine, could have made her true and clear and fine as a sword, could have tramped with her desert and starfield ... Work! She was light to my clumsy groping and I've lost her –'

But I had heard another sound through the hushed morning. I caught his sleeve.

'Listen!' I said.

X

De Bruyn and Pamela, you must understand, had planned to arrive at Alexandria, where was de Bruyn's yacht, early in the forenoon. They danced till as late as the three o'clock at the ball on Ghezireh Island. Then Pamela sent off the letter to Ravelston by the native messenger, and they went out to the car which had been awaiting them.

De Bruyn came flushed with wine and dancing, and as he wrapped the rugs about Pamela he was of the over-affectionate. This she told him, with the usual fearless insolence, and he sat beside her sulkily, driving out of Cairo.

But he was the skilled driver, steering with reckless care, and in the little they were clear even of the grey mud suburbs and the stars were a splendour above them. Pamela Ravelston yawned, and sank deep in rugs, and presently was asleep.

For an hour the great racer fled westwards, along the Alexandria road. Then de Bruyn suddenly swore, and the car bumped and shuddered and fell to a crawl. They were in the midst of a village, shuttered and sleeping, and the roadway was pitted with uneven holes.

The searchlight rays of the headlamps shook and made a standstill. For the moment, amongst the narrow lanes branching from the roadway, the noise of the car was deafening.

'Curse it. Puncture,' said de Bruyn. 'Stay there, Pam. No need for you to get down.'

Pamela stirred sleepily and murmured something the while he got down and fumbled with the lamps. Above the silent, mud-walled village the sky glimmered amethyst [40] in the false dawn.

And then from a mud-hut near at hand a child began to cry, and shrill and clear, awakened by the noise of the car, misled by the false light in the sky, a cock crew and others throughout the village took up the call till de Bruyn lifted a dawn-greyed face, and laughed and swore.

'Those infernal birds! They would waken the dead. [41] Eh?'

And as he stared in amazement at one who sat and wept there in the flickering light, and then sprang to vivid life, and swore at him and made the unreasonable demand, he did not know that that clamour about them had indeed awakened the dead.

XI

'What?' said Ravelston.

But I was looking out of the window as the great car of de Bruyn halted in front of the house, its noise deafening. Out of it leapt someone in the whirl of dance-draperies, someone whose key slotted urgently in the street-door, who came up the stairs with flying feet.

'Ravelston. ... Old Stealthy Terror. ... I've come back. ...' White-faced, but the scared and shivering repentant not at all, she stood in front of him. Not the fear or safety brought her back, but remembrance of that lover with the lost-boy stare. 'Oh, I've been such a fool! Dirty and a coward. ... My dear, I forgot!'

'We both forgot,' he said, and took her in his arms – those arms in which perhaps she is sleeping tonight in some desert of the Hadramaut.

But I turned away and went down to the street. As I opened the door, de Bruyn, starting up his car, glanced at me with a wry, white smile.

'Morning, St Peter.'

And then I had the sudden sense of a moment dramatic, of the story told and retold the many times, in many ways.

'Poor Judas,' [42] I said.

VIII

VERNAL [1]

I

Noon and April and eighty-four in the shade! [2] Who would dream it, here in the Khalig-el- Masri, that the Spring [3] is in our northern lands, and the wind and the rain? ... Grey clouds and shadows and the whoop-whoop-whoop of birds in mist and the calling of lost sheep. God mine, how today the Volga must be crying through the willows! [4] There are boatmen singing there, [5] and the dance of the waters, and all the earth coming so green. ...

And nowhere such foolish ache of heart as mine in Cairo!

How does it stir us so, here where Spring is a day and a night, more fugitive than a dream? No mere season, surely, but the mood universal that comes every year to cry of the things undone and unachieved. ... Eh? Oh, the lips unkissed and the poems unwritten and the mountains unsealed and the sins unforgiven and the hearts unfrozen. ... We stir from the dreamless sleep of the day-to-day and wake and stare – even here in Cairo where the Spring is as a girl who passes with hasting feet and urgent eyes. ... As once I saw her pass.

Beat on the table for the little Simon, my friend, and I – God mine, if only I may forget my Volga and the willows! – will tell you the story that for me still haunts each Cairene Spring.

II

In the beginning was God, and He created James Freeman. [6] And James Freeman served Him all the days of his life. [7] ...

This is not the blasphemy. It is paraphrase on the wording quaint of that English Bible [8] wherein I sought to master style in the Gymnasium of Kazan. So of himself always I think believed James Freeman. Long before we met here in Polychromata, and watched the little drama unfold to that evening in Spring, was he assured of the standing with his God. Since childhood had that standing been certain below his feet.

Of your English sects I know but little, and that from the Dickens and Trollope [9] and the casual mention and the tale without footnotes – as told me it was by Norla [10] and Adrian, and ultimately James Freeman himself. But it seems he was born of parents who early designed him as priest, and themselves held by the faith of some church that conforms not to your national belief. [11] This in the English provincial town where was smoke and glare of furnaces night and day to furnish the so-ready similes for the hell of the conforming wicked.

When I met him he was tall and thick-browed, with white hair and stooping shoulders and a rasp of voice. He had the face that seemed to me as the face of a lion – if one might think of a lion that had forsaken meat for other food – perhaps because the meat had disagreed with him. ...

But this is the description unfair. He was of type outside my comprehension and love – surely the priest-type that goes fast from the world. Since the age of twenty he had preached and believed the ancient, cruel god of sacrifice and supplication and the bitter codes. By the age of twenty-five he had had the church of his own, and in the glare of those furnaces, himself already twisted and bitter and white-earnest, preached salvation and damnation in name of his God.

And then, in that twenty-fifth year, he had loved and desired and married.

How comes love to such as those? I think it moved and shook him, and perhaps he was the lion he had forgone, and there were the nights of stars and the scents of the veldt [12] when the world and its sins fell from him, and he and his mate were alone and splendid under splendid skies. ... Surely, surely. And then –

I think he came out of the love ecstasy suddenly – looked at himself, and through the strange, distorting mirrors of his beliefs saw himself one unclean and lustful, a sinner in the jargon of his creed. Perhaps in a night his restraints and taboos came back on him again. And with them must have come that harshness of demeanour and expression bred of his own repressions and tortured inhibitions. ... To one who had known him only as lover he became the cold and affrighting fanatic.

She must have lived in the hell he was incapable of imagining, spite his furnaces and sin-creed. Of her kind there have been the pitiful many. They have gone uncomplaining and unrecorded to the dead: but for their slow fate was not Mary Freeman.

I never knew her, and to me she is but a name. But I think of her as one awakened to wonder and desire, and then starved. For nearly six years she endured that life – or had it ceased to be endurance till there came reawakening and the call of the stars again? They had one child, the girl of five, Norla, and perhaps that tie had held her. They lived in your London by then, in some suburb where was church of their sect.

And suddenly, without note or notification, she was gone. The mystery was not a mystery for long. Near at hand had lived the political, a Russian, an artist, and he was gone also.

It was Spring, in March, and Freeman met her leaving by the gate of his house, and singing the little song. He spoke to her and she said strange words, not looking at him. 'I am going out to seek the Spring.'

He turned and looked after her, I think, in the moment of astonishment, and watched her out of sight. Nor did she ever return.

III

She wrote him from the south of France, [13] asking that she might be divorced and so marry the Russian. Again, at end of a year, she wrote, the pitiful letter saying that the Russian was dead. To neither letter was a reply sent by James Freeman. He brought his sister to rear his child and barred out into the night that pitiful face that surely came to haunt him after the second letter.

He became preacher of the savage purity, persecutor of the poor outcasts of the streets. Throughout the War he preached a God of Battles tied to the gun-carriages, and in the after-War ecstasy of self-flagellation your London took him to its heart. He addressed the great demonstrations, organised the violent crusades. From denouncing sins of the age in the little, unknown church he was invited as preacher in your cathedrals and made the divine doctor and given the great church.

But he was already an old man. The bitterness had overflowed from his heart to his body. There came on him the chronic rheumatism and he was ordered to the sun and the south of France by the so-assiduous doctors.

But to go to the south of France he refused with the surprising outbreak of violence. He handed over the great London church to a substitute, and came to Egypt, to Helwan, [14] and later to Cairo.

With him he brought his daughter Norla.

IV

I may never think of the Spring but I remember Norla Freeman; I may never read in your little gazettes of the modern women who lack the seemly dullness and virtues but I think of this English girl. For she was refutation of all the printed spite of us of the superseded generation. Cold and stark and vivid. ... And yet the Spring!

My friend, the Dr Adrian, took me to the Pension Avallaire [15] and made the introductions between us. She sat in the garden, in a dream, when we came upon her. She had that red hair known to the old painters and it was the sudden flame of colour against the Pension greenery.

'Miss Freeman, this is Colonel Anton Saloney, of the Russian White Army and the Republic of Plato.' [16]

This is the good Adrian's jest, because I am unmarried and hold belief in men yet upbuilding the ultimate wise state.

'I am from Utopia [17] myself.' She was tall and slender, standing so, red-crowned, with serene purity of laughter in opal eyes. She sighed. 'Dr Adrian will have explained to you. My father is an invalid and can't take me round Cairo. I –' she considered the garden '– sketch. My father insists that someone go with me, and Dr Adrian suggested you.'

She had the aloofness that puzzled me, but that later I was to know so well. Defence it was she had erected – she who found sunsets of more interest than souls – against that world of meaningless enthusiasm and denunciation and hysteria in which she had been reared.

'I shall be honoured,' I said, 'if you think me suitable.'

Then was the sudden smile again and the peep of friendliness.

'I like you. Will you come and talk to my father?'

I followed her to where Dr Freeman sat on the balcony of his room, with below it the garden of Esbekiyeh [18] and the sunshine and the changing colours of our Cairo. He peered at me from beneath the heavy brows. He did not offer to shake hands. I was only the dragoman.

She turned to leave us, then bent over her father, adjusting the cushions, and in that so-simple action I had a sudden glimpse of vivid strength and certitude of character, the reality like the current below the surface-serene river. Dr Freeman looked after her and then spoke in the pulpit voice.

'Dr Adrian tells me you are reliable, which is not the case with natives. Are you a gentleman?'

I made him the bow. 'My ancestors have cut throats for nine centuries.'

He crouched in his chair, the old priest with twinging bones, humourless and cold, considering me. 'You will be required to select the places fit for Miss Freeman to visit. I do not wish her to see the filthy and unclean sights of Cairo. Understand? Nor to make chance acquaintances amongst strangers or your friends. You will remember that you are my employee and hers.'

I, the ex-Professor of English Literature, have withstood much of this, my friend, and also have built my defence. I take refuge in the irrelevant conjecture and fantasy. ... That daughter of his – surely I had seen her many times before?

Out in the garden of the Pension she waved me au revoir. And suddenly I remembered.

One might see her face in the hundred prints and pictures. For so, the girl unawakened, the Lady of Serenity, is portrayed on the ikons the Sitt Miriam, the Virgin Mary of the Coptic Church. [19]

V

You must bear that picture of her, my friend: early dawn in the northland Spring. Never the bird-song or the morning wind or the flying clouds yet had she known; she did not dream that a soul may flame splendid as never a sunrise.

Between us came very quickly the friendship. [20] For was I not of the Republic of Plato and a dragoman to the boot? [21] Not that she made consideration of these things. Cairo was hers, and all its sights and colours and sounds, and the funny Russian to make an occasional jest and order the taxi and row the boat and see to the provided lunch.

'But you have ... talent,' I said, that first morning I took her to the Gamaliyeh bazaar, [22] and was allowed to look in her book of sketches. They were the pencillings and the charcoal work, the tentative touchings and limnings, and they caught my breath. Yet I had been to say something else before I looked closer. She knew it and the smile peeped from her eyes.

'But not "genius", Colonel Saloney?'

'Some day that will come.'

She meditated a subject, eager and young and alien and wonderful against that brownness and flame of savage colour, where the traders come with spices from the Red Sea lands [23] and Arabia, and the camels droop in long rows, and the air is sick with the smell of attar of roses. [24] Then: 'If it doesn't come now, it never will. ... That woman there, with the yellow skin and the jade earrings! Do you think she would allow me?' [25]

I looked and saw a woman of the painted streets. 'I think a camelier would be better.'

So one was found and posed and sketched, and she forgot the woman. Then we were threading the bazaars to the next view of interest, the next face that caught attention, the next vivid glimpse of blue mosque against burnished sky, those lines and traceries that nowhere as in Cairo stand and threaten and then faint and crumble in the yellow haze of sun.

In the next days I took her to the Khan Khalil, to the restaurant in the Muski, to Old Cairo and the sleeping walls of Citadel. At Citadel it was, while she sat and sketched and I smoked my pipe, that she uncovered for me the little history-chapter of that life that seemed to run with such swift serenity: the battle with her father before she could take the drawing lessons, before she could attend the colleges and lectures. They had fought this battle to an end, and she had won.

I took her to my Pyramids one morning, when they stood against the dawn, lonely, and with mournful beauty, impressive not at all, but infinitely sad. I took her to the Museum [26] one afternoon, and watched her stand amidst the bright flight of pigeons like one out of Plato or an old Greek myth. [27] One afternoon I rowed her out from the bank of Dubara, down past el Roda, [28] to a place in the afternoon sunlight where were the long reeds standing sentinel, and the water of crystal clarity, and presently the sunset amber upon all Cairo.

'It is as though the world were listening,' she said, and listened herself, like a child. And then, very far and remote in that silence, as though we were in the valley of the Avalon, [29] came on the Nile a nameless undermurmur.

'What is it, Colonel Anton?'

'Cairo,' I said. 'Life.'

We turned downstream, [30] past the island, to the right bank, where the lines of houses amidst the water-lanes lifted in broken serration red against the sunset. I rowed the boat to the bank, to the shed of the Greek who leased it – a cousin of the little Simon, and also of the incredible surname Papadrapoulnakophitos – and in a little we were walking up from the waterfront through a street that had seemed silent enough three hours before.

But it was silent no longer, and I suddenly understood, and hurried the English girl who would have loitered. Faces everywhere, seeming to have no bodies: faces in doorways, grey faces in windows, faces in apathetic groupings from which came the apathetic calling and twitter. ...

Women's faces – there were only women, women of all ages and surely all nations – painted faces with dead eyes, and in all that street not a stir or breath of air, but only the high, unreal voices and the dead laughter that comes from far back in the throat.

'Colonel Anton – all these women – we must come here again. What is this place?'

I looked at her and saw the answer to her own question dawn in horror in her eyes. I said nothing and in silence we passed up through that street of shame.

VI

The last day of my engagement by the Dr Freeman Norla and I and the sketch-book spent far by the Bab-el-Futtuh. [31] We returned early to the Muski, to have tea together as the parting feast, and in the old arabiyeh would have passed down the street to a restaurant we had before used when opposite a new café we heard the sound of a violin. Thereat Norla stopped the arabiyeh and turned to me with eager eyes.

'That music, Colonel Anton – can we go there?'

'But of course,' I said, though with secret doubts. Yet it was the last day and there could come little harm. ...

So presently we were seated at a little table, in the packed restaurant, with the honey-cakes and Norla pouring tea, and the stout Egyptian women of the freed harems [32] sitting near us, and the little Jew-men of the blue serge and yellow boots. [33] Here and there was the Greek and once I saw an American. The band at the far end played with raggedness.

'I hope that violinist plays again,' said Norla, and hardly had she spoken but the tanking of the piano ceased and the violinist stood up in the little hush.

I recognised him at once, and me also he recognised and smiled at, with his eyes straying to her who sat beside me. Then he began to play. As often, he was now making the improvisations, the little tunes that presently faded and altered, the ripple and the cadence and the strum. ... He flung his gifts in our faces with the same carelessness that he flung himself in the face of life.

Alexandr Sergeyvich, who called himself Utro – of the Morning. [34] Thirty years of age, ex-aristo, [35] revolutionist, anarchist. He had shed the name older in Russia even than mine, had at the age of eighteen written a successful opera, had in the civil war hoisted the Black Flag of Anarchy [36] and held a country the size of your Scotland against all comers – White, Green and Red [37] – for the full three months. Then he had passed to the Sovyeti, to Lunacharsky and the Department of Education and Culture, [38] and the planning of a gigantic Palace of Music [39] and the writing of a revolutionary song-cycle. But his anarchism was of the soul, and there was no discipline that might tame him. Within two years he was making his way from Russia while the Cheka [40] watched the ports for his arrest. He and his violin had thenceafter wandered most of south Europe before he came to Cairo and greeted me one day in the Muski. ... He had once been a student of mine in the English lectures at far Kazan.

Black of hair and eyes, with the brown face and the long, swift smile, and tall and slender. ... Alexandr of the Morning, dreamer of dreams, born out of his due time. ...

I awoke from reverie and was suddenly conscious of one who sat beside me, stirred and transformed. I had glimpse of white face and rapt eyes, and then followed her look. Alexandr Sergeyvich, his eyes fixed on our table in a look that shocked me to realisation, was playing as never before I had heard him play.

He was playing my Volga and its willows and the shouting waters in the sun. Life in the morning he was playing, life running swift and sweet, and its call ringing and ringing like far laughter. He was playing that life that never was but always may be, love young and eternal and with ecstasy unquenched, love with shining feet and unbraided hair. ...

He had finished and stood beside us. He had come threading the tables without hesitation or doubt.

'Miss Freeman,' I said, 'this is M. Utro.'

She looked up at him. Dawning in the opal eyes was that which I had never seen before. They made none of the conventional greetings, but looked at each other in white wonder.

'It was wonderful,' she whispered. 'I never knew life could be like that.'

He spoke in a half-whisper also. 'Nor did I,' he said.

VII

In the week's time, while I was tramping the Ghizeh sands or helping the stout lady tourist to surmount the steps of Kheops' Pyramid, Alexandr Sergeyvich, a little worried over the proprieties – he, the leader of the Black Bands! [41] – was kissing the hands of his Norla in the garden of the Pension Avallaire.

'If you will take me to your father, I will ask of him the permission.'

'Oh, my dear! ...' And then gravity. For they had met three times already, and after the third meeting he had written to her. 'That letter of yours – about all the happenings since you were a boy, and – and other women. ... What is the past to me? I am not an auditor.'

'You are divine,' he said, very humbly. And then, with his shattering earnestness: 'When will you marry me?'

'Whenever you will. But there's my father – he's an invalid still. ... And I love him also.'

He had been a gentleman before he was an anarchist. Which of them was it that kissed her hands then? 'I shall write to your father and explain every thing.'

And the next day this he did. He was a Russian of the Revolution, you will remember. He told Dr Freeman of his love for Norla and his desire to marry her, he told of whom he was, of his life, his sins, his poverty. He wrote of those things with the starkness and simplicity of a Gladkov [42] – that simplicity that leaves even the liberal of the older generation shocked and agape; he wrote with that devastating earnestness that was of his soul-fibre, and made no decorous attempts to gloss. ...

To Dr Freeman, the preacher of the purity crusades in your London, it must have seemed as though he had received a letter from an evil fiend. He read it at breakfast, in the private room, and Norla was startled at the pallor on his face. He tried to get up, and made the unsuccessful attempts, with the rheumatism twinging his bones.

'This Russian anarchist and seducer' – he glared across the table with the cruel eyes – 'how long have you known him?'

She herself was to tell me of this conversation, and the little lie she told then to shield me. 'A week. I met him by chance when I was separated from Colonel Saloney.'

He raved at her. 'You will not see him again, do you hear? Whatever the loose blood you inherit from your mother, I'll see that it's held in check.'

Once she would have kept a serene silence. But it was a new Norla whom Alexandr Sergeyvich was evoking.

'I will see him when I choose.'

He choked, with empurpling face. He made another effort to rise, then sank back with a groan. Their eyes met. In the moment, contrite, she was kneeling beside him.

'Daddy, Daddy – I didn't mean that. ... Let me help.'

And this he suffered her. I think he believed he had won, and that night he wrote to Alexandr Sergeyvich the letter which I will not quote. There is an obscenity of suspicion which goes with the dark old sacrifice-cults. [43]

But while he wrote Norla also was writing. She had sat a long while in the self-struggle, remembering that half-promise given to her father. But the old standards and the old allegiances – they were fading from her like the garments of gossamer.

Across in the Esbekiyeh Gardens was a dance and the scraping of violins. A night in mid-March it was, with the Cairene scents and the Cairene lights. But in the air a premonition of something else that brought to her heart the sharp, sweet ache.

Far away, through miles and miles of your English lanes, the Spring was burgeoning that night.

VIII

At two o'clock next day, in response to the letter she had sent me, I was at the Pension Avallaire, and in the quarter of an hour, with Dr Freeman's consent, we were driving to the Nile in a taxi.

She had found it urgent to be rowed down to el Roda again, to make the final reed-sketches.

'We will go to the other place for a boat,' I said, with troubled remembrance of that street that led to the wharf of Simon's cousin.

She shook her head. 'I wrote reserving a boat – to the Papadrapoulnakophitos man.' She twinkled the opal eyes. 'His name covered three lines on the envelope.' But she was grave. 'Colonel, I want to tell you ...'

And so of the whole business I was told. I sat in stunned silence, and also a little horror, for am I not of my generation? Utro, the Black Anarchist – and this English girl!

'What are you to do?' I asked. We were on the Nile by then, and I was rowing up-river. She shaded her eyes with her hand, looking into the heat-haze by left bank.

She did not answer my question. Suddenly were the little flags of excitement waving in her cheeks. 'Turn in by that jetty, please.'

Unthinking, I drew up by a line of green timbers. In a moment someone was in the boat, and it rocking under his weight. While I stared at Alexandr Sergeyvich bend to the swift kiss of the English girl I made realisation of a story-plot in which I figured as the false clue. [44]

IX

'This is unfair to me, Alexandr Sergeyvich,' I said.

I had rowed them up to the place of reeds, and they sat opposite me in that still place where once Norla had listened to the call of Cairo. It was she who answered.

'There is nothing unfair, Colonel Anton. For you didn't know. You can tell my father as soon as we go back. By then Sashka [45] and I will have decided.'

'Sashka?' How had she come to that name already? And then I saw on his face, as he looked at her, that which stilled for ever some of the doubts that had been on me.

'We'll marry,' he said, 'if you can love such fool as I. I'll work myself to a shadow for you. And I know we will win.'

She trailed her hand in the water, not looking at him, but across at the sun above Moqattam. 'And your anarchism and your dreams and your faith in freedom – all these you'll give up?'

He set his face and looked at her not either. [46] 'All these.'

She turned to him very swiftly. 'You'll give up nothing for me. My dear, do you think I don't love you for your dreams as well? You'll put them in music that'll shake the world yet – and I'll paint them in pictures that'll light it for ever! ... Remember that thing you played in the Muski Café? We'll live like that, you and I, and never grow old!'

'Listen!' I said.

They turned their faces towards me in surprise. And then, far away, from some hidden cote, it echoed down the river again – that calling that Solomon heard these three thousand years ago in the hills of Palestine and set for ever in words undying. [47]

A rainbow sprang and vanished against the shores of el Roda. Trailingly went by a thin curtain of rain. Half-hidden behind the hills was already the disc of the sun.

I turned the boat and we drifted down the Nile between the tinted shores. Never-ceasing in that sunset silence was the calling of doves. Norla and Sashka had ceased to whisper, and sat hand in hand. And then Norla spoke in the serene voice that yet held a golden tremor.

'Colonel Anton, will you go back to the Pension Avallaire and tell my father not to worry? I am going with Sashka.'

I stared in stupefaction. 'But you cannot have the consulate marriage [48] for many days. ...'

Over Bulaq hung already the evening star. Already were the ghosts of shadows. And through them, answer to me, Norla Freeman's laughter, very low and tender.

And then, in helplessness, I understood. They had passed beyond the hold and restraint of me or anyone. The world and wonder was theirs tonight. ...

The jetty. I pulled in, and in a moment we were on shore, walking up through that street where once I had hurried Norla. Towards the river was coming an arabiyeh, and we drew aside to let it pass.

But it did not pass. There came a sudden order in English, a groan of pain, and Dr Freeman was in the street beside us.

X

The false clue, you understand, had not misled him. From the first he had doubted Norla's story of the sudden necessity of the reed-sketch, and with the passing of the day his doubts had become certainty. After we had gone from the Pension Avallaire he had driven to Sashka's address, and, finding the Russian so-abominable neither there nor at his café, directed his arabiyeh to the boat-shed of Simon's cousin. They had had difficulty in finding the street of approach, and the anger of his passenger had but seemed to increase the stupidity of the driver.

Of these things we learnt afterwards, but at the moment we stood and stared at him in that twilight street – I, at least, in the consternation. He stood a moment in silence, leaning on the heavy stick, glaring from one to the other of us, with for background the loitering, weary-faced women crowding in doorway and at window.

'So you have been for the "final sketch" – you and the Russian "gentleman"? And who is this?'

Norla was white-faced, but she spoke in a voice as quiet as his. 'This is Alexandr Utro, whom I am going to marry.'

'Another Russian "gentleman"?' He glared at her like the beast and then made the foul sneer, standing there with quivering hand upon his stick.

'M'sieu' –' [49]

Sashka with smouldering eyes confronting him. And then Dr Freeman gave evidence of that passion that seethed in him. He lifted his stick and struck with it, blindly, and like a savage. ...

For a moment was a foolish scrimmage in the street strangely hushed. Then I was holding Dr Freeman's wrist the while he raved at us and in the eyes of Sashka glowed murder.

'My God, my God!'

I thought it a cry of pain and released his wrist. He was staring up the street, and we followed his gaze. Even the eyes in the dim faces that backgrounded him turned to follow it. And in the street, though Dr Freeman was shivering as one in an ague, [50] was nothing.

I caught his arm to support him. Some current seemed to shiver through me. And then I saw.

Down the street, emerged from a middle house, was coming a woman, fair and young and with red-coiled hair. With noiseless feet she came, looking neither to the left nor right, but ahead, with shining eyes, and for the wonderful moment I could smell the fragrance of the primrose pinned at her throat. With hasting feet, clad in the trailing robes, she went by, down to the shadows and the glow of the Nile, and as she passed I heard on her lips the murmur of a little song. ...

'Mary!' [51]

We lifted Dr Freeman into the arabiyeh, and then Norla was shaking my shoulder.

'What was he looking at? ... Colonel Anton, you're dazed also. What did he see come down the street?'

I looked, as one coming out of sleep, at the dimming Nile, at Sashka, at Norla, at the crowding faces.

'I think it was the Spring,' I said.

XI

I shall not tell you of the talk I had the next evening with an old priest [52] very broken and frightened, nor of the little gathering a fortnight later at the Presbyterian Church, [53] where Alexandr Sergeyvich Utro was married by the father of the bride to a Norla who bore a great bunch of English primroses, and stood with shining eyes, there, surely at the Gate of Spring. [54] ...

But within twelve hours of that happening in the street of shame I had gone back there, making enquiries at the middle house on the right side of the street. For a little they would give me no answer, those women with the dead eyes, and I was turning away, when one in the doorway leaned and whispered to me.

'Yes, there was one who died in this house yesterday. In the evening, at sunset.' There came the high, toneless laughter from far back in the throat. 'An Englishwoman. We called her the Sitt Miriam.' [55]

IX

East is West

I

See to the dip and play of them above Heliopolis! [1] They are as birds, despite the good Mogara. ... Fighting machines, I think.

Incongruous over Cairo – those the aeroplanes? They outrage the atmosphere Eastern? But why? Was not Dædalus of the East – of Crete and Crete prehellenic [2] at that? Was it into La Manche [3] so-admired that the first of the aeronaut martyrs fell? ... Yours the geography unreliable, my friend. The Icarian Sea lies not in Western Europe! [4]

East is East and West is West [5] – the heresy pitiful, the concept pre-Copernican. [6] Those fighting birds of steel: they were made in your England – and are numbered with symbols evolved in the East two thousand years ago; [7] your aeronauts [8] – they bear on their tunics the winged crests of ancient Egypt! [9]

For East is West and West is East; they merge and flow and are the compass-points of a dream. And the little jingo men [10] who walk the world, lifting here the banner Nordic and there the flag Mongolian – in the white hands that raise the banner is the blood of cannibals pre-Aryan, the banner itself is a-flutter with symbols obscene first painted in the jungle-towns of Cambodia; [11] the little Jap is a White, a mongrel Ainu, [12] and salutes on his flag the design first graved on the ancient stones of Cuzco! [13] ...

Then of race or culture-barriers – I would recognise none? God mine, I can recognise nothing else! Like Simon Mogara, like all of us, my life is fenced about with tribe-taboos, my ears deafened with the whining rhymes of cultures troglodyte! [14] Like Simon –

II

But I will tell you of Mogara the while we sit and watch the aeroplanes. And the haughty tourists that pass us by this dusty Abbassieh roadway will think us tramps or Europeans gone native!

Mogara. It is almost four years ago since I first met him, the one evening in January. I had gone to live in Heliopolis that I might be near the clients of the hotels, and that day had spent the many and wearying hours indoors, in the Cairo Museum, explaining to a party indifferent and irreverent the unauthentic history of King Oonas. [15] Returned at sunset, I set out to walk across the sands towards Helmieh, so that I might meet the evening wind.

I remember that evening very well. There was a thin ghostplay of lightning on the horizon and presently a little wind stirring to whorling [16] puffs the tops of the sand-hillocks. I had stopped to light my pipe in a miniature nullah [17] and from that climbed out, and so came abruptly on Mogara, a silhouette.

'Good evening,' I said, in uncertainty.

He also spoke in the accent un-English. 'Good evening.' He wheeled slowly on his heels till almost he faced me. Then: 'Would you mind stepping aside – or falling flat? The wind's just coming behind you and I'm going to launch her.'

I stepped aside in the hurriedness and some bewilderment. A little film of mist-powder came drifting over the tundra. Mogara raised his arms and flung a glittering bird into the air.

For a moment it swayed perilously, as if about to fall. Then came a little click and sputter, and with the flapping of great wings the fowl amazing soared upwards. So, for perhaps a hundred yards, it soared, in a long curve towards Cairo. Then, unaccountably – for the wings beat quickly as ever – it began to fall, but backwards, and towards us, like a boomerang. Mogara ran forward and I followed him. The bird slipped down into his arms the moment I came to his side.

'This bird,' I said, 'it is –'

He turned on me a face deep-scowling in thought, and with a little start I realised that he was no European. It was a face of the heavy and even bronze, with thin nose, straight brows and lips, and with the startling disfigurement of two long-healed scars stamped darkly from right eye to ear. For a little we looked at each other, and then he smiled slowly.

'It is, God willing, an ornithopter.' [18]

III

I grew to know him well and made occasional visits to his hut in Zeitoun. It was little more than a hut, being the American bungalow set in a little garden. One half of it he used as workshop and study, the other he slept in and therein cooked the much of eggs and rice, being inexpert in the preparations of foods more ambitious.

'Flying? There has been no flying yet. Aeroplanes are not flying machines. They're structures of cambered planes [19] juggling with artificially-created currents of air. The aeroplane is a mistake – no true forerunner of the flying-machine. Like the pterodactyl, [20] it's only a tentative air experiment, destined to die childless. ...'

'And this,' I would say, pointing to the bird-winged model, with its little petrol engine and gleam of aluminium, boat-shaped body, 'this ornithopter – presently it will fly?'

He would scowl and laugh at that, then jump to his feet and stride to the window and watch a flight of desert-making birds. 'Damn it, colonel, it flies already. You've seen it. Only –' he would peer upwards unfriendlily at the dots that were birds – 'it doesn't keep flying. There's something –'

There was something, some law of flight still insoluble, which brought his models to ground after every first hundred yards or so, albeit their wings still beat. Model after model he had tried out. In itself a tremendous achievement, he had solved the initial difficulty of the ornithopter – the building of wings strong, yet flexible, capable of the under-sweep and the poising blow, capable of lifting the machine into air. But in the air it refused to stop.

He would expound these things to me, the child in matters aeronautic, with great logic and clarity, and in the swing of exposition would a strange thing occur. His voice would lose its mechanic staccato and acquire an alien lilt and rhythm. Once, in the midst of such converse, he pulled himself up and laughed.

'Did you notice that – the half-caste sing-song? [21] Funny. And quite ineradicable.'

He had a genuine, impersonal amusement in these traits betrayed by his own personality. But it was the same half-sardonic, half-impatient amusement which personalities ever stirred in him. He had none of the half-breed's resentments or enthusiastic championings – 'perhaps because I'm a quarter-breed. The snarling of the bleached and the coloured go over my head. People don't count. Aeronautics is my job.'

He was of the lesser breeds intermingled enough. His grandfather, a Goanese half-caste, had settled down in Jaffa [22] after wanderings dim and inexplicable. There, as an orange merchant, he had flourished, acquired a Cretan wife, and, in the course of time and nature, a son. This son, exported to France for education, married, and returned to Jaffa after several years with a Parisian lady who took life as a jest and the circles orange-growing by storm. ... Such Mogara family history and social advancement till the appearance of the little Simon.

His appearance seemed to his father the event retrogressive. The Parisian lady, true to character, found him an oddity amusing. They had expected a child who would show no trace of the Goanese grandfather. Instead, they found themselves parents to an atavistic little infant who might have been a Hindu undiluted. As soon as he was old enough his father, in some disgust, exiled him to school and university in Lyons, [23] where colour is little bar and they of the skins dark-pigmented accounted of God's creatures.

He was twenty-nine years of age that evening I encountered him on the Helmieh sands. In that interval from the Jaffa days he had become the French citizen, had during the War served in a French air regiment and acquired a high Legion [24] decoration, had succeeded to and sold the business orange-exporting on the death of his father and mother, had travelled to America –

Of those American days I heard only in the disjointed, sardonic outline. Early after the War, dissatisfied with aeroplanes, he had set about experimenting with helicopter models, and, abandoning that second stage, with flexible gliders and winged kites. He might have remained in France to this day but for the lack of readily-procurable apparatus in that country immediately after its exhausting triumph. The experimenter's needs drove him to America to work and study.

There he found himself, to his own amusement, treated as servant and inferior. Even from other experimenters and aeronauts was the occasional jibe at the 'nigger birdman'. Settled in the new town built on the aircraft trade, he went out one night and found the streets in excitement and turmoil. The usual story had spread of the negro and white woman. Presently was the negro, also as usual, dragged out of jail by the crowd and lynched. Ensued a kind of anti-colour pogrom. [25] ...

Mogara brought out of that turmoil a scarred face and a week in hospital. A citizen of France, apologies were made through stiff consular representations and an indemnity [26] offered. ... I can see the light of amusement flicker on that brooding brown face as he lay in hospital and heard of the indemnity.

For he was as completely indifferent to revenge as to reconciliation. Mankind I think he envisaged largely as straying packs of parti-coloured puppies, baying unaccountably at the moon and indulging in dog-squabbles equally unaccountable. Amidst all this canine pride and uproar his the 'job' to find a corner obscure and pacific where he could build an ornithopter that flew. ...

I remember making the interjection.

'But for whom, then, do you work – for whom add to the sum of knowledge? If such is humanity, why seek to build this flying machine?'

'For my own private pride, I suppose. ... To visit the moon and see what all the howling's about.' He shrugged. 'How should I know? ... Anyhow, I decided against returning even to France, and came to Egypt instead, where there are other browny men in charge. Being the shade they are I calculated they'd probably neither hinder nor mutilate me nor look askance at my feet.'

'Your feet?'

He grinned, the scars creasing in dark serrations on his cheek. 'Yes. You see, I have the half-caste's passion for yellow boots.' [27]

So, with the jest indifferent, to switch to other matters. I remember he told me these things at his garden entrance on the Zeitoun road one evening, the while we smoked the parting pipe. When he had ceased speaking there was a little clatter and cloud of white dust far up the road towards Cairo, and

I watched it idly.

They were the man and girl on horseback, and as they cantered near I drew the breath of admiration. The young man, of the thirty-forties, with the soldier's shoulders, the cold, narrow face with clean-cut features, the cold stare of blue eyes. But the girl – like her companion English, like him result of that fineness of breeding and the much nursery-scrubbing that has made the English aristocrat. And the something – as so often in the feminine of that type, and never in the masculine – it had brought to flower in her: beauty indefinable as the grace of a lily. Very young, bareheaded with the shock of the tidily-untidy hair, slim and upright and with easy hands she rode, head a little thrown back. As she went by her eyes passed over us in the momentary scrutiny, distant, indifferent, impersonal – and bored.

So they passed into the evening, and I, who love types and so seldom find them, [28] had a sting of gratification. These the English, the Aryans ultra-bred, [29] dominant, blood-proud, apart. How apart from all the lesser breeds, they of the pigmentation, 'without the Law'! [30]

I glanced at Mogara in the little shame for my own thoughts. And then I saw that he had scarcely noted their passing. He was staring up into the sky at the inevitable flight of sunset-winging birds.

IV

All next day he worked on a new modification of the keel [31] of his model, and about five of the afternoon went out across the ranges beyond Helmieh to test it anew. For a little, near the original mound where I had found him, perhaps, he stood awaiting the coming of the wind. Deep in thought and the calculation of mathematical minutiae he saw the sand-heaps at length begin to puff, and, setting a dial, launched the bird-machine into the air. It beat upwards with stiffer motion than formerly. A clatter of stones behind him drew his scowling attention. He glanced over his shoulder.

Not a dozen feet away a bare-headed girl sat on horseback, her eyes fixed on the flight of the ornithopter. So only for the moment he noted, then his attention also went back to the model. It flew perhaps two yards further than usual, then commenced its usual boomerang descent.

He swore, ran forward and caught it, and heard behind him an amazed intake of breath. The girl had dismounted, and as he turned with the bird machine in his arms her eyes were very bright with excitement.

'Oh ... sorry if I'm spying. But that was wonderful!'

'It was rotten,' he said, neither graciously nor ungraciously, but with complete indifference to either her apologies or applause. Undiscouraged, she came nearer, her horse following with downbent, snuffling head.

'But why? It's an ornithopter, and it flew. Real flying, not just aeroplane gliding. ... And my brother argues we'll never have ornithopters [32] – never anything more than a lop-sided helicopter or so. Wish he could have seen that! It wasn't a secret test, was it?'

He had been aware of a slight surprise at meeting someone who knew the difference between an ornithopter and a helicopter. Now, still with absent-minded scowl, but half-heeding her presence, he answered the question.

'No. Why should it be?'

'I thought all experimenters did these things secretly and then pestered Governments.' This with flippancy, but then the return to excitement. 'I say! Most thrilling thing I've seen in this boring country – most thrilling thing I've ever seen, I think. ... Do you know the old Frost ornithopter in the London Science? [33] Is yours on the same principle?'

'If you've seen the Frost –' He was launched more successfully than ever had been his model. He set the bird-machine on the ground, demonstrating its build and principal departures from the Frost model. He brought out a pencil and scrap of paper and dashed off lines of the calculations dizzying and algebraic.

The girl remained undizzied. Still holding the bridle she knelt down in the interest, and the horse extended over her shoulder the inquisitive head. ... They must have made an amusing grouping there on the sands.

She had flown many times in aeroplanes, had the English Aero Club's pilot certificate, [34] had, like himself, the obsession that the aeroplane was traitor to aviation and that Romance which had lured men to the conquest of the skies since the days of Cretan Dædalus.

'It wasn't for the sake of a world of super-engined kites that Icarus and Egremont and Lilienthal [35] died. But real flying. ... And you won't sell your model to any Government, or make it a war machine?'

'Good Lord, no.'

'Good man!'

He saw a hand stretched out towards him, and stared at it. His thoughts came hurtling down from rarefied heights like an aeroplane disabled. He found himself kneeling side by side not with a pleasant voice and a disembodied enthusiasm, but an English girl. ...

That stare and silence of his drew her eyes. So, for a little, they looked at each other in mutual wonder: the girl, white and gold, radiant and aloof even in excitement; Mogara, lithe and slight, with the slightness un-European, the dark, scarred face, the scowl of thin-pencilled brows. ... He saw the girl's eyes widen, and at that, with a sardonic little laugh, he was on his feet.

'Yes, I'm a native. But you're quite safe.'

And then, dimly, indifferently, he realised that he had made a mistake. The girl's eyes looked through him as she too rose to her feet.

He had ceased to exist.

V

At nine o'clock that evening passing down the Sharia Kamil, [36] my eyes fell on the small car unmistakable. It was a yellow runabout, the property of my friend Adrian, and it stood in front of a little open-air café with many tables. And at one of those tables, deep in the usual self-game with dominoes, sat Adrian himself.

This is to him relief and narcotic in one, this game played with great seriousness. To me recurred the wonder whimsical: is [37] he ever victor – and over whom? ... He looked up and saw me and swept aside the pieces.

'Hello, colonel. Haven't seen you for ages. Sit down and gossip. How's Heliopolis?'

'It is the dry place,' I said, and at that he ordered me wine. Then:

'Seen anything of the Melforts there? Cousins of mine – air-people, newly come from Malta?' [38]

'I did not know you possessed cousins,' I said. He grinned and yawned, having passed the toilsome day.

'Knowledge that was never kept from me, unfortunately. I was forced to punch the aristocratic Melfort nose quite early in my career.' He was reminiscent. 'And was getting as good as I gave till Joyce, in a pinafore and a white wrath, separated us with a shower of stones and pelted us impartially. ... Murderous little pacifist.'

He expounded the brief and irreverent family history the while I drank the wine. These Melforts were remote cousins only: the grandmother of Adrian had been sister of the grandfather of Reginald and Joyce Melfort.

'But we come from the same county town, you see, and there's been a kind of family friendship – patronising on both sides – kept going for three generations. The Adrians have been the medical and impoverished branch; they've assisted new Melforts into the world and signed their certificates of departure [39] for the last seventy years or so. Know more of Melfort history than the Melforts themselves, who've only passed on the high lights to their descendants.' He chuckled as at some secret jest. 'Grandfather Melfort went out to Jamaica, raised rum and a great deal of money, and returned to perpetuate a military and gentlemanly stock. Put his son into the army, and grandson Reginald followed in his father's footsteps. ... It was he whose nose I punched.

'Not a bad chap really, I suppose. Only – he never had a chance. Born in India and reared on the usual pap. A Nordic snub-man [40] with highly-scrubbed virtues and a disposition to pronounce what as hwaw. [41] Transferred to the Air Force during the War and is a squadron leader [42] or something now. Has taken the latest wonder of science and made of it a means for forming fours [43] in the air and inspecting engines to see if they're properly shaved. [44] ... That kind.'

He broke off, as in conversation he so often did, to refute his own exaggerations. 'No. That's damned unfair. A very good airman, I believe. Straight as a die, efficient, proud of the service, an excellent example of the breeding of an aristocrat in three generations. ... Let's be unfair. Impartiality's too much of a strain. He has less imagination than a wombat, and the colour, caste and class prejudices of a taboo-ridden Brahmin. [45] In his secret soul he believes the Anglo-Saxon sahib [46] evolved from a special type of ape which always cleaned its teeth in the morning and even in the early Miocene [47] wore badges of rank on its fur. ... I've been invited to dinner in ten days' time and if Reginald and I don't quarrel and bandy authorities [48] and sneers, it'll be the first occasion since the nose-punching episode. Joyce'll better stand by with an armful of stones.'

'She is the sister?'

'Occasionally. When she remembers. Keeps house nominally for Reginald: keeps him on tenterhooks in reality. Modern and unmodern. A romantic's idealisation of English womanhood in appearance – she'd delight your eyes, Saloney – and in mind a Gypsy adventurer. [49] Flies aeroplanes and innumerable outrageous opinions, waxes hot over all kinds of unexpected things and cold over everything which her appearance warrants. ... By the seven gates of Egypt [50] – Hi!'

He leapt from his chair with beaming face and a startling shout, and seized the arm of a passer-by – the man bareheaded, absorbed, chest-clasping the large and ungainly parcel. Thus assaulted, the stranger dropped the parcel – which split, grocery-disgorging – and turned scowlingly upon Adrian. Almost immediately vanished the scowl.

'God, the doctor of Chaumont!' [51]

'Air-ambulance 30Q!'

They fell to the hand-shaking, the enquiries innumerable, the laughter of men who had shared a war-episode unforgettable. Adrian turned to make introductions, but I forestalled him.

'I am acquainted,' I said, 'with M. Mogara.'

VI

For four days after his meeting with the unknown girl on the sands, and with the little Adrian and myself in the Sharia Kamil, Mogara kept to his workshop, fitting a new keel to his ornithopter. On the fourth evening he tramped out beyond Helmieh again to put his modification to test. As usual he walked in the study brown, [52] and so almost dashed his head against horse and rider – both of whom had been regarding his approach for over a mile.

It was the girl, and she surveyed him insolently. 'What is your name, Mr – Native?'

He was in a good humour, expecting better results from his model. He twinkled at her sardonically. 'Mogara – memsahib. ... And my grandfather was a Goanese.'

She flushed angrily. 'He may have been a Chinese albino for all I care. You are very concerned with your own family history, M. Mogara. Hasn't it ever struck you that it may be boring to others? Or your assumption the other evening of the role of the dark and dangerous male – wasn't it rather cowardly?'

He was sardonically undisturbed. 'No doubt I'm both a bore and a coward. Meantime my job's not psycho-analysis but amateur aeronautics.'

'Of course it is! And since the tests aren't secret why mayn't I come and watch them? Why have you kept away from the trial-ground these last three evenings? Can't you see that I want to learn, that it's your ornithopter I'm interested in, not you, you –'

He stared at her. It was the one appeal which could have touched him. On his face, dark and scarred, she saw come something like wonder. Followed the slow smile. Then:

'"Blithering ass" are the words you want. ... I'm sorry.' He held out a tentative hand. 'If –'

Her fingers touched his. They regarded each other gravely for a moment, laughed together; then Joyce Melfort dismounted, sat down, clasped her hands about her knees, and watched. ...

You must figure her so, evening after evening. For the meetings went on. Almost every evening she rode across the sands to find Mogara, with some new modification imposed upon his model, waiting for the sunset wind.

And presently, in between times of the test-flying and calculations abstruse, they would find themselves deep in talk – talk that ranged away from aeronautics and back to it and away again. She found his mind the encyclopædia of sheer fact, the mind of the scientist, a little warped, almost passionless but for that the desire and pursuit of knowledge; hers was to him revelation of how knowledge may be transmuted to idealism and hope and purpose. ...

Except a sardonic scepticism for all enthusiasms nationalist and religious he had the no-philosophy of life. She made him see all human existence in the terms of high Adventure – the adventure scarce begun, the struggle from the slime to the stars. *Per ardua ad astra.* [53] Every scrap of new knowledge was equipment for that Adventure; every man who fought the beast in himself and others, who kept honest ledgers and an open mind, who knew the ache of wonder and a desire beyond fulfilment – he fought in the spear-head of the Adventure. ...

And Mogara, his model half-forgotten, would brood and listen till he too glimpsed faith and belief in that Republic in the skies which lies beyond our shadowed uncertainties, which sometimes seems but a generation away.

Sometimes, as they talked, they would lift their heads and see the wheel and glitter of Squadron-Leader Melfort's aeroplanes practising dusk landings at Heliopolis.

VII

'A nigger chappie with a bee in his bonnet [54] and one of those helicopter-thingummys. He's been at it for months, they say, practising out on the sands beyond Helmieh. Saw him myself last night when I went up to do a spot of night flying.'

Joyce Melfort came riding against the sunset of the tenth day since her first encounter with Mogara. Fragments from the chatter at her brother's table the previous evening rode with her, like buzzing gnats. ... She had been coldly angry, then wondering and amused. Now, with an amazement, she found herself angry again.

From far across the sands Mogara waved to her, absent-mindedly. As she rode towards him the buzzing of an aeroplane engine grew loud overhead. She glanced upwards, saw one of the machines of her brother's squadron dip towards her and Mogara as though they were a bombing target, and then rise and wheel back towards Heliopolis.

'Now that that anachronism's [55] gone –'

She reined in, dismounted, and stood watching in silence. Mogara clicked out the wings of the much-tried model, set revolving the little dial and pointer in its heart, and then launched the contrivance into the air.

He did not stop to watch its progress, but turned round towards her with the now not infrequent smile. '"Hope springs eternal – "' [56] he patted the neck of her nuzzling mount. '– If you're not bored with the performance by now, I think your horse must be. ... Eh?'

She had caught his arm in a grip that was painful. 'Quick! Look!'

Mogara wheeled round and stared skywards, stared at a flapping-winged model which neither failed nor descended, which rose and rose with steady purr of miniature engine and then began to wheel overhead in great circles. ...

Its inventor gulped, swore inadequately, and then found Joyce Melfort's hands gripping his, shaking them up and down.

'Why, you've won, you've won!' She glanced up for reassurance and then executed a little dance. 'My dear man, can't you realise it? Waken up! [57] Aren't you glad? ...'

Her voice died away. There came in her eyes the terror and expectation. Unaccountably in his arms, she saw his scarred face bent dark-flushed above her. So, a moment she would remember for ever, and then, kissed by him, there awoke in her something like a dream forgotten. ... That – then they were apart, and she had slashed him across the face with her riding whip.

He staggered a little under her blow, and then, in a queer silence, not looking at her, brought out a handkerchief, and dabbed at the blood-pringling [58] weal which flushed angrily on his unscarred cheek. He lowered the scrap of linen, looking at it in a kind of wonder, and at that Joyce Melfort's stricken remorse found voice.

'Oh, I'm sorry. ... I was a beast. But you shouldn't –'

He smiled at her, without a hint of mockery, with dull eyes. He was very quiet – dazedly quiet.

'I know I shouldn't.' That was the only possible reply. He turned away uncertainly, fumbling with the handkerchief. 'And now you'd better go.'

He expected to hear the sound of her footsteps going towards the horse. Instead, there was complete silence. He glanced round again. She stood where he had kissed her, in her eyes a mounting flame of courage and resolution. She began to speak.

'Listen: I'm sorry – because I hit you. Not because you kissed me. Why shouldn't you?' Her voice quivered a little, but her eyes were very brave. 'I – I wanted you to.'

They stared at each other. Overhead, absurdly, and in circles drawing gradually earthwards, wheeled the unheeded ornithopter model. Mogara shook his head. ...

She found herself listening to an impossible renunciation from an impossible lover, the while the darkness came flowing across the sands.

'... You're splendid to have said that. But tomorrow – and the next day – it'll sound impossible. To you it sounds half-impossible even now. ... English – and I'm a mongrel. Your people –' He seemed to forget what he had intended to say. His voice trailed off. He shrugged, and held out his hand, and was oddly shy, and stammered for the first time since she had known him. 'Thanks for you – for it.' Her limp fingers touched his. They smiled at each other strainedly. 'This isn't anything, you know. We aren't anything. And there's still your Adventure. For both of us. Always there's the Adventure. ...' [59]

She found herself mounted and riding towards Heliopolis. A hundred yards away she looked back and saw Mogara snatch a magic bird out of the darkness, like a boy playing with a dream.

VIII

And less than a dream was it presently to seem to him. In the Zeitoun hut he sat and stared at the ornithopter model. Successful. He had won. Successful.

He went to a mirror and saw the ghostly reflection of his own face, scarred on both cheeks. ... So it had actually happened.

He began, mechanically, to prepare a meal. What was it he had said? The Adventure: still the Adventure. ... Aeronautics not enough now. Something to follow and believe in. She had believed in it. ...

He heard the galloping horse stop at his garden-gate; heard hasting footsteps come up to the open door of the hut. For a moment was a figure dim against the night dimness, and then Joyce Melfort was in the room.

They stood facing each other a moment, and he saw her breast rise and fall, as might one who had run a race.

'M. Mogara – did you or did you not kiss me out there?'

He nodded whitely.[60] Thereat she gave a sigh, and suddenly collapsed, limply, happily, into a chair.

'Then that's all right. Because you'll have to marry me now, in spite of my deplorable ancestors. Where can I throw my hat?' She jumped up in expostulation. 'My dear, whoever told you that was the way to cook a sausage?'

She knelt over the sputtering oil-stove, and, so kneeling, wheeled round and laughed up at him. 'Poor brother Reginald! ...' She stopped to make mirthful appraisement of her fingernails. She was incoherently light-hearted. 'Knew as soon as I got home that he knew. That was *his* machine that came bombing us this afternoon. He'd heard about us – came down to spy, my dear. ... Was waiting for me, he and Adrian – they'd been quarrelling – and oh! what does it matter what he said? I felt too sick to notice much till Adrian broke in with a kind of shout. "Who? *Simon Mogara?*" Stared from one to other of us and then laughed and laughed, and then grew white and furious. *"Nigger?* Why, damn your impudence – !" and it all came out, and so did I, and made for the stables, leaving Reggie like a ghost and Adrian shouting wishes to you. ... What an evening! Who'd have guessed it? Who ever? And now –'

His queer, frozen silence made her glance up. In a moment she was beside him. 'Why, why – Simon! ...'

IX

It was some time before either of them stirred from that position wherein she had told her eager secret amazing. Smell of burning sausage roused Joyce. She broke away and danced to the oil-stove, and Mogara, released from necessity to hold her in his arms, sank down into the chair she had vacated and stared at his yellow boots as though they were the footwear unbelievable. ...

An hour later, on parting under the stars at the garden-gate, he heard her gay answer to his question come out of the dimness: 'Why, soon as ever, my dear!' Dimly from her saddle she bent towards him to give him the ghostly kiss. Then had a whimsical thought and laughed a grave little laugh.

'But our children – whatever'll they be citizens of?'

Her hand, warm and assured, in his, he stood and looked up at her, and beyond her at the stars, at the years he saw with their difficulties and disillusionments and perhaps the bitter shames for her to face. But in his voice she heard only tenderness as he answered with the jest that was more than jest, that would cry its promise through all their lives.

'Why – the Republic in the skies!'

X

For East is West and West is East and the little fascistic German blesses as the Aryan symbol exclusive the swastika they worship in the Mountains of the Moon. [61] ... Eh? You see, the good Adrian, until provoked beyond endurance, had held it as a dark and mirthful secret that the Melfort grandmother, wealth-bringing, had been a 'white mulatto' [62] of Jamaica.

X

Gift of the River

I

Keith Landward [1] seen in Athens? And you have heard of Landward? Read of him in the Egyptian Gazette? [2] ... The story scandalous, I make no doubt.

An abduction charge initiated by the Greek Institution? [3] And with hastiness dropped, though it was sufficient to bring about ostracism of Landward and his unwed victim – if one may ostracise those who walk unaware of both laws and law-givers!

To Landward I think a marriage ceremony would have seemed a gross sacrilege. ...

Eh? But how? ... Let me tease you for moral, my friend, you who are young, the realist declared – though where was ever yet realist who dipped pen in the inks of reality? I, Anton Saloney, the much and foolishly over-read, have met him never!

Love – is desire, possession – satiety. Are not these the axioms realist?

Yet Heloise walks a garden still, and tonight – who knows the agony of Abelard [4] under these stars? Who knows the face of Paolo [5] in the Khalig throngs? Yet I have seen him pass. I have seen in a Nileward [6] window the light set by one who waits and weeps Leander [7] – dust and legend these three thousand years!

Polychromata – the City of Many Colours. But there is one colour that abides and changes not. Gift of the River is our Cairo, and what gifts but the miraculous does the Nile bring? Who may say, knowing Keith Landward and his tale, knowing romance and miracle for the children of faith and necessity, that even Hero waits in vain?

II

And his tale fantastic that I have pieced together – it begins as indeed no tale should begin, when Joan Landward died in the Nile house beyond Bulaq Bridge.

She had spent a bare five months in Cairo, brought here for health, and for portrait you must make imagining of one with dark hair and grey eyes and the white cheeks stained with bright blood-ovals. As though painted on the pallor of her skin were those ovals.

Keith Landward, the husband, brought her here in late November, and I took them the explorations of the bazaars. She had in these explorations much delight. Life she found continually a wonder and delight. ... Laughing, she would cough and stop, and the bright blood-ovals flame in her cheeks, and Landward's eyes leap to her in startled fear. It was, you understand, hers the lung-wasting [8] that had brought them to Egypt.

'Insane climate. Treacherous,' he would storm, with that startled look still in his eyes. 'Dr Adrian says so. We'll go back to Majorca.' [9]

'Not yet. Not until the Spring. I'm in love with Colonel Saloney's Cairo – *and* the Nile. So's Steadfast. Bark yes, Steadfast. Do it in Esperanto!' [10]

She had a dog, the little solemn, thick-coated beast, called Steadfast, and to him she had taught the many little solemn tricks. In the narrow, high-walled garden of their house, with the water-steps leading down to the River, she would prevail on Steadfast to make the ludicrous evolutions for my delectation, and on her never did the exquisite funniness of those pall. Landward, laughing and scowling, would shake her shoulders.

'Stop it, Joan! You'll exhaust yourself.'

'Sorry, but it's Steadfast to blame.' Seated, she would lean back against Landward's hands and look up into his face with just such solemnity of tenderness as was in the eyes of the dog looking up at her. So sitting, she would reach her arms round his neck, her fingers twisting in his hair in the mock-cruel caress, and be very still.

'Listen to the River!'

She loved the Nile, and I think listened much to it in that garden the while she worked and translated with Landward. He was a linguist, the master of many tongues – never have I known anyone master of so many – and language-study was his life-work. It was his the dream to build up the scientific international language – not one of the easy elisions and evasions, but a tongue founded on the broad evolutions of human speech, a flexible, synthetic World-Speech [11] that would presently be taught the earth over. ...

He was a Scotsman of the far Western Islands, of that Celtic fringe that is now denied by your historians. [12] Dark as Joan herself, quick and emotional and subtle, he worked not ploddingly, but in the sudden flares of inspiration and enthusiasm. But that men turn now from romantic dreamings as from childhood's toys, he might have been poet or painter of the twilight melancholy. The poet, I think, for words, the power and beauty and terror of words, could move him as stars or music another. His Joan and his World-Speech – these his two loves, grown inextricably one.

'There won't be a frontier or a fort in Europe fifty years after we've finished,' he would declaim, and she would look at him with shining eyes. Swift herself in the learning of languages, this dream of the World-Speech had grown as vivid for her as for Landward.

But presently he was in difficulties. The framework of the World-Speech was already planned, but how to garb it in living flesh?

'Accent – intonation – some common denominator of word-rhythm and music. ... Damn it, Joan, it's an impasse. Take another twenty years of work. ... Oh, curse all fools since the Tower of Babel!'

And he got up, tramping to and fro in one of his sudden rages. Then her silence, the fact that she did not laugh at him as usual, brought his gaze to her. She sat very still, with eyes closed.

'Joan!'

Fear for her haunted his life, though he hid it even from himself, except at such moments. She roused and looked up at him.

'What? ... Oh Keith, my dear, don't look like that! I'm ever so well. Only lazy.... And this accent-business won't take twenty years: nor twenty months. You'll find it long before then – I'll find it myself! ...' Her arms round his neck, the solemnity in her eyes as he bent over her. 'Lazy this afternoon, my dear. And the sound of the River –'

That night, lying wakeful in the darkness over this matter of the World-Speech accent, he heard Joan cough and turn restlessly and the sound of her hand come out to seek him. ... He sat up in panic and turned on the lights, for the hand had ceased to seek and the noise of the River below had suddenly grown to the noise of a torrent.

III

That shining room in the crematorium [13] of Al Fostat – always shall I remember the smell of the mimosa wreaths that blinded the white coffin, and the still, dark face of Landward, and that strange burial-service of your Church, [14] at once so beautiful and grotesque. ... Then Adrian and I, with uneasiness for what might happen if we left him, drove back with Keith Landward to the house above the Nile.

He went with us in silence, but suddenly, in the garden of the house, at sight of the solemn little dog, Steadfast, padding to and fro, burst into one of the rages that with him were temperamental.

'That infernal dog – can't have it here. Interrupt my work. ... Must go on with my work. Do you hear? ... Take it away, Saloney. Eh? Anywhere you like. What the devil does it matter to me? Never want to see it again.' He raised his voice. 'Ibrahim! That fool Ibrahim – why hasn't he set my table out here? Does he think this is a national fête?' [15]

He darted into the house, there was presently the sound of cursing and commotion, and he appeared again, driving the scared and laden Ibrahim Garas, his Egyptian servant.

'Down there. In the usual place. And take away that other chair – *that* chair, you fool! ... Anything you two want? Eh? Oh yes. Goodbye.'

IV

The little dog trotted beside us, making the heartbreaking whine, and to me he was a worry, for Landward in such mood might order him to be drowned. Adrian had no place to keep him, nor had I.

Then I remembered my friends, the Freligraths, and that they perhaps could help. After parting with Adrian I took the electric train out to Kubbah, and at the domed house of the Freligraths [16] waited in a downstairs room for her who had been Flore Gellion to descend from the immersements astronomical.

'Anton, my friend! Ages since you came to see me. And who is this?'

The little beast, Steadfast, whined up at her with pricked ears, and then drooped his head again. I made explanations.

'*Quelle honte!* [17] But of course he may stay here.' She knelt and encircled him in her arms. 'It is but right, since your mistress is with the stars, [18] is she not? ... Stay to tea, my colonel. I've delayed for Friedrich, but cannot wait longer. Ribaddi, [19] in Rome, and I are doing the Venus transit together, [20] just after sunset.'

Already was that sunset near and I bidding farewell, when we heard the car of Friedrich Freligrath, the Nile engineer, coming from Cairo. He came in haste and we waited for him.

'Am I very late, Flore? Hello, colonel! ... Gods, what's this? A doormat?'

He made the embrace of Flore, and the little beast, Steadfast, growled at him, but without spirit. Still standing, Friedrich drank tea.

'Going, colonel? If you'll wait a minute I'll drive you back. I've to go into Cairo again, Flore – there has been an accident a little way up-river. That was what delayed me. One of our launches ran into a crowded Greek pleasure-boat and spilled half the passengers into the Nile.'

V

Keith Landward sat in his garden and listened to the sound of the River.

That first agony of desolation – the awakening agony of a wound realised which had led to the violent scene in the presence of Adrian and myself – had passed. He sat now and looked down the future, the corridors of the days and nights he would tramp alone, without hope or heroism, vision or God. These things he had left behind in Al Fostat with the ashes of Joan.

He closed his eyes, and the dull ache passed from these to his heart. Agony had done its utmost, and now was merely tiredness unutterable with him; that, and the sound of the River.

And suddenly, listening there, a verse of your Swinburne's, that he had not read or thought of for many years, came into his mind.

From too much love of living,
  From hope and fear set free,
We thank with brief thanksgiving
  Whatever gods may be,
That no life lives forever,
  That dead men rise up never,
That even the weariest river
  Winds somewhere safe to sea. [21]

'Even the weariest river. ...' He looked round about him in slow amazement. The ache passed from his mind. *Why had he not thought of that before?*

He thrust aside the pages that had once spelt vision and achievement but seemed now petrification of the idle and inane chatter. Very calmly and deliberately he walked up the garden and into the house. His revolver required cleaning, and he took it out to the balcony of carved mushrabiyeh work [22] that overhung the Nile, and sat there smoking and cleaning with the River below him.

Both fear and agony had fallen from him. It was a very lovely evening. Waiting for the sunset, the River was the hushed blue expectancy, except where a launch that went by against the further shore clove the water in a furrow of gold.

'That is lovely,' he said to himself.

His senses were sharp and vivid as never before. He finished loading the revolver and laid it aside, and sat, head in hands, thinking of all the beautiful things he had ever known. Sunsets and sunrises and ripple of water; music heard at night; a naked bather in a Majorca cove; Joan; her laughter; singing; the beauty of words. ...

Below him and the balcony was a continual whisper.

'The River. ... How she loved it! Tired. It called her.'

He raised his head. The sunset was raining darkness over Cairo. Below him the River flushed and paled and dimmed. He picked up the revolver and twirled its barrel, set the hammer [23] – and dropped it clattering to his feet.

In the lower rooms Ibrahim had switched on the electric lights, and their radiance was flung upon the Nile. But it was beyond that radiance, the thing he had seen. He closed his eyes in unbelief, opened them again, and then –

Out of the darkness it swirled into the light, going seawards, rising and falling on the slow current, a thing white and unmistakable.

It was the body of a woman.

VI

From Adrian, met on his rounds the next day, I heard of the happening at the Landward house.

'Keith saw her from his balcony, ran downstairs, jumped in, and pulled her ashore. ... Must have cost him a vile expenditure of temper! A girl of seventeen or eighteen, unconscious, but alive. She had banged herself somehow. Hair clotted with blood at the base of the skull. ... Another casualty of that pleasure-boat accident?

'Of it I have heard,' I said. 'She has been identified?'

'Not yet, though that won't be any difficulty. I've supplied descriptions to the Police, the Greek consulate, and the Nile people. Greek quite certainly. Spoke a few words of it this morning, and apparently doesn't know any other language. ... Some dialect of the Islands, Landward says, and very pure. ... Yes, said that! Thank the Lord, in one way, the poor girl was nearly drowned. Her intrusion has jolted Landward into one of those towering rages of his – and I was afraid of something else.'

'She has told her name?'

'Not yet. The pure Greek stream is – or was this morning – only a tricklet. Too exhausted to do anything but sleep. Probably been reclaimed and taken away by now.' He mused a little. 'Something wrong with her eyes, I think. Eh? Oh, white and gold – like a Greek out of Wilde. [24] Or a *koré* of the vases.' [25]

VII

But neither that day nor the next came anyone to identify Landward's salvage. The captain of the pleasure-boat, interviewed, swore that all the people flung overboard in the River accident had been rescued by himself or the launch. He was a man shifty and untrustworthy, and frightened that he might earn a reputation for the reckless handling of his boat.

'Obviously a liar,' said Adrian. 'Don't suppose he had the least idea how many passengers were on his precious boat. It was a three hours' jaunt up and down the River.'

'There are no relatives – the police have no information?'

'No, that's the devil of it. The girl must have been friendless. Meanwhile Landward's going about like a roaring multi-lingual lion. Went up to the Greek consulate yesterday and kicked up Hades. [26] Swears his work's interrupted and disorganised. ... Hope it's only his work. I went out on that balcony this morning, looking for him, and found this lying on the floor.'

He displayed the revolver, of which, and other things, I was afterwards to hear from Landward himself the full tale.

'And that's not the worst of it. I thought there was something funny about her eyes. That blow on the head's responsible, of course. ... She doesn't remember any of the happenings before the accident. Doesn't remember even her own name. Pass in time, naturally. Amnesia never lasts.'

VIII

To Keith Landward he made presently a suggestion.

'There is, of course, a Greek Institution for the destitute. She can be handed over to that.'

'Eh? Pauper's home? No, she can stay here till she's better; if she wants to.'

And with this ungracious and unreasonable invitation – for she was as yet unable fully to understand the situation – the nameless Greek girl stayed on at the Nile house. Adrian has a sardonic wit. That day, when he decided the girl should be taken out of doors, he called Landward from the book-strewn balcony to which the latter had retreated on hearing the garden was about to be invaded.

'She'll have to be carried to the garden. As you carried her up you may as well take her down. She might object to Ibrahim.'

'He swore, but went up the stairs to her room and knocked at the door,' Adrian was to relate to me. 'I was climbing up from below and heard and saw most of the comic incident. I know a little Greek. She called out "Who is it?" and Landward replied "It is I" – a statement possible in Greek, but just as idiotic as in English. [27] Her voice came back – surprised and amused, I thought – "Oh, come in. I am almost ready." In he went ... to come striding out again in an instant, banging the door. You see, the Egyptian women-servants had taken up some clothes a minute or two before, and Landward, going in, found his protégée in quite an unnecessary state of negligée.' [28]

'It was an accident.'

'Oh, innocent enough, I imagine; but a bit surprising, seeing she tucks herself up to the chin even when speaking to her medical adviser. Anyhow, she wasn't in the least embarrassed when he did carry her down. Doesn't seem in the least aware of the upset to the Landward regime. She's the confidence of an infant, or –' He shrugged.

'Eh?'

'Quite. A friendless Greek girl in Cairo – starvation and worse send scores south from Smyrna and the Archipelago [29] each winter. This memory-obscuring may be a fairy-tale. One never knows. ... If it is, she must envisage the situation as one of heaven-sent opportunity. Poor thing!'

IX

Next day I called at the Nile house – I who had not been there since the funeral of Joan Landward – and in the garden saw a sight unexpected. Under the great green umbrella Keith Landward sat with table and books. In a chair beside him, much-wrapped and with the yellow-gold flame of hair, was a girl. Landward's face was lighted and eager with excitement, and he was alternately listening and writing with rapidity. At sound of the door closing they looked round and Landward, with no appearance of cordiality, made the brusque introduction.

I know a little of the ancient speech – which is to the modern Romaic as Virgil to the twitterings of the little d'Annunzio [30] – and that it seemed to me would have been the fitting speech for her. And then I had a surprise. For, though with accent and quantities unfamiliar, it was verily almost in the ancient tongue that she spoke.

'You see, I have no name.'

I cannot hope to convey to you the ring and beauty of those words she spoke. I stood and stared at her with the mists of strange questioning and wonder rising in my mind. Somewhere, somewhere –

And then I knew. A figure on a vase I had once seen, made when the world was young, in the dawn of Europe. Even to line of nose and forehead so beloved by Athenian craftsmen she was that figure. I groped for name and memory, and, unembarrassed under my rude stare, she smiled with slow-widening eyes.

Eyes like sunflowers. And suddenly I heard myself speak.

'I think it should be Kora,' [31] I said, with the utter conviction that in a moment was gone, leaving me foolish and self-wondering. The wonderful eyes budded a question, but Landward broke in with impatience.

'Eh? What's that? Kora? It'll do as well as any other, won't it? Must have a name. ... And now we'll get on – if you'll excuse us, Saloney.'

X

With enthusiasm Landward set to the teaching of English to his River-salvage, though for other reasons his interest had first awakened in her. They had both accepted my christening, and neither was embarrassed by the fact that as yet she possessed no surname.

One afternoon I collided with the hurrying and book-laden figure in Esbekiyeh. It was Landward, happy, with the face of a boy.

'... Intonation – that was the root difficulty of the World-Speech. But I believe I've fixed it in phonetics at last. Kora has just the requisite tone and accent. ... Natural enough. Greek is the oldest and purest of the Aryan dialects, [32] and in whatever out-of-the-way spot of the Archipelago she or her people originated the spoken tongue must remain amazingly archaic.'

'The mind-obscuring – the amnesia – it is going?' I asked.

'Eh? No, I don't think so.' He shrugged aside this triviality. 'I haven't asked. I've been too busy.'

He had accepted her as an accent and intonation, not as an individual. Compilation of the World-Speech again obscured his every horizon. Kora could now walk to and from the garden unaided. She still went clad in the absurd Egyptian clothes. Unless questioned, she never spoke to Landward in his long spells of work, but would sit under the green umbrella, head to one side, apparently lost in day-dreams.

And then, a thing disturbing to the contentment of toil and achievement, he was conscious in himself of a vague uneasiness, of vague, unworded questions whenever he raised his head and met those sunflower eyes fixed upon him. Drugged with work, living betwixt sleep and wakefulness, as he knew himself – what when he awoke?

XI

And then into their garden came an official from the Greek Institution.

He was the young-old man, the American-cultured Greek, and was shown to Landward, under the green umbrella, at the moment when the latter sat alone.

'You are the Mister Landward?' he asked in the American English.

'I am,' snapped the linguist, in Romaic, and for a moment this seemed to disconcert the young-old man. ... But he made a quick recovery. He was directed to enquire into the conditions under which a young Greek girl was living in the house. The circumstances of her rescue were well known to the Institution. But there had been rumours. Was or was not this girl living with him as his mistress?

Landward had listened in the daze, and now sat staring his dazement. The young-old man became confidential and made the greasy smile. ... The girl was, no doubt, a stray from some unlicensed house, [33] and there need be no difficulty. Between friends. Providing she was not being forcibly detained. And even then, if it was certain there would be no scandal – ?

Landward had looked beyond him. The American-Greek turned round. The girl was coming down the garden towards them.

If he had had any hesitations with Landward, he had none with Kora, presuming her to be what Adrian had suspected. She stared at him with wondering eyes as he made the easy greeting in Romaic, and then, pulling out his notebook, put the coarse questions.

But at even the first of these the rapidly-fraying temper of Landward, until then held marvellously in one, snapped. Like most of those who toil for the ultimate brotherhood of all men, he was one with the intense prejudices and dislikes; amongst these, his hatred of nasal Americanisms. Questions apart, the Greek's accent had already undone him, and for Landward to seize him abruptly and urgently, rush him to the garden-gate, tear that open, and kick out into the dust and the street the young-old convert to transatlantic acumen and intonation was the work of a moment. ... He returned to find a wondering Kora awaiting him.

'You are very hot.' She considered him gravely, brought out the scrap of handkerchief, and, with an air absorbed, dabbed his forehead. Then:

'But what did he mean? How does it concern him? Of course we live together. Though at night – ?'

She shook her head, puzzled, her eyes raised to him. Then the puzzlement slowly faded and remote amongst the cornflowers [34] came hurrying strange lights. ... Landward turned his head away.

'There are such men,' he said, lamely, avoiding her eyes, shamed by that white innocence.

He went away on pretended business, but returned to the garden that evening, tramping to and fro for hours. The evil chatter of the Helleno-American should have stirred him to disgust alone, but now, in an agony of self-hatred and remorse, he shuddered away from the thoughts suddenly uncovered in his mind. ... My God, and Joan – Joan who had taken the light from the world – she had not been dead two weeks. ...

In the bright moonlight of his room, long after the rest of the house was quiet, he undressed, trying not to hear that haunting song of the River below his window.

Somewhere, out of the swift, strange dream, near to dawn, he awoke, and as realisation came to him it seemed that the noise of the River below grew to the sound of a torrent.

In his arms, very fast asleep as a child might sleep, one arm around his neck, a shoulder white to the moon-dazzle, lay the girl Kora.

XII

That morning I awoke to the free and lazy day. I had no clients. At the Freligrath house the week before had occurred that happening eternally miraculous, and I went out to the Kubbah house to make the call. Flore Freligrath, the very young and modern mother, I discovered hard at work in her study, with Thibaut August [35] asleep in a portable cot and the dog, Steadfast, outstretched in boredom upon the floor. At sight of me he leapt up with a whine.

After I had admired the sleeper, doubtlessly miraculous but hardly of himself admirable, I found the solemn little dog attempting to follow me from the room.

'I am afraid Thibaut August and I bore him,' said Flore. 'He has never displayed those tricks of which you spoke.'

'He is the lover steadfast,' [36] I said, and patted him, and took my leave. But I did not return to Cairo; instead, tramped to the hut of Mogara, and there remained a little while, and then struck across the roads and so presently the dusty Cairene streets to the house of Landward on Nile bank.

I did not go through the house, for the garden-gate hung loose, and by it I went in, half-expecting to see under the green umbrella the heads dark and golden bent in collaboration over the typescripts of the World-Speech.

But Keith Landward sat alone, and as I crossed the garden to him he raised a livid face. I stopped. It was the face of a man horrified and self-tortured. He spoke in a whisper, as though I had been standing there for hours.

'Saloney, how is it a Greek drab [37] from the River can have the face of a saint?'

'I do not –' I began, and then understood at once, glancing to the house and then back at his face.

Adrian had been right.

Beyond the garden gate was the sudden snuffling and low whine. We both looked round. In the opening, padding into view, was the little dog Steadfast.

He had followed me from the Kubbah observatory, you understand. I did not care to look at Landward. And then we heard another sound and looked towards the house.

Down the path was coming the girl Kora, and at sight of her Landward sprang to his feet and flamed red and swore aloud.

'By God, but *that* I won't stand!'

XIII

She had been rummaging in the room of his dead wife and wore the red frock, absurd and yet becoming to her white Greek beauty, in which I had last seen clad the dark slenderness of Joan Landward. She halted in front of us, pleased and unembarrassed and smiled at us with the sunflower eyes, and spread the short skirts for our inspection.

'Like my frock?'

Landward swallowed, made to answer, and in that moment something hurtled past us like an animated ball from a catapault. [38]

It was the little dog Steadfast. He had suddenly gone mad, was barking and sobbing in a delirium of joy. Again and again he leapt to lick the hands of the girl, then spun round in dizzying circles, then rolled in abasement at her feet. She looked down at him in the lighted wonder.

'It is the frock –' I began, and then stopped.

The little beast had reared himself up, in the culminating pride of performance, and at that her delighted laughter rang clear.

'*Look, look, the fairy dance!*'

XIV

In two strides he was beside her, his face ashen, the face of one whose sanity toppled, his eyes ablaze.

'"The fairy dance" – where did you hear that, where?'

She stared up at him, lips quivering, eyes suddenly clouded and frightened. In their depths struggled effort at that memory neither of them was ever again to seek. She put her hand to her head and stammered in the little broken English.

'I ... Oh, once ... Steadfast ... I do not know.'

Then fear and questioning went from her eyes. Compassion came there. In a moment she was in his arms.

'Keith ...Oh! Keith, my dear, don't look like that!'

XV

Somehow I was out of that garden; I have forgotten how I went; they did not hear me go. In his arms, her fingers twining in his hair in the caress. ... My friend, I am no realist. I fled: such coward as he who looked on Kora in Eleusis. [39]

XI

It is Written

I

First sunset after Ramadan! [1] Our Cairo is painting herself in the red tonight – that is the phrase, is it not? ... Hark to the drumming with which the little Muslim celebrates the reprieve of his stomach!

Eh? The religion vigorous – Islam? It is a withered tree that creaks and falls; this shouting and show is but the last wind in its branches. Nor falls it alone. In all the Forest of Faith is a rending and overthrow. [2] The specialised creed and the specialised god – what plants amazing and monstrous they will seem to the future generations who excavate in the strata carboniferous! [3]

Yet they pass not alone, I think. The Disciples Twelve, the priests and worshippers – in their company passes even the Thirteenth Disciple [4] – the infidel who feared and doubted and disbelieved. Doubt and devoutness, faith and fear – they pass in a drift of twigs and leaves on that slow wind that beats through the dying Forest. And in their place – ?

How should I know? Perhaps there comes the era of God Himself, creedless and testamentless, without priest or shrine, triumphant slowly amidst the darkness – as once Godfrey Steyn glimpsed him in the eyes and speech of an unbeliever.

II

Steyn! It was an evening in May when I first met him. I had passed through the dusty drooping of trees in the garden Esbekiyeh when on the sidewalk, near to the little café, I was hailed by name. I turned and saw my friend, the Dr Adrian, seated at a little table, intent on the game of dominoes. But it was not the usual self-game he played. He had an opponent.

'Oh, colonel. I've been waiting for you to pass. Knew you'd come this way sooner or later. Here's someone who wants to know you. Mr Steyn: Colonel Saloney.'

I made the bow and at that Adrian's companion also rose and bowed, and smiled with an absent friendliness. He had the hair too long and the face too pale, and for a little I thought him one of Adrian's patients. His face I seemed to know and made the rude and puzzled consideration of it. This he endured without embarrassment. And indeed I may have stared not so long as I thought before I remembered his prototype. He had such face as one sees in the portraits of your Shelley – comely and kindly and the face of youth, yet not weak at all.

He might have been thirty years of age. He had the soft brown hair like silk, and eyes that were also a shade of brown. His voice in conversation was the voice very clear and accentless – this perhaps because he was a trained elocutionist, and sought to conceal the fact.

'Won't you sit down, Colonel Saloney? And have a drink?'

I murmured thanks. Adrian, sweeping the dominoes-game to himself, grinned. 'Mr Steyn is a parson, colonel, so you'll have to forgive him his lemonade.' [5]

The brown eyes twinkled. 'My constitution, not my profession, you'll have to forgive, you know. I've no objection to wine – except being forced to drink it. Makes me sick. ... Colonel, Dr Adrian has been telling me about you. Oh, lots to your credit! Have you any important engagements during the next few weeks?'

I was a little disappointed and bored. ... So he was a tourist and wished me to show him Cairo and expound the Sphinx and crawl the pyramid-tunnels in his company. 'None of importance.'

He cupped the lean, pale face in a brown hand. 'That's good, if I may say so. Because I want you to act as my guide and general assistant on an archæological expedition to the Wadi Faregh.' [6]

'Faregh?'I shook my head. 'That is the bare stretch of the hills fifty miles west of the Pyramids? But I know nothing of it. And I am no archæologist, whatever the good Adrian may have been saying. ... Faregh? But surely there are no remains there?'

Adrian glanced up the sardonic moment from his game, but said nothing. Godfrey Steyn sipped the sickly lemonade and turned on me again his charming smile.

'Doesn't matter though you aren't an archæologist. I'm not, either. Nor though you've never been to Wadi Faregh. I want someone who knows the country and people generally, and can organise a small expedition for me. I'm going out to Faregh to look for the tomb of one Polyorthes, a Hellenised Egyptian [7] who was buried there seventeen hundred years ago.'

I was a little intrigued. 'A tomb of importance? There were but bare burials, seldom with either mummification or inscription, so late as that. And even of such tombs in the Wadi Faregh I have never heard.'

He was silent for a little, looking out into the street. His face changed from the face of the polite and gracious youth to that of the fanatic, the enthusiast. He spoke with a quietness of voice that stilled me.

'I have almost certain evidence that this Polyorthes was buried in Faregh, and that buried with him is a document, a Lost Testament, in the handwriting of our Saviour Himself.' [8]

III

This he actually believed. The while Adrian, sardonic and indifferent, immersed himself in the game of dominoes, and I, a little uncomfortable, drank of the wine he had ordered me, this priest with the face Shelleyan proceeded to relate the story that was in reality thirteen years' autobiography.

I may summarise it for you with brevity, though indeed was the original brief enough. Too brief in places so that I had difficulty in comprehending the chemic [9] structure of a personality at once fantastically medieval and pleasantly modern.

For both these things was Steyn, he who had landed at Basrah [10] as the clergyman-missionary in March of 1914. Twenty years of age, newly out from England, the mystic that was the essential part of him a little overlaid by the muscular Christian of the theological college, he had stood on the hotel verandah that first afternoon and watched the mirage-sway of the jungle-walls across the Shatt-el-Arab. [11] Within twenty months there came rolling up against those walls another mirage, [12] and he stood and stared at it aghast. ...

The boy Shelley in a world of Anarchs, [13] he saw evil and cruelty, crowned and robed and acclaimed in an incense of blood, stalk the Mesopotamian days and nights. As an Army clergyman he went through the campaigns of sunglare and horror, fighting not Turks, but something greater than these – belief in that dark Consciousness now unleashed and triumphant across all the world. Belief in it would make of him a cheat and impostor; disbelief – to deny the evidence of his senses. ...

That mind medieval of his is outside your comprehension – as once so completely outside Gillyflower Arnold's. But I think he endured an agony Gethsemane-like. [14] God – the all-powerful, the all-good, the creator – a super-ape bending in amusement [15] over the foetid scum that writhed and fought on this rotting mud-ball that was his creation. ...

He was but one of many in those years startled to some such horrific vision. And, like many, he refused that vision. Somewhere was explanation, somewhere recoverable that faith in goodness which was more necessary to his existence than sunlight or food. Meantime, work.

It was the after-war years by then, and he fled from his own thoughts into relief-work amidst the refugees and refuse scattered in the Anatolian hinterlands – the straying tribes war-uprooted, the starving thousands who drifted over mountains and deserts without country or home or mandatory power to own them: Chaldeans, Armenians, unprosperous Jews, Nestorians. [16]

And amongst these latter it was, in 1925, [17] that he made that discovery which was to lead him to Egypt and the Wadi Faregh.

He had been sick with fever, and was nursed by monks, some half-dozen of whom still inhabited the portion of a ruined Nestorian monastery in the mountains beyond Lake Van. [18] Once had it been a great monastery-citadel, the sanctuary of Asiatic Christians; now, ruined by centuries of war and earthquake, it remained half-forgotten by the world beyond the encircling mountains. Towards the end of his convalescence Steyn had proof of the local earthquake force when throughout a night the ground heaved under his bed and the ancient buildings creaked and groaned.

Next morning, assisting the monks in rebuilding the living-quarters damaged in the tremor, he came on the centuries-lost library of the monastery, and, amidst its earthquake-uncovered scrolls, of which he was made temporary curator, the writings of a fifth-century monk, one Nicolaos of Corinth. [19]

Those writings formed the beginning of the monastery record, diversified with moralisings and rebuttals of heresy. Steyn spent many curious hours deciphering the monkish Greek and trying to reach at meanings in fears and formulæ long dead – even to him. And then, somewhere near the end of the entries in the hand of Nicolaos, he came on these words:

'*But of those who have corrupted our faith with the teachings of the heathen Mani,* [20] *it is told that Polyorthes, the Egyptian, he who lived within the life-time of his own false prophet, bore with him for many years a writing which the Manichaeans believed to be in the hand of Christ Himself. And this document they told, in their heretical blasphemy, revealed teachings other than those recorded by the Fathers* [21] *– teachings which would yet be made known to men in an age when the world was ripe to receive them. But Polyorthes, the Christian Manichaean, disappeared, and was heard of no more, neither he nor the false testament.*'

IV

To you or me this might have seemed but the curious reference to an ancient fiction. But it lighted the life of Godfrey Steyn as might the personal revelation. He abandoned all his work – there were a score of American missions to tend to his refugees by then – and set out to search for other records regarding Polyorthes, the ancient Egyptian with the Greek name that was perhaps the nickname, him who had been the Christian Manichaean.

His researches led him to Trebizond, to the lines of ancient monasteries fringing the south Black Sea, [22] to Mevr, [23] into Sovyet Russia, where the Tovarishii, with much courtesy and irreverence, believing him to be an atheistic historian, made free of every ecclesiastical document in their possession. And in eighteen months, pieced together from a score of sources, he had the full record of the fate of Egyptian Polyorthes. The Manichaean had died in his native land, in a solitary house in the Egyptian hills: undoubtedly the Wadi Faregh. Together with 'an heretical script' he had been buried in a secret tomb by two negro slaves who subsequently disappeared. ...

'And that is why I have come to Egypt. If archæological remains are unknown in the Wadi Faregh, so much the better. It'll never have attracted graverobbers. For I believe that lost script to be the Last Testament of Christ Himself.'

Before that fantastic faith I might have known my objections trivial. 'But even if the tomb exists – Surely there is no mention anywhere else of Christ Himself having written anything? I know nothing of your Christian Mysteries, but is not the complete doctrine revealed in the New Testament – complete and final, as miraculously made known to the Council of Nicaea?' [24]

He laughed aloud, the pleasant modern who could so suddenly replace the medieval mystic. 'For one who knows nothing of the "Mysteries", colonel, you're too ingenuous! ...' His eyes shone Shelleyan again. 'Nicaea and the New Testament final? They've left unexplained that which God's Messenger came to explain and justify – the *conscious* cruelty and darkness which rules the universe, against which the forces of light and pity fight so feebly. If God be God, how do these things persist?'

I am no theologian. I made the bewildered shrug. 'Perhaps they are character-tests in the purpose inscrutable. Perhaps resultant on the workings of impersonal natural forces.'

'And my agony and despair of those years – my groping after that God without whom sanity is impossible? What impersonal natural force is that resultant on? ... Character-tests? Purposes moulding us? These ancient lies! Three million lie and rot in France [25] and what meaning had their tortured deaths? To what betterment did agony mould each individual of them?'

To that I had no answer. It was the thing outside my mental range. But there began to stir in me a wondering imagining.

'An authentic message from Christ Himself! That would be wonderful!'

I had hardly known I spoke aloud till I saw their faces, Steyn's and Adrian's, turned on me. Then Steyn held out his hand.

'And you will come with me to Faregh?'

'I will come,' I said.

V

Within a week, fifty miles away from Cairo, we were setting up our encampment on the lower spurs of the Wadi Faregh. I had engaged five labourers – one to act as cook – for our little expedition and had obtained from the Ministry of the Interior the permits necessary and a good map of the Ordnance Survey. [26] So equipped, we had journeyed out to those hills to seek the tomb of the lost Egyptian.

Above, and curving away into the west, stretched the limestone ridges, rowelled [27] here and there by the sudden nullahs which we were to explore. They were cloaked in a thin growth of bush and desert-grass that June. South of our encampment an ancient well still yielded water – perhaps it had yielded water to Polyorthes and his slaves seventeen hundred years before.

Crowning the western foothills, hill-climbing a little, was the thin row of date palms, and the second evening of our arrival Steyn and I sat at the door of our tent and watched those palms stencil their unquiet shapes against the coming of the sunset.

So sitting, Steyn began to quote from that Ave of Rossetti's – lines very beautiful in that stillness and flowing light under the hand of darkness:

> 'Mind'st thou not (when June's heavy breath
> Warmed the long days in Nazareth,)
> That eve thou didst go forth to give
> Thy flowers some drink that they might live
> One faint night more amid the sands?
> Far off the trees were as pale wands
> Against the fervid sky –' [28]

They moved me strangely, those words, and that picture of the Virgin, [29] in some such setting as the night-threatened Faregh, going forth to revelation of her miraculous destiny. Moved me as beauty may always move me. For I have been too much the romantic to be ever the conscientious Not-Knower. I am not more remote from the Old Believer than I am from the English or German agnostic – him who sees all anthropomorphism [30] as merely the ridiculous garbing of idealism in an extra-terrestrial brain and heart and lips and lungs gigantic.

To believe that a human maid once bore into the world an incarnation of the Consciousness which set the Galaxy in the sky and may hear the undersong of life in the world within the electron! To believe such thing, to have proof of it! A message from that strange prophet, human or divine, who still for all of us stands a figure sky-whelming [31] at the gateway of all spiritual endeavour that has meaning. ...

The darkness came striding from the desert over the shoulder of the Wadi. Steyn had finished his quotation. He leant forward and shaded his eyes, and I followed his gaze. Betwixt two palms, far off, minute, something moved.

'What is it? '

And so into our encampment strolled Gillyflower Arnold, [32] geologist, atheist, and lawn tennis champion.

VI

'I'm a stray female,' she said, 'but you needn't bother to light a lantern for me. [33] My camp? Over there, half a mile beyond that hog-back. [34] I'm prospecting for oil – Government commission.'

Thus, succinctly, our visitor, the while I offered her a camp-stool and Steyn bent to the lighting of a lantern. Beyond, at a little distance, was the singing of our labourers about their fire, and now it was almost complete darkness.

'You are of an expedition?' I said.

She sat down, removed from her face the tortoiseshell glasses, [35] and rubbed her eyes. Her voice had the faint accent, but to me easily recognisable – I who have assisted at the pyramidal priming and mal-education archæological of so much transatlantic femininity. 'I *am* the expedition – or at least, I lead it. Myself, an Egyptian surveyor, and three servants.'

I made noises of apology, and at these Steyn and the girl chuckled together, and at that moment the lantern flared up.

She was indeed but the merest girl, no middle-aged and mosquito-salted explorer, as her voice had seemed to warrant. In the dusty breeches, puttees and boots she sat; but her shirt was dusty not at all and very unmasculine, the fine silk shirt. Bare-headed, her hair in lamplight and sunlight alike had that blue raven-wing sheen I had met only once before in Egypt – such hair as possessed the little madame who once lived at Daybreak House. [36] But her eyebrows were almost fair, very fine brows, of one line of tinting, like the brows of a Japanese.

She had a face thin and humorous, redeemed from severity by the girlish curve of chin, even as it was denied beauty by the spectacles American and absurd. She sat cross-legged, cigarette-smoking, and nodded an easy acknowledgment of our introductions. She talked about herself and her work without apologies, because her work seemed to her the most important thing on earth.

A mineralogist, she was already apparently of such note as to be sent out to Egypt by an important American company to consult the Government with regard to exploring and mapping the putative oil-centres in the Bahaira. [37] To such good effect had she carried out those consultations that the Cairene Government had fitted out an expedition for her and sent her to the Wadi Faregh for preliminary investigations.

'Of course, oil shouldn't be a matter for exploitation by any single company. Or any single Government. But what's one to do, seeing we're such fools we haven't got a world board of control yet? [38] ... And my people are the sanest and cleanest of the lot. Great work, you know. The world's fuel is growing scarcer every year.' She laughed. 'So in depressed moments I dramatise the business and prefigure myself fighting silence and primordial darkness, the last Ice Age [39] and the extinction of the human species! ... You people – archæologists? I'm afraid you'll find the Wadi disappointing.'

It was Steyn who answered her. He gave a little laugh and looked away from us, out into the night, which was moonless but with the soft splendour of starshine.

'Archæologists? No. We also have come to fight the Darkness.' [40]

VII

Each evening of the days that followed it became the custom for Gillyflower Arnold to visit our camp or we hers. The latter was the more common occurrence, for the leader of the oil expedition had brought net and rackets into the desert and nightly, up to the time of our arrival, had insisted on impressing her stout surveyor as partner for the mystic gambollings of tennis. Except in the infrequently-ordered doubles, he now escaped these objectionable activities, as I did, and we and the massed camps would sit and watch Gillyflower and Godfrey Steyn executing the manoeuvres agile and enthusiastic. Steyn was discovered as a player extraordinarily good; and, occasionally beaten, Gillyflower would stand and marvel at him.

It was as though she had discovered a Stone Age shaman making miraculous breaks on a billiards table. [41]

Palæolithic indeed was the cultured period in which she placed him. 'Medieval? My dear man, you're pre-Adamic. This worship of light and fear of darkness – it's the mumbo-jumbo of the carrion caves. Saints and ministers! [42] And in the twentieth century, too!'

'Even in the twentieth century – when a young woman comes five thousand miles to dig in the earth for weapons to fight that same Darkness! [43] Do you think it's any the less real because you call it Cosmic Chance or something equally nebulous?'

'My *dear* shaman! You're not in the pits of Neanderthal [44] now! Why personify the thing? What good has belief in gods ever done? Isn't our job in this age plain enough – to bring order and decency into human life for the first time and bring adventure back?'

I left them, both flushed and arguing but good-tempered, and walked away into the starlight to smoke a pipe alone on a Faregh brow, with below me the murmur of their young voices. And beyond the hills and sands – Cairo – Egypt – the world that had known so many creeds and faiths, where the young have sat and talked and debated through the million evenings, loving and hating and questioning the gods who shine and pass. ...

But indeed, when I had gone up to my hill-brow and pipe, there had fallen the quieter spell on them – these two with the philosophies apparently irreconcilable. You imagine Steyn sitting there, facing her, talking, with for background the dusking desert, and Gillyflower Arnold bending on both the finely-pencilled brows. ...

He did not argue then: merely told her of the world and life as he had seen it, the necessity of a guiding Consciousness to account for his own consciousness. ... And then the blood and agony of the rotting migrant-treks in the Anatolian hinterlands, the butchery and cruelty of the War, evil exultant under the shams of plenty and peace, evil that crawls in the shape of vile and loathsome disease and unmeaning suffering and torture through all life. ... Darkness. Everywhere the hand of a Consciousness, surely – but a Consciousness that, without explanation, was surely vile.

'You are fair and wise and brave and eager,' he said, 'and do you think that is equipment enough to believe in the triumph of the Adventure which you see all life to be? A natural law might kill or crush you – but what of the Darkness that may maim and torture you horribly, that may wipe the cleanest and most selfless of your work from all record as a slate is wiped clean, that may even vilify the fairest things of your memory till that memory disgusts the world? ... For all those things have been.'

'I never thought of it that way,' she confessed. And then: 'Oh, but I won't believe it! It's only a horrible dream. ... Even if it were true, how would the finding of this lost script help?'

'Don't you see – Christ, the Messenger, the Captain of the Adventure – *He* knew what He came to lead men against, He must have known why Darkness, the stark denial of God's Godhead, so prevailed. ... The script – it must be explanation and plan of campaign in one, the Lost Message of the Christ!'

She sat and looked at him with scornful, troubled eyes. Reared in a dogma of unbelief as stern and uncompromising as any Calvinist's creed, she felt her no-faith crumbling and dissolving even as the world of the ancient materialist has crumbled and dissolved into the unchartable atom-swirl of the modern physicist. ... Words and symbols and dreams – and yet – and yet –

'Christ – the Great Captain.[45] ... Of course it's only dramatisation – hero-personification of the Adventure's essence. But splendid enough, Steyn! Thrilling to think we may have had a Leader, Someone who saw the beginning and the end!'

He looked at her, glad – and a little startled, I think. For perhaps his world was also blurring and losing outline a little. That heroic explorer-spirit in which she saw life and the universe – it blew now and then as a sharp, keen wind amidst the cloudy veils of his mysticism. And in its blowing he would glimpse with a strange amaze and fear a Christ he had never dreamt. ...

VIII

There was no oil in the Wadi Faregh.

So Gillyflower informed me, one dusty noon we met, each accompanied by a labourer, in a nullah of the Wadi.

'I'm packing up in a day or so and reporting back to Cairo. There isn't a drop in the whole range.'

'Nor a god-script either, I fear.'

She laughed and then frowned. 'I haven't seen a trace of anything that looked like a tomb. How's Mr Steyn?'

'He is in bed with the touch of fever,' I said. And added: 'He takes this failure to heart.'

We looked at each other in some helplessness, for somehow he had grown the mutual charge. [46] With the passing of day on day of fruitless excavation and exploration, the strain on him had begun to show. His face thinned, and the charming smile and boyish laughter were less frequent. At first Gillyflower Arnold and her tennis-games had had the power to bring him out of his trances of brooding, as had her laughter and irreverence and American exuberance. But of late he had shown the disposition to avoid her encampment, or, when there, to avoid anything but the talk most trivial. ...

He had fallen in love with her, as was almost inevitable. But there was the something more than belief in the hopelessness of his love that made him avoid her presence. And that thing it seemed to me was fear – fear that after all he had followed only an ancient fiction, that no script had ever existed, that his very vision of life was false. He had outlived and outfaced his belief in the divinity of that consciousness which ruled the universe, but either to outface the scorn and pity of Gillyflower Arnold or to go forth into the stark deserts of atheism were the thoughts from which he shuddered away.

Yet I did not care to think what would happen when the oil expedition had left the Wadi.

And then next day Gillyflower Arnold discovered the tomb of Polyorthes.

IX

She became visible at half-past two in the afternoon, on the brow of the hill, waving, an excited silhouette. She cupped her hands and called, 'Bring your people and pick-axes. I've discovered a passage that looks like a tomb-entrance. ...'

Yet when we reached the ridge beside her she regarded Steyn doubtfully.

'You can't come like that.'

He was newly up from his bed, the fever still upon him, staggering, white-faced. He laughed.

'Do you think anything can hurt me *now*?'

She stared at him, seemed about to say something, changed her mind, shrugged, and turned and led the way.

On the extreme western edge of the Wadi a precipice-shelf that faced the desert; at the foot of it still standing the gleaming apparatus of the oil-boring; three feet away, the rock-covering crumbled aside by the drum of the apparatus, the partially-uncovered mouth of a brick-walled passage. ...

At half-past three Godfrey Steyn and I, having had cleared from the entrance the fallen rubble of rock, pushed a lantern in front of us and crawled into the passage.

X

We crept sweating in the foul air, but the passage was of the shortest. Within eighteen feet of the entrance [47] it emerged upon a rock-hewn chamber, plain and undecorated, dry and cool. Set in the midst of that chamber was a rock kist [48] – a great stone box on which rested the unhinged lid of stone.

We seized that lid, and, panting, lifted it aside. Then I held up the lantern.

A mummy-coffin of the simplest: for a moment the wood still smelt fresh. Upon it inscriptions in the Persian and the Greek, the latter of which I read and remembered, and will always remember:

'*Polyorthes, the traveller, son of Thi-Hetep: I, who pass to the darkness, yet have seen the light of Ormuzd: I, whom the Prophet Mani blessed at Ctesiphon in the names of the Christ and the Buddha: To any who in after years follow a tale and rumour and find these bones, let them seek that which is written even in the darkness of Ahriman.*' [49]

Within the coffin: An unmummified body which fell to flaking shreds and brown bones even as we looked at it. Under the head of that body a roll of what might have been either parchment or papyrus – a roll that crumbled like an ash and rose in the little puff of dust. ...

XI

She came across to our encampment at sunset, went into Steyn's tent, and emerged from it a moment later.

'Steyn – where is he?'

He had fainted outside the rock-tomb where we had left the Manichaean Polyorthes and his unread script. We had had him carried to the camp, and then Gillyflower Arnold had gone back to the precipice-shelf to see to the resealing of the tomb.

Now I stared at her in surprise. 'He was there but the short time ago. Tossing in fever. I looked in.'

'He's gone.'

I went to his tent, pulled aside the flap, and looked in. Then I had the sudden thought. I began to search. Gillyflower Arnold stood in the doorway and I heard her quick breathing.

'Anything missing?'

I turned and nodded. She clenched her hands.

'Not – ?'

We stood outside and looked at the familiar fall of the Wadi evening. It was very silent and very desolate. Suddenly Gillyflower Arnold began to speak in a quick, high voice.

'Darkness. ... Perhaps he was right after all, colonel; perhaps there's something. ... Oh, it's a lie, it's a lie, anyway. Cowardly even if true. ...' She laughed a little hysterically, then shook my shoulder. 'What are we standing here for? We should be searching. We must find him.'

I do not know how long we searched amidst those reddened hill-slopes and sudden valleys. It seemed that we called and clambered and stumbled for hours, though it may have been only a few minutes. Once Gillyflower Arnold stopped and laughed and looked at me queerly.

'"Seek in the darkness of Ahriman –" wasn't that the phrase ...?' She became rigid. 'There. Look.'

He sat bowed of shoulders like the Rodin Thinker, 50 his face in shadow, the night almost upon him. He moved his hands, and in those hands something glinted and flashed red as with blood.

XII

'Wait!'

The other searcher was gone from my side. Steyn half-started to his feet, and in that moment the revolver was snatched from his hand and sent hurtling down the hill-slope. Dazed, he faced in the half-darkness a raging accuser.

'Coward! You beastly coward! Christ – the Captain – do you think He came in triumph or that He won? Do you think He lost because He seemed to lose, do you think He's lost now because a mouldy script has crumbled to dust? Had He no terrors of the Darkness to face, foes to out-fight, that He might leave select campaign instructions to you? ... You coward! Deserter!'

He was motionless. She made a despairing gesture. The passion in her voice was very near to tears.

'Steyn – listen! Can't you see, don't you understand? It is God who fights to reclaim the world! What does it matter the fable we accept or reject?

Perhaps the old stories are all wrong, perhaps it was God, not Satan, who was overthrown in the beginning of time. [51] ... Wonderful to think – Christ – you – I – *we're the champions of the dethroned God!* ... That lost script – it's written wherever there's pity and courage in the world. ... Oh, my dear, help me ...'

He seemed like a man emerging from a trance. He stared at her, then reached out and caught the hands extended to him.

'Why, I've been blind! ... *Gillyflower!* ...' [52]

XII

The Passage of the Dawn

I

What is it? A camel-train with *bersím*, I think. ... Unpleasant? He smells not sweetly, the camel. ... You have startled the driver; he thought us *jinni*, [1] perhaps!

That tinkling? You did not notice it as they passed? It requires distance for effect. To have your heart rise in your throat you must hear it ring across dusk miles of desert – or as Oliver Gault once heard it beyond the fairy mountains of Mesheen. [2]

Sit here in this doorstep and rest, my friend. Young men should dream their loves at night, not wander the streets of Cairo with a middle-aged and prosy Russian! Even though it is your last Egyptian night, [3] and tomorrow await you sea and ship and weeks wherein your Cairene days and I will fade to the merest names – and even those of uncertain orthography!

... Very soon the morning now. See that greyness above the roofs? In an hour we will go down past 'Abbas Pasha [4] and stir the little Simon to provide a last Greek breakfast in the Khalig. Meantime –

Eh? Gault? Mesheen? I had forgotten both till that camel went by. In the self-defence I have forgotten. ... Weeks now since I went out to that desert-house of his – coward and fool that I am!

But I will go again: this very morning I will go! Somehow I will find the courage. ... Oh, dreamer of dreams, fantastic fool though I am – who knows, who knows – ?

... Bear with me a little, my friend. A camel's bell – that it should stir one so! Yet perhaps this very night in Abu Zabal [5] another heard it go by – one who may find forgetfulness never, unless – unless –

II

And for beginnings of all this strange haunting of three lives is to go back across a year and eight hundred miles of desert to the last outpost of the company Trans-Saharan Transport. [6] A stifling night of February, far beyond Kufra, in the regions where the oases ceased and the raiding Tuareg of Air and Tibesti [7] came but seldom. And in his tent, on the edge of the encampment, Oliver Gault, the sick and fevered surveyor, hating his work, his companions, his life.

'Mosquitoes crawling battalions deep on my face, and my stomach rotten with fever. I was at the last stage: I'd have broken down before morning. Next tent that infernal Caprotti was jerking out a tune on a sand-clogged gramophone – the needle seemed to be playing round and round on my brain-tracks. Air thick as soup, and yet cold. ... And that greasy blaze of stars!' [8]

So to me he was to describe that place, in the uncouth jargon that is the modern English colloquial – the speech-debasement from which is yet smitten the occasional vivid phrase. ...

The year before that I had known him in Cairo. Slight, quick, restless, with the strange flare of light in pale eyes, the mouth unevenly cut, and a face tanned almost negro-black: Oliver Gault. He was then in negotiation with Trans-Saharan Transport for the post of desert surveyor. This was the new American company proposing, after the planning of routes and roads, to run the constant caravans of caterpillar automobiles [9] throughout Sahara, linking in trade and travel Cairo to Air, Algiers to Timbuctoo. [10] ... The project florid and magnificent, and one that had fired the quick imagination of Gault, though he would speak of it in the humour as twisted as his mouth.

'In a year we'll have the Tuareg talking through his nose, dancing to jazz and uplift, [11] and holding Monkeyville trials. [12] ... Nothing can withstand the progress of nasalisation.' [13]

Young though he was, he had already reputation as Saharan explorer and geologist. With Hassanein Bey [14] he shared credit for first traversement of the stony deserts – though this credit he would claim for himself, and jeer the Bey from the field. ... Not a gentleman, you understand, either in birth or outlook. But I think the gentleman passes from the world. Up in his place rise the Gaults, cruel and crude, restless of outlook, tenacious of purpose, without honour and without faith – yet stirred by the gleam occasional of a vision and a new selflessness that no knighthood of the world has ever known. ...

But that new vision is still but a mirage-picture in the dusk. From Gault that evening he was to describe it was more remote than belief in the articles thirty-nine of your Church. [15] He was a man frantic with fatigue and disgust, his nerves frayed to twisted rags by months of self-overwork and discomfort and monotony.

'I think I'd have gone mad in a minute – I was reaching for my Webley [16] to go out and settle the hash of [17] either Caprotti or his gramophone when I heard our sentry shouting a challenge, and an angel of God, disguised as a Sudanese and smelling like a cholera epidemic, came clumping into the camp on a camel. All the way from Kufra. He'd brought the mail-bag – three letters. ... I opened the single personal one, read it, and gave a croak. Like an overcome bull-frog. ... And then I was laughing and crying, in hysterics, the pages slipping and falling from my heat-rawed hands and being picked up and being lost again. ...'

The father whom he had hated – the war profitmaker in England whom he had regarded always with the savage contempt, even before the days of their final quarrel, whose life of safety and security his own aching restlessness and bitter no-content had despised – was dead.

'I found myself chanting an insane sing-song – "Saved from hell, saved from hell!" And then I grew calmer. Hell – of my own choosing. Whatever for? *Whatever* for? Why hadn't I stayed in England and wallowed in war-profits? ... And then I was scrambling for my boots and weeping and singing again. Sand and dirt and discomfort, prickly heat and Baghdad boils and potted [18] meat – finished and done with! The world waiting there in the east – if I didn't die first! – the world where I could laze and laze and laze ... bathe and bathe and bathe ... spend and spend and spend ... live like a lord ... sleep like a hog ... go clad in sin and shining raiment [19] ... drink of life like a fly in a tumbler! ...

'And women – oh, my God, were there still women with white, white skins, and would any of them be alive when I got back?

'They must have thought me a raving lunatic, the roadmen. In an hour I'd chucked my billet, [20] handed over the road-survey to little Savraut – who did foolish things and tried to stop me with a revolver, not knowing that I was a soul reprieved. Then I grabbed the camel, some food and water, and was on the way to Kufra before midnight. ... Reached it in three days. Rode most of them delirious, I think, with an insane conviction that the world in the east was a mirage that I must overtake.

'A mile from the first oasis the camel gave a ping like a clockwork toy with the works gone wonk, and doubled up. [21] I staggered into Kufra just ahead of the sunset.'

III

Six weeks later, all unconscious of that happening, in the last days of spring and the tourist season, I was preparing for myself a short holiday. Three weeks on the beach at Mustapha I planned, where none would question me as to whether the good antiques of Frankfort [22] were genuine or your Mr Wells an incarnation of Akhnaton. [23] ... I had saved a little money, you understand, and was sick of Cairo, the Mediterranean calling me like a pleasant friend a year neglected.

And then one morning I was handed the letter brought by a messenger over-night. I opened it, recognised the handwriting, and read:

'DEAR SALONEY,

Come and talk to me. I learnt the other night that you were still in Cairo. I myself have been here a month and a half, but I'm going to Alexandria next week – thank God! for I'm very bored.

Any time this afternoon if you can manage it.

OLIVER GAULT.'

I stared at the notepaper in stupefaction. Oliver Gault – whom I had believed to be in the Sahara beyond Siwa – he was in Cairo and staying at Shepheard's Hotel! [24]

I had no commissions to carry out, and no engagements that afternoon. So, in the some curiosity, I dressed myself in tourist drill and sun-helmet, playing the little game that I was the English tripper arrived for the hasty week in Cairo. In a taxi I rode to Shepheard's, speaking to the driver in the loud and inaccurate French, as only an Englishman may speak. At the entrance, where I had so many times waited for custom amongst other dragomans, I handed the card and was shown to the cool lounge to await the coming of Gault.

He was taking a bath, they told me, in the tone respectful, as was proper to my bad French and the cut of my drill. [25] It was the room deserted and I leant back in my seat and closed my eyes and heard the sound of the little waves come racing up the beach at Mustapha. ...

'Anton!' In the voice of amazement, the voice half-choked. 'Oh, Anton Kyrilovich!' [26]

IV

I opened my eyes at that. As one confronted by a ghost I sat staring, myself white-faced I think, as she was. Then I came to my feet and stood at attention and kissed her hands.

'*Princess!*'

She looked round the room the swift moment, then flung her arms about my neck and kissed me. Then laughed and wrung my hands, and for a little we stood breathless. Slowly the colour came back to her face and to her lips the amused smile – amusement at herself and me.

'Anton! I thought you dead or a gay commissar [27] all these years! ... In Cairo for nine of them? [28] And since we met – oh, I don't want to remember how long!'

'Twelve years,' I said, and tried to smile. We Russians have learnt to smile at much which is unamusing. We sat down and looked at each other, I and she who had been the Princess Pelagueya Bourrin. [29] ...

Of those far days in Kazan, when I was still Professor of English Literature in the Gymnasium and – though this you may find hard to believe! – without suspicion that in twelve years' time I would be a middle-aged dragoman sitting on a Cairene doorstep at dawn – of those there is no need for you to know. She was the girl of eighteen then, and I, though the mere professor, had yet my personal dreams, for I came of a family as old and noble as hers – we could still consider that of importance, we whom the soldier-groom, Budenni, [30] was to sweep from South [31] Russia as so many vermin!

So distant in the years from that quiet room at Shepheard's. ...

She was changed unbelievably – and yet hardly at all! – she whom I had always found strange pleasure in addressing by the formal title. And of this my princess – even now I do not know the colour of her hair and eyes. I think they are both that black that is on occasion the brown: when the sun comes on them. In unexpected lights and moments the sun comes on the hair and eyes of Pelagueya. ...

Short-cut hair; in the absurd, short skirts, the dress of white over-stamped with the whorls of gold; with still that clear pallor of brow and cheek that is Russian, and the smooth out-jut of cheek-bones, and the long, sweet fall of lips. ... Unchanged, except that the sunlight in her eyes brought a different picture: like spring sun on a Ural river [32] when the ice lies frozen beneath.

'Of course you look older, Anton. But handsome as ever. Oh, Anton Kyrilovich, it's so long since I saw a man blush! and with a beard – I hardly knew you a moment because of that beard.'

The beard was safe topic. 'All Russians are bearded – outside Russia. Without it I would not have been the refugee authentic, nor the guide interesting.'

Of my profession for nine years I told a little. There came the swift pity and anger in her face.

'A dragoman! How horrible! If we had known, we might have helped – at least at first. But they said you were killed at Perekop. Some other Saloney, of course. We escaped to France and lived – I will not tell you how we lived. Then Boris went back to Russia secretly three years ago, and was arrested and shot. That broke father's heart. He died and left hardly a sou – Poor father!

'And then, on that awful strip of coast – Oh, Anton, you escaped much by becoming a dragoman! – I began two years as companion, teacher, nursery-maid. Once I loved children. ... Amongst nouveaux riches, [33] Brazilians, French bourgeois. ... Why isn't there a revolution in France? *We* at least had pleasant manners!

'And then this January –'

She had looked one night at the pearl necklace she had hoarded, and all the pleasant life forgone – the life of ease and consideration, laughter and gay song and cultured voices – had cried in her ears to take the mad risks. She had gone to Paris, had had the orgy of purchasing pretty clothes. Then south to Marseilles and so a passage to Egypt. [34]

'But why Egypt?'

'They said the bigger and more brilliant Brazilians came here. I came after them, Anton, to sell myself as advantageously as possible. [35] ... I'm glad he's not a Brazilian, though.'

She had looked away whilst she was speaking, but now she turned her head directly towards me again, a little spot of blood flaming below each cheekbone, but with the cool irony still in her eyes.

'I'm glad to have seen you again, just once, Anton. It's been the final and artistic touch. You see, I'm leaving Cairo in a week's time as the mistress of a millionaire.'

'Pelagueya!' And then, at sight of the laughter still in her eyes: 'You are joking.'

The laughter was suddenly gone. 'Joking! Anton, I'd have sold myself to a Jew from the ghetto – if he'd had money. Shameless? You haven't known those last two years – condescension and mean rooms and the life of a servant. The nursery-maid emigrée, the pauper princess! ... Rather than face that again I'd go back to Russia and turn tovarish. But I'm to do neither. And my millionaire's not a Jew. Of the canaille, [36] of course, but rather amusing. ... Especially now that he hates me.'

'Hates you?'

She laughed. 'It was comic. He explained that of course he had no romantic love, that I was, in fact, just something he wanted and could afford. Nevertheless, he offered marriage. I told him that the price was too small and that in Russia we Bourrins did not wed with the gutter. ... How easy to sting the vanity of those animals! He's accepted my counter-proposal, but every moment I think he swears that I'll pay to the uttermost for that acceptance. ... The bargaining instinct, I suppose. We've had the terms and endurance of the association drawn up by a lawyer!'

She clasped her hands round her knees, the defiance leaping in her eyes. 'Shocked, Anton? But me – Oh, I'm to have the things that haven't been mine for years except as desperate luxuries: money and laziness, leisure; clean food, clean hands, and long, long bathes; books and jewels and pretty clothes. Clothes! The loveliness of clothes, Anton! If I could only take you upstairs and show you the things I've been buying!'

I found my voice strange and high-pitched.

'And the price?'

She suddenly wrung her hands. I thought she was going to weep.

'The price! What cowards you are – men! Liars and cowards and cheats, weak and emotional! Greedy liars, greedy cheats! ... If I came to share your dragoman's room would I not pay the same price?'

I had nothing to say to that, nor looked at her, the princess who had strayed from a fairy story into the legend of Gomorrah. And then her hand on mine.

'I didn't mean that. Or I did. Oh, Anton, it's too late. If this was 1917 and Kazan and yours wasn't a dragoman's room. ... All our faiths were futilities, and before I grow old – oh, my friend, I must *live!*'

She withdrew her hand, laughed again a little unsteadily, and sought for her cigarette-case. Then she paused with lighted match, and the amused scorn flickered on her lips.

'The exhibit. Here comes my millionaire.'

I did not look over my shoulder, hearing the footsteps approach. I sat with a grip on myself, trying to believe that all our faiths had not been futilities, our codes cowardice. And then she spoke, in English, in the insolent drawl.

'This is a countryman of mine, Mr Millionaire. Mr Oliver Gault: Colonel Anton Saloney.'

V

I can still hear her gay laugh, a trifle breathless, as she glanced from one to other of us, and learnt that I had come to Shepheard's to meet him.

'Then I will leave you,' and, with the smile to me and the nod patronising to Gault, she was gone. I had stood up, but Gault turned a casual back to her nod and looked out through the window. He was clad in the soft and expensive flannels, the clothes well chosen and seemly, but for one detail. This was a tie of the vivid red, and, still in the dazement of his revelation as Pelagueya's millionaire, I stared at it foolishly.

'Why do you wear that?'

He turned his sun-blackened face and grinned at me, twistedly. 'Oh, to show my kinship with Budenni! ... Coming upstairs?'

And there, upstairs in the gorgeous suite, I sat and listened to him, with all the time at back of my mind the thought: this [37] is Pelagueya's millionaire. But I made no interruptions or denunciations heroic. ... It was a very evil and unkind dream I was dreaming, and through it all I heard forgetfulness and the Mediterranean calling on the beaches of Mustapha.

'... And only a month since I rode into Kufra, Saloney. Like a bad nightmare badly remembered. Lord, how the mosquitoes must be mourning my passing!'

'How have you passed this six weeks?' I asked.

He grinned and sprawled in a chair. 'In bed, largely. Clad in silk. Look at these socks. ... God bless my parental profiteer and his forgiving last testament. [38] ... A little man comes and shaves me each morning, and another finds my braces, and three bring my boots – one to each boot and one with the laces. They'd fetch a palanquin [39] and carry me down to lunch, if I asked for it.' He yawned suddenly and jumped to his feet and swore.

'And I'm bored, Saloney – oh, fed to the teeth! Dances and outings and chatter and opera – Lord, that opera! I've escaped to heaven from hell – St Peter himself shook hands with me on arrival: I think it was St Peter, though it may have been the manager – and the harping and the company celestial bore me. Or is it only Cairo – your Polychromata? I'd rather live in a damn dye-factory. ...'

He prowled to and fro, restlessly. 'The peasant in the palace, the Zulu in Versailles [40] – the unimpressed Zulu. Is it that, or do we just outgrow these things, along with wigs and patches and gibbets and powder? [41] ... He stopped and grinned again, his face a satyr's. [42] 'Anyhow, there's one thing we don't outgrow. Still that.' He stared at me a sudden curiosity. 'Are you in love with this Princess Pelagueya, colonel?'

How the sea was calling out beyond Pharillon! [43]

'Told you of our relations – our prospective relations? She has! ... And the price? I'll see she pays it. By God, I'll see to that!'

But not even in a dream – I made to rise. 'This is the beastliness.'

He caught my arm. 'Oh, sit down, colonel. Beastliness? Of course I'm a beast – a starved beast, a beast hungry for beauty and tenderness. What else is there to grope after? And I'm to buy it, and in a week. ... To think I might have been still in Sahara!'

I could not hate him, even in a dream; they are the kind beyond hate, those. He sat down and yawned again, and stretched.

'Sahara ... the old company. Wonder where they are, little Savraut and Caprotti and Ba Daghshar and the rest? Somewhere north of the Mesheen massif. [44] ... Pity that infernal detour was necessary.'

He seemed to await the question. He began to scatter cigarette ash on the gorgeous carpet in idle illustration.

'Mesheen. A mountain block beyond Kufra. Lies north to south thirty or forty miles. Block in several senses. Terra incognita [45] and absolutely impassable – a wilderness of closed gulleys. Every nullah we tried ended in a cul-de-sac. [46] There's no pass at all through the massif and the road'll have to wheel up north by a long detour to carry on towards Air. We searched for days. ...'

He dropped his cigarette and absent-mindedly ground it into the floriferous [47] carpet. 'Funny thing happened there. We hadn't a single camel with us, the range seemed uninhabited – couldn't be inhabited. No oases anywhere near at hand. And yet – one night, at the other side of the impassable walls, I heard a camel's bell.'

The ice-flare in his eyes. 'Clear and distinct – and no possible camel-train could be there. Later I heard a yarn amongst the Arabs of the road-gang that a pass through the mountains had once existed. ... An old chap told me of it – some crazy legend of a *Madhiq el Fiqr*, with guarded entrance, that traversed Mesheen from east to west.'

'Madhiq el Fiqr?' I sought in inadequate English and Arabic vocabularies of my mind for translation. 'The Passage of the Dawn?'

'Eh? ... That funny Russian twist! Morning Pass I called it. You're the better poet.' There came on his dark face the sudden strange dreaming look. 'The Corridor of the Morning – the Passage of the Dawn!'

He leapt to his feet, and swore. 'Gods, almost I thought myself back there! Waken up, [48] Saloney. A drink to celebrate my beatification?' [49]

VI

Next day I went to Alexandria. Behind, in Shepheard's, the Princess Pelagueya Bourrin, descendant of boyars, prepared to consummate her bargain with Oliver Gault.

There was no shame between them, you understand, no embarrassment and no pretence of affection. Rather the reverse. They were each conscious of a bright, sharp enmity. Pelagueya made no concealment of her scorn, nor Gault of the fact that for that scorn she would pay dearly. As he had paid.

'A heavy price, Mr Millionaire,' she had said, when they came out together from the office of the shocked and amazed little lawyer in the Sharia el Manakh.

'It is worth it,' he had answered, looking at her, the derisive grin for once vanishing from his twisted mouth. And at that look, so far from love, somehow not lust, she had shivered a little.

But there is no courage like to that of their generation – the generation to which the gods are foolishness and the codes and restraints but maunderings of dull dotards. They cry for life without veils or reticences, and face it without veils themselves. In that last week Pelagueya and Gault evolved a strange friendliness – mocking on her part, sardonic on his, though they would meet but seldom, and then as casual acquaintances.

On the Monday they were to go together to Alexandria, where Gault had already bought a house. But on the Saturday he came to her with the proposal that this plan should be altered. There was an old Turkish castle out in Abu Zabal [50] which he had once seen. An acquaintance had told him it was lately renovated, and to let. If the Princess Bourrin was agreeable, they would go there, instead of Alexandria, for the first few weeks.

'But why? We'll be very bored. It's on the edge of the desert, isn't it?'

'That's the chief attraction. I want to get out of a comfortable bed each morning and make faces at the Sahara.'

She laughed at that, for once unguardedly. 'Yes, I think I can make the concession.'

He called for her early on the Monday afternoon, bringing the great touring car. Her luggage was loaded into it, and together they drove out of Cairo. She lighted a cigarette, and sat watching him for a little, then made a request. Might she drive?

'Why not?' he said, and relinquished the wheel to her. The car ran through the long afternoon into the Egyptian country. Once he looked at her with his twisted grin.

'Honeymoon.'

Canaille.

It was nearly two hours before he spoke again. 'Five miles now.'

Now they came to a slope where the road zigzagged ruttily and steeply away beneath them. Little stones pattered on the wind-screen. Out of a field by the side of the road a heavy cart, single-poled, wooden-wheeled, was being drawn by oxen. Two boys in charge stared up at the nearing car and beat the indifferent beasts. Their shouts came up the evening.

Gault looked at Pelagueya, saw the puckering of her brows, the tinge of colour mount to each cheekbone. He hesitated only a second.

'Shall I – ?'

He leant over, slipped his right arm under her left, put both hands over hers, and grinned at the road. A wisp of her short hair clouded his eyes an irritable moment. He felt her fingers strain under the pressure of his. ...

It was a difficult moment. The oxen laboured aside, clumsily, up the steep mud-bank sheered the off-side wheels of the car. [51] Then, with a breath-catching swerve, they were on the road again, with the sunset-reddened incline sloping away before them.

It was as if that sunset would never die. In front and behind the road glowed in gold and red. Under the dim clumps of date-palms fled painted shadows. Gault's hands still remained on the wheel and to Pelagueya it seemed that in a moment she would weep.

Then she heard him speak, jerkily.

'Look here, that contract. ... You'll be all right, but you needn't – We'll go back to Cairo.'

They glanced at each other, whitely, queerly, strangers trapped by wonder. The car sped on. Then, the fairy princess, she turned her face to him.

'Do you know you've never kissed me? ... And it's only three miles to Abu Zabal.'

VII

They spent two halcyon [52] and amazing months in the old Turkish castle, the while the summer waxed. [53] They talked the sun out of the sky each day and never lost interest in the talking. They had waited all their lives to talk to each other.

'We'll buy a yacht and go drowsing through the Mediterranean. To Greece. To Crete. South through the Red Sea to India – Java – Sumatra. ... Wander together for ever, princess. ... Was there ever a man so lucky as I am?'

They sat listening that evening to a nightingale that sang in the cypress grove at the end of the garden. And Gault, listening, was aware that his love had already changed from a romantic passion to something akin to a vivid pain.

‘When are you going to marry me, Pelagueya? Sometime? Why not now? I’ll make Saloney persuade you when he comes tomorrow.’

But on the morrow, when I came to kiss the hand of my lost princess, she would not be persuaded by me either.

‘Some time. When we know each other.’

He swore at that. ‘Don’t you know me by now? Every secret of body and soul?’

She laughed and kissed him, gaily. ‘You English boy!’

But that afternoon Gault was restless, and together we tramped into the village, leaving Pelagueya sitting in the shade of the cypress grove. Coming back at sunset we could still see her there. And suddenly he was talking to me with a strange passion.

‘Lord, Saloney, what fools we are! Wanting even when we’ve the world in our hands! Wanting something we cannot name. ... Pelagueya – God, she’s wonder itself, life and love and God to me. And yet – and yet – sometimes I feel I could sell my soul for the gift of an hour’s sheer unhappiness! What is it, Saloney, what is it? Marriage – the world’s sanction we’ve forgone and she refuses. [54] ... Is it that?’

We were within hearing of Pelagueya by then, and she waved to us. He knelt beside her and laid his head in her lap.

‘On edge today, princess – like a fool! Don’t go away, Saloney. I shan’t make more love in public than I can help. Sit down and listen for our nightingale.’

That velvet silence of the Egyptian evening closed in on us. Suddenly Gault started and cursed, and moved his head restlessly. Pelagueya put her arms around his neck, silencing him, and we listened.

From far across the tundra it came, on the Cairo road, sweet and remote, a faint music growing clearer and clearer, then fading into the gathering dusk – the tinkling of a camel’s bell.

VIII

Next morning he came into Cairo with me, and it was late in the day before he returned to Pelagueya in Abu Zabal. At the first look at the flame in his eyes she shivered. But he caught her hands, like a man in desperation.

‘Pelagueya, will you come into Cairo and marry me tomorrow?’

She shook her head, smiling with trembling lips. He laughed queerly, brought something from his pocket, and tore it into little scraps. Then, looking away from her, he spoke.

‘I’ve been into the offices of Trans-Saharan Transport. They’ve a caravan leaving Sollum [55] in four days, and I’m going with it – paying part of the expenses, on a special expedition. I’ve been commissioned to make a detailed investigation of the Mesheen massif.’

'I knew,' she said, and smiled at him, weeping.

'You knew? But how? ... Have you tired of me, then? ... I'm a fool. Don't cry, princess. ... What have I done?'

'Tired of you? Oh my dear! ... Of course you must go. And I'll wait for you, and perhaps –'

He was holding her close, the old ice-flame in his eyes. 'You'll marry me when I come back? Fairy and reward! ... It's that infernal mountain range that's worried me. Mesheen. I'm to find the pass I know lies through it – the Passage of the Dawn. Little Savraut and Caprotti are to be detached to assist. Be back again inside six months. ... And then – !'

IX

Within six months he was dead, killed in a manner very horrible by a raiding band of the Tuareg of Air, he and two others of the special expedition which was exploring the mountain passes of Mesheen.

Pelagueya sent me news of it from the castle at Abu Zabal to which she had returned after the passing of the hot season. I went out to her and she greeted me with the old, kind smile and the easy talk, till we stood together near that cypress grove. And then, suddenly, she broke down.

'Oh, Anton Kyrilovich! I sent him back there. Did I do right after all? I could have married him; perhaps I could have kept him –'

She wrung her hands, staring across the tundra. 'Only – there was something else. Always – haunting him. And I loved him so. He could never hear a camel's bell go by but he remembered.' She turned to me with groping hands. 'My friend, my friend, what took him back there? What was it that I could not give him, that was not mine to give?'

And then she gripped my hand and stood rigid.

'Oh, listen!'

There are many camel-trains go by Abu Zabal. From far across the tundra, as once before I had heard it, it came, sweet and faint, growing clearer and clearer, then fading till it died remote on the Cairo road.

And suddenly, for the vivid moment, it seemed to me that I understood that aching restlessness that had driven Gault to his death in Mesheen, that Pelagueya herself had shared when she let him go. As in a vision, I saw again that room at Shepheard's, the dreaming look on a dark, still face –

The Passage of the Dawn! All his life he had sought for it – and who does not share that search? Somewhere, he dreamt, beyond the twilights of love and hate, ease and unease, there was the morning. Somewhere, beyond the mountain-walls, there was wonder and the morning.

(*And this is the last of the Saloney stories.*) [56]

L'Envoi [1]

To Colonel Saloney

A warm wind from the great steel bridge, [2]
    A swift tremendous Nile below,
And Cairo drowsing in the dusk
    Reluctant that the day should go,

And close for us another day
    Where Simon planned, and Andrei came,
And Kora loved beyond the Gates,
    And Connan [3] hymned the Way of Shame –

Saloney dreams beside the Nile:
    O dreamer of the camel's bell!
Shall we not hear your voice again –
    We who have known and loved you well?

Arthur John Hall [4]

Cairo, 1930

Full bibliographical citations are generally provided on first mention only in cases in which texts are directly quoted or which are by Mitchell/Gibbon (in his case quotation and page citation are nearly always from the first British editions) or which are cited in order to provide evidence of the availability in Mitchell's time of an English translation of a foreign-language work. The abbreviation "Bold, *Smeddum*" is used in citations of the following large and readily available collection of Mitchell's less well-known work, some of which was published only posthumously: Valentina Bold (ed.), *Smeddum: A Lewis Grassic Gibbon Anthology* (Edinburgh: Canongate, 2001). All quotations from the Bible are from the Authorised Version (1611), but the italics now customarily used to indicate non-manuscript interpolations by its original translators have been ignored. The life dates and significant details of historical persons are given only on their initial mention. The meanings of unusual words are similarly explained only on first, not subsequent, occurrences in the text. "*OED*" signifies *The Oxford English Dictionary*.

Dedication

[1] **MY FATHER AND MOTHER** James McIntosh Mitchell (1862-1936) and (*née*) Lilias Grant Gibbon (1873-1953).

Mr H. G. Wells to Mr Leslie Mitchell

[1] **H. G. Wells** Wells (1866-1946) was genuflected to in every early Mitchell book, one reason being his personal patronage, although Mitchell had been a lifelong Wells fan. In an article entitled "Author of 'Sunset Song'" by Louis Katin in the Glasgow *Evening News* of 16 February 1933, Mitchell explained Wells's involvement in the publication thus: "Wrote a romantic story with Egyptian background – 'For Ten's Sake' – which sent up the dividends for the Post Office but earned me nothing but rejection slips. So I sent it to H. G. Wells. He advised me to try the *Cornhill*." Wells also referred Mitchell helpfully to A. P. Watt and Son, his own agent, which really does suggest that he genuinely considered Mitchell to have promise. The story at that point was called "The Ten Men of Sodom". It was published under the amended title in *The Cornhill* in January 1929 (vol. 66, pp. 38-51) almost two years after Wells's suggestion. Wells later read *Stained Radiance* (London: Jarrolds, 1930) and wrote to Mitchell approvingly about it in October 1930 (see Ian S. Munro, *Leslie Mitchell: Lewis Grassic Gibbon* [Edinburgh: Oliver and Boyd, 1966], p. 58). When he came to collect the stories in *The Calends of Cairo*, Mitchell wrote again to Wells, at the very last moment (5 June 1931), a month before the book was published, perhaps a sign that even now after two published novels he was not very well-connected in the

literary world. He included all the stories in proof and expressed his earnest hope "that as the series' godfather you'll pen a short forenote to it". While Wells was past his best as a writer at this time, he was still as ever extraordinarily productive and had considerable power in the world of English letters, so his repeated generosity to Mitchell is notable.

[2] **I never write prefaces** This was not entirely true. Wells had written a four-page "Introduction" to W. N. P. Barbellion, *The Journal of a Disappointed Man* (London: Chatto & Windus, 1919). That had not turned out well: "W. N. P. Barbellion" was a pseudonym of the entirely unknown Englishman Bruce Frederick Cummings (1889-1919) and some consequently thought the entire book (actually the diaries of a man with multiple sclerosis) to be a fiction of Wells's own authorship. The issue could not be clarified until the real author's early death, which happened a mere seven months after publication. (Mitchell was to live less than five years longer than Cummings.) But of course Wells would also want to pre-empt being badgered (just as Mitchell was now badgering him) too often for his much sought-after, market-pleasing endorsement. He could have been forgiven for not replying at all.

Introduction

[1] **the *Cornhill Magazine*** *The Cornhill Magazine* was a literary monthly which ran for over a century (1860-1975). At its Victorian height it first published what were to become many of the nineteenth-century classics of English Literature. By the early twentieth century its fortunes were in decline and the title was acquired by the London-based Scottish publisher John Murray, which since 1904 had also overseen a long-running book series called "Wisdom of the East". In 1929, for example, it published Rev. James Robson, *Christ in Islam* (Robson was at the time Lecturer in Arabic at the University of Glasgow).

[2] **'Polychromata', which duly appeared in the *Cornhill*** "Polychromata" simply means "many colours" (Greek, *polý + chrómata*). In the stories the word is often used as a substitute for "Cairo" itself. Twelve of the stories were first published in *The Cornhill* under this catch-all title, six in vol. 67 (1929) and six in vol. 68 (1930). These had been preceded by "For Ten's Sake", published as a stand-alone story in vol. 66 (1929), set apart in *The Calends* as "Proem". The order of the stories was different in *The Cornhill* and one, "The Road", was in *The Calends* retitled "The Lost Prophetess". The *Cornhill* texts are reprinted in their original order in Bold, *Smeddum*, pp. 224-419, with the exception of the *Cornhill* version of "For Ten's Sake", which is reprinted separately (pp. 460-77).

[3] ***Calends*** "Calends" (Latin: *kalendae*) was the word given by the Romans to the first day of every month, the beginning of a new phase of the moon. It is not a plural and would usually only be followed by the name of a month (cf. "the Ides of March"). Literally the title means, somewhat oddly, "The first day of the month of Cairo". In the USA the book was less arcanely entitled *Cairo Dawns* (one of the variant titles

Mitchell himself proposed), but to it was added the explanatory subtitle *A Story Cycle with a Proem*. There are twelve "Calends" stories ("For Ten's Sake" is categorised separately as the "Proem" and is not located in Egypt), so each might seem to stand for a month of the year, and the original *Cornhill* stories had virtually been published monthly across the extent of a calendar year.

4 **Leonard Huxley** Mitchell's *Cornhill* editor (1860-1933) was the son of the evolutionary biologist Thomas H. Huxley (1825-1895) and father of Aldous Huxley (1894-1963), the last one of the most talked-about living English novelists since the triumph of his *Point Counter Point* (1928). Leonard Huxley became the assistant editor of *The Cornhill* in 1901 and editor in 1916. He was a rather orthodox establishment figure, the author of many forgotten non-fiction books. Likewise, *The Cornhill* under him was no flagship of experimental modernism. Its roll-call of writers at this time – those whom Mitchell found himself alongside between its covers – is a catalogue of names literary history has almost completely forgotten.

For Ten's Sake

1 **Easter Day** Easter Sunday, a moveable Christian feast which commemorates the resurrection of Christ from the dead. Easter normally falls between late March and late April (potentially as late as early May in the Eastern Orthodox Church).

2 **Mevr, the Hell-Gate of the East** Mevr is fictional. It reappears in Mitchell's *Persian Dawns, Egyptian Nights* (London: Jarrolds, 1932).

3 **siesta** Afternoon nap (Spanish).

4 **in the days of Asoka** Ashoka (c. 304-232 BC), Mauryan Emperor of Magadha in the Indian subcontinent between approximately 268-232 BC. Mevr appears to be a very old and important city on a major trade route between Africa and Asia.

5 **caravans** The English word derives from the Persian *karwan*, signifying a group of desert travellers.

6 **the Kablurz Beg** A fictional mountain range, which also reappears in *Persian Dawns, Egyptian Nights*: "the desolate mountain-jumble that crept upon Persia from out the wild wastes of Baluchistan. [...] it was land unexplored and unknown, the great range of the Kablurz Beg" (p. 93).

7 **across the dun tundra ... Persia and far Iraq ... Baluchistan** Tundra is a treeless plain and "dun" means dull greyish-brown. Persia is what we would now call Iran, which Iraq borders on the west. Balochistan is the largest province of present-day Pakistan, but geologically speaking it is also part of the Iranian plateau and occupies parts of neighbouring Iran and Afghanistan. Mevr, from this description, would appear to be situated in what is now south Iran.

8 **the City of the Plain** The "cities of the plain" are biblical (they also appear in the Qur᾽ān), and comprise Sodom, Gomorrah, Admah, Zeboiim, and Zoar. The plain is "the plain of Jordan" in what is today Israel (Genesis 13, 10). Abraham and his nephew Lot settle there when "it was well watered every where, before the Lord

destroyed Sodom and Gomorrah, even as the garden of the Lord, like the land of Egypt, as thou comest unto Zoar" (Genesis 13, 10). Zoar was in fact the only one of the five cities on which God did not rain down fire so that "the whole land thereof is brimstone, and salt, and burning, that it is not sown, nor beareth, nor any grass groweth therein, like the overthrow of Sodom, and Gomorrah, Admah, and Zeboim, which the Lord overthrew in his anger, and in his wrath" (Deuteronomy 29, 23). Despite the fact that the story was originally called "The Ten Men of Sodom", we might consider Mevr as a modern equivalent of Zoar, a last remaining sinkhole of depravity and vice, like Sodom seemingly deserving of divine punishment, but spared, at least for the nonce. In the Bible Lot pleads with God not to destroy Zoar so that he can have a place of refuge (Genesis 19, 20), and a terrifyingly destructive and vengeful and frankly anger-management-deficient God stops seeing red for a moment and okays Lot's despairing request before going totally Hiroshima-Nagasaki on the other four cities. He then ensures that Lot's suffering will nonetheless be ratcheted up by turning his wife into a pillar of salt for an offence no greater than looking back at a burning city (a prohibition God announced without explaining the flesh-and-bone-mineralising consequences of transgressing it, an extreme penalty compared to the mild exile visited a few chapters earlier in Genesis on the more fundamentally law-breaking Adam and Eve). It is this maniacal, irrational, psychotic, literally earth-shattering God that is about to be invoked.

[9] **'How long, O Lord?'** "How long wilt thou forget me, O Lord? for ever? how long wilt thou hide thy face from me? How long shall I take counsel in my soul, having sorrow in my heart daily? how long shall mine enemy be exalted over me?" (Psalms 13, 1-2). The face of the Lord remains expressly hidden at the story's end. The actual phrase "How long, O Lord?" is found in the poem "Ave" (1870) by Dante Gabriel Rossetti (1828-1882), to which Mitchell will allude at least twice more in the stories.

[10] **Osmanli** The Turkish word for the ruling class in the Ottoman Empire, deriving from the name of its founder, Osman I (d. 1323/4).

[11] **hakim** An Arabic word generally used to refer to wise men, professionals, leaders.

[12] **In'sh allah!** Arabic, variously spelled: "If God wills".

[13] **djibbah** The long outer garment worn in many Muslim countries (also variously spelled).

[14] **viper** Vipers are common snakes in Iran.

[15] **effendi** A respectful form of address to a man, "Sir".

[16] **M.D.** This abbreviation for "Doctor of Medicine" means different things in different countries. It had once in Scotland signified an undergraduate medical degree, but by the twentieth century throughout the UK this had become Bachelor of Medicine. "M.D." persisted as undergraduate nomenclature elsewhere, notably in the USA. In Britain M.D. became uniformly a postgraduate degree.

[17] **to the great bazaar of the Suq es Iraq** "Suq" or "souk" signifies a marketplace.

[18] **Bokhara** Bukhara is a city in modern Uzbekistan. It was on the Silk Road, a major trading route which until the mid-fifteenth century ran from the Middle East to the east of China. The rise of the Ottoman Empire diminished its importance around this

time because it greatly reduced the international passage of goods between East and West.

[19] **babel of many tongues** Another glance at the Bible, in which early humanity speaks a single language. They build a tower that will reach to the sky. God confuses their speech and disperses them. The city is left unfinished: "Therefore is the name of it called Babel; because the Lord did there confound the language of all the earth: and from thence did the Lord scatter them abroad upon the face of all the earth" (Genesis 11, 9). Cf. English "babble".

[20] **camelier** A driver of camels.

[21] **arrack** An alcoholic drink, mostly found in India and southeast Asia.

[22] **gendarmes** The use of the French name for a policeman may appear puzzling because the French had never been involved in Persia, and after the Great War it was entirely in British control. But in fact what is being translated is the word used in the Ottoman Empire after 1879 to designate such forces (*jandarma*).

[23] **pock-marked** The suggestion is that the pock-marks may derive from some disease, like chicken pox or the worse smallpox.

[24] **who sold the services of his knife to any who sought them** We soon learn that his name is Ali.

[25] **Selim of Damascus** Selim is an Arabic name; Damascus is the capital of modern-day Syria.

[26] **scatheless** I.e. without injury.

[27] **cotes** A cote is a dovecote, a man-made structure designed for pigeons or doves to rest in.

[28] **flirr** An onomatopoeic Mitchell coinage.

[29] **Two horsemen ... to the Street of Ten** Cf. Genesis 19,1: "there came two angels to Sodom at even". The biblical angels are there to destroy the city, but warn Abraham and his family to leave so that they can be spared – a task that will in this story fall to the protagonist. The arrival of these two cynical and worldly white men (one of whom "called himself a doctor") nonetheless does at first reading seem fittingly portentous, and certainly heightens the stress on Mevr as a decadent den of iniquity. In fact, their function here is primarily to drive the plot, as their conversation tells us much that we need to know of Southcote's past, but the man who calls himself "Mitri" will be integral in what follows.

[30] **Alexandria** On Egypt's Mediterranean coast.

[31] **ducks** Flannel trousers.

[32] **Herr Consul** "Herr" is German for "Mr".

[33] **'Twixt** Betwixt (i.e. between).

[34] **the English Society** There were many award-giving learned societies in England, so this is somewhat non-specific.

[35] **Calvinist** A strict Protestant after the manner of the French theologian John Calvin (1509-1564).

[36] **Pfuu!** An exclamation of disgust.

[37] **Me the old Southcote ... on some Old Testament authority** It would appear

that Southcote mistook the Greek for a Muslim and thus as a worshipper of a false idol.

[38] **Midan** Also *maidan* (Persian): any open space in or near a town, like a town square.

[39] **festa** This word usually designates a religious feast day like the present Easter Sunday, but the Greek seems take the religion out of it and rather concentrates on the eating part.

[40] **Auf wiedersehen** Goodbye (German). In the first edition the previous sentence lacked a closing quotation mark. On the likely assumption that there is then meant to be a change of speaker (i.e. that the German says goodbye first) a closing quotation mark has been added to it.

[41] **the evil eye** Fear of "the evil eye" is a belief in the supernatural power that someone can curse you by looking at you in a particular way (which is "to give the evil eye"). The Qurʾān contains "The Verse of Evil Eye", Al-Qalam, 51-52.

[42] **Kuchik Khan** Mirza Kuchik Khan (1880-1921), President of the Iranian Soviet Socialist Republic, a short-lived and unofficial state (May 1920 to September 1921). His brief revolutionary career did not involve anything like "sweeping down from the north with his army raised on Soviet gold".

[43] **sword of Tamerlane** Tamerlane (*c.* 1336-1405) founded the Timurid Empire in Central Asia, and was known as a great warrior. He called himself the "Sword of Islam". English readers knew of him mostly from the two-part Elizabethan play *Tamburlaine the Great* (1587/8) by Christopher Marlowe (1564-1593).

[44] **spite** I.e. despite.

[45] **the San Francisco earthquake** On 18 April 1906 (three days after Easter Sunday) what was to be the deadliest earthquake in US history hit San Francisco. The Richter scale which we now use to measure earthquakes was not developed until 1935, but it has been estimated that the San Francisco quake would have measured around 8. Damage was extensive and it is now thought that more than 3,000 people died. Many thousands were left homeless.

[46] **Peradventure there be ... for ten's sake** The quotation is from Genesis 18, 24 and 32 (Mitchell quotes the Authorised Version with some slight differences). Abraham queries God's decision to destroy Sodom and Gomorrah entirely, given that there may be righteous people among them. With all the persistence of a skilled bazaar-haggler, Abraham doggedly bargains God down until He promises not to destroy Sodom and Gomorrah if He finds ten righteous inhabitants there. It is a moment of rare humour in the Old Testament.

[47] **chaffering** Haggling.

[48] **bravo** Used in the sense of "a daring villain, a hired soldier or assassin" (*OED*), but also echoing the earlier description of him as "a murderer who killed openly, with bravado".

[49] **Hope and Faith and Charity** Cf. I Corinthians, 13: "And now abideth faith, hope, charity, these three; but the greatest of these is charity."

[50] **forehead** "forhead" in the first edition.

[51] **One with bleeding hands and feet and hidden face** This can only be a vision of Christ, whose resurrection, the first words of the story tell us, is commemorated on this day. Of course Southcote, devout Calvinist, might *in extremis* readily believe he saw a vision of Christ (he is, let us remind ourselves, deranged), so we need not entertain the idea of any work of the divinity actually having taken place.
[52] **the message brought to the Governor from a brothel in the slums** Southcote has presumably given warning of the imminent earthquake. Hence the order to evacuate. He has saved himself and everyone else by means of a descent into the meanest circumstances, where it seems both truth and virtue are to be found. The biblical parallels, then, seem to have been established only to be redrawn, for the result of Southcote's warning is to save the people of Mevr from an "act of God" (in the legal sense of the term), whereas the populace of Sodom and three other cities was exterminated. The story rewrites Genesis by *secularising* salvation and redemption: the message brought to the reader from Mitchell would seem to be a not unusual Christian Socialist one that Christian virtues, if applied, will save us in the earthly here and now, even if there is no hereafter.
[53] **a murderer and a thief, two of those reckoned in the sum of the righteous Ten** In Luke's gospel one of the two thieves crucified alongside Christ asks to be remembered "when thou comest into thy kingdom. And Jesus said unto him, Verily I say unto thee, Today shalt thou be with me in paradise" (Luke 23, 42-3).

He Who Seeks

[1] **the Gift of the River ... the Khalig el Masri** "The Gift of the River" is the title of one of the later stories in the volume. The Khalij al-Misri (there are variant spellings) was an ancient canal in Cairo and was at one time vital to the city's water supply. "Masri" can denote "Egyptians" or the Egyptian language. The canal was discontinued in the late 1890s (probably 1899) and converted to a street of the same name. Later, in "The Epic", it will be accurately described as "this street young in Cairo, this street where once was a canal and one may still see the tide-markings of the waters". It was renamed after the Egyptian July revolution of 1952 and the road is now called Port Said, which is extremely long and extends from north to central Cairo.
[2] **Key-colour ... master-note ... it is Quest** In other words, the dominant theme of this part of Cairo (or the main concern of life) is also that of a literary genre, the quest narrative, which deals, one might say, with "He Who Seeks". The quest narrative is as old as literature: Homer's *Odyssey* (which simply means "long adventurous journey") is, for example, a quest of epic length. It is usually a romantic (as opposed to realist) tale in which the hero journeys in search of something valuable, more often than not spiritual in nature. We have already witnessed in "For Ten's Sake" a hero who seeks mass vengeance but, instead of finding it, discovers

something more enlightening to his soul ("Happy he who finds not what he seeks").
[3] **that mirage-orchard that flourishes by the Dead Sea** The "Dead Sea Apple" (also known as the "Apple of Sodom") was described by the ancient writers Josephus (37-*c*. 100) and Tacitus (56-*c*. 120). The orchard in which it supposedly grew is perhaps here called a "mirage" because the soil around the destroyed Sodom was, according to the Bible, thereafter barren, but the Garden of Eden and its fateful apple is obviously being evoked too. The general suggestion which follows is that the knowing quester might expect to be more than frustrated: he may discover the opposite of his wish.
[4] **dragoman** A guide in Arabic-speaking countries. Anthony Sattin, *Lifting the veil: British society in Egypt, 1768-1956* (London: Dent, 1988), p. 126, writes informatively about the tourist's dependency on this hired help. "The first thing to be done, usually even before hiring a boat, was to find a dragoman. The word is derived from the Arabic *targuman*, which literally means 'interpreter'. The dragoman, however, was more than merely a linguist; he was also a guide and organizer. He knew better than his employers where they wanted to go and how they were going to get there; and along with the *rais* or captain of the boat he was the person who left the greatest impression on the traveller. A dragoman was usually indispensable, but the relationship between him and his employer was a delicate one: he had the knowledge but they had the money; they were the masters but he was their leader. Obviously it was important to get on with him from the start. Cook's *Handbook* for 1906 advised that 'It often requires considerable moral courage to keep these individuals in their proper places, for the more useful and capable they are the more easy it is for their employers to lose control over them.'"
[5] **Olympus** Mount Olympus, in Greece: the mythological seat of twelve ancient Greek gods.
[6] **when they have laid aside their bowler hats** In other words, like an English civil servant after a long day's work, though John Garland in Mitchell's first novel, *Stained Radiance* (London: Jarrolds, 1930), encounters "Four dragomen [*sic*], wearing bowler hats and the tunics of colonels" (p. 188) as he tries to make his way to the pyramids near Cairo. (The technically correct plural is "dragomans", not "dragomen": Mitchell gets it right in "The Passage of the Dawn".) The British had occupied Egypt (ruling it as a "protectorate" rather than a colony) since the Anglo-Egyptian War of 1882, and it did not become formally independent until 1922, with many British troops still stationed in the country afterwards. Mitchell himself was among the occupying forces.
[7] **The little Simon** Simon is an occasional character who appears in several of the stories.
[8] **the Anglo-Saxon** The English.
[9] **Anton Saloney ... the army of Deniken ... the Gymnasium of Kazan** Saloney is our narrator henceforth, and he often speaks to us directly and as if we are physically present before him, as here. He is our dragoman, our guide, explaining Cairo to us in his very good but slightly idiosyncratic English ("this book-English of

mine", he calls it in "The Epic"), and we are presumably tourists or visitors. He has fought on the losing side in the Great War and in the "White" counter-revolutionary southern Russian army of General Anton Denikin (1872-1947) in the Russian Civil War of 1917-23 (Denikin had been a Russian General in World War I). Calling himself "Professor of English Literature in the Gymnasium of Kazan" (a city about 500 miles or 830 km due east of Moscow) is grandiloquent: a "gymnasium" in this context is simply a secondary school, and while he may have taught English there, one can doubt that his job title really was "Professor of English Literature". We learn more details about him later in dribs and drabs. For example, he tells us that he has never been to London or Scotland, that he is unmarried, and that he has spent at least nine years in Cairo. He had a real-world original: Mitchell jointly dedicated his later novel *The Lost Trumpet* (London: Jarrolds, 1932) "TO/COLONEL GRIGORI SALIAEFF/ON WHOM I MODELLED SALONEY".

[10] **the dynastic tables** Records of the Pharaonic dynasties which ruled ancient Egypt, going as far back as approximately 3000 BC. These are among the oldest surviving written records in the world.

[11] **Rameses II ... Kheops' Pyramid** Ramesses II (*c.* 1303 BC-1213 BC), an ancient Egyptian Pharaoh. In *Stained Radiance*, Garland "sat on the top of Cheops and ate peanuts" (p. 189). The Pyramid of Cheops, the pharaoh who commissioned it, built in the 26th century BC, stands in a complex of ancient monuments in Giza, close to the city boundary of Cairo, on the west side of the Nile river. It is also known as the Great Pyramid. The tale of Ramesses committing suicide by throwing himself off the Pyramid is entirely a concoction of Saloney's to excite a gullible western tourist. Thus Saloney plainly confesses that he makes up fictions for transient visitors, a *caveat emptor* for the implied reader as to his veracity.

[12] **Morris** The English writer and utopian socialist William Morris (1834-1896). Literary history has not been as kind to him as Mitchell often was: he is hardly lauded today as "subtle tale-smith", but rather as a minor writer more notable for his influence on political thought and interior design than literature.

[13] **the Hollow Land ... faery-knight ... faery-saint** "The Hollow Land" (1856) is an early story by William Morris. It is a quest narrative with a medieval setting which begins, "Do you know where it is, the Hollow Land? I have been looking for it now so long, trying to find it again, the Hollow Land; for there I saw my love first. I wish to tell you how I found it first of all; but I am old, my memory fails me: you must wait and let me think if I perchance can tell you how it happened" (*The Hollow Land and other contributions to The Oxford and Cambridge Magazine by William Morris* [London: Chiswick Press, 1903], p. 154). The Hollow Land of the story is a kind of purgatory. "Faery" (as adjective) is defined by the *OED* as "[h]aving the ethereal or magical qualities associated with faeries, or with the realm or world in which they are supposed to live; enchanted; illusory": the very stuff of romance.

[14] **Perekop, on the bridge** The Soviet Red Army besieged and destroyed the town of Perekop (in east Crimea) during the Russian Civil War (7-17 November 1920). The Whites had previously held Crimea, which is a peninsula separated from the rest of

Russia on its east coast by the Kerch Strait. There was no bridge across the Strait in Mitchell's time, though there is one now. The assault was conducted by crossing the water in boats. Mitchell may be trying to use the term figuratively (that is to say, taking Crimea was the "bridge" to Red Army victory). We learn that both Saloney and Andrei Bal'mont have fled the reprisals likely to be meted out by the Reds to the Whites who rose up against the revolution. Egypt was one common destination for such Russian refugees (later in the story we learn that Saloney has actually founded the Cairo refugee committee), but they are notably not the Communists one would expect Mitchell to favour. The Andrei Bal'mont of this story was to become the Dutchman Koupa in *Stained Radiance*, but there Koupa claims to be on the winning Bolshevik side: "I have fought under the Hammer and Sickle and seen the Red Battalions storm impregnable Perekop" (p. 101). He too nonetheless has a spell in Cairo, but beginning a little later (1921). He revolts against Soviet atrocities and escapes on a boat to Latvia, thence to England. He gets "a position with a company which specialized in conducted tours to the East" (p. 62), which he deserts in Cairo.

15 **Sovyets** Mitchell used the unusual spelling "Sovyets" elsewhere (but also the more common "Soviets").

16 **whoom** "Whoom" is a felicitously onomatopoeic verb (here a noun) that Mitchell invented. "Only in Gibbon" say Scots dictionaries, which nonetheless appropriate its effectivity for Scots, although there is nothing particularly Scots about it. It is used also in *Stained Radiance* and *The Thirteenth Disciple* (London: Jarrolds, 1931).

17 **Yalta ... Black Sea** Yalta is a port on the Black Sea to the very south of Crimea. From there Bal'mont could sail to Turkey.

18 **Sovyeti** Mitchell means to indicate a Russian-sounding plural of "Soviet", i.e. the Bolsheviks.

19 **veter, the wail-wind of the Russian winter** The Russian "ветер" simply means "wind".

20 **Stamboul** Istanbul, until 1923 the capital of Turkey (not officially its name until March 1930).

21 **French money** This may imply that Bal'mont's wages were paid by one of the Allied governments that helped sponsor the White uprising. A French cruiser will soon appear, as if to repeat the point. This is historically accurate: the French had sent a military force to Crimea in 1918. Once they had been defeated the White Army retreated to the Crimean ports, where a massive evacuation of 150,000 people by ship – mostly to Istanbul – took place.

22 **Tovarishii** Comrades (Russian, used by Bolsheviks as a form of address).

23 **screw** A colloquialism for a propeller.

24 **the Holy Grail** The staple of much Arthurian romance (of the kind which suffuses Morris's "The Hollow Land" and much of his other work), the Holy Grail is an archetypal quest-object: variously a stone, a cup or a dish possessed of magical or spiritual properties.

25 **God mine!** Not "My God!" This exhibits one of the slight quirks of Saloney's English, several of which he curiously shares with a fictional Dutchman: Koupa in

Stained Radiance says "God mine" more than thirty times. Another mild linguistic flaw the two have in common is occasional misuse of the definite article.

[26] **the Golden Horn** An estuary which flows into the Bosphorus river in Istanbul.

[27] **the Imperial Army ... the Mosque Sophia** "Imperial Army" indicates the Russian army which had fought in the Great War. The Hagia Sophia Grand Mosque is an impressive Byzantine place of worship in Istanbul, near the Golden Horn.

[28] **kennels** Not doghouses but (in archaic usage) the drainage ditches ("channels") at the side of a thoroughfare. Bal'mont is experiencing life in the gutter.

[29] **the pity of the Christ** "The Christ of Pity" was something of a favoured Byzantine devotional genre, an image to inspire thoughts about the death of Jesus.

[30] **Jaffa ... the Russian colony in Palestine** Another presumed Russian emigré hangout of the time. Jaffa is now in Israel, which did not exist until 1948.

[31] **the Levant** Hardly anyone uses the term "the Levant" anymore, but it basically signified the region of the eastern Mediterranean.

[32] **Greek consul** In "For Ten's Sake" the title "German Consul" is given with a capital c, but it has not been regularised here.

[33] **Jerusalem** Around 40 miles (66 km) south-east from Jaffa by road.

[34] **a convent of the Irish nuns** Of course there were convents of Irish nuns everywhere, so one would expect there to be a few in the Holy Land of the 1920s.

[35] **Mountains of Moab** A range of mountains on the eastern edge of the Dead Sea, a course of water which historically separated the Kingdom of Judah (where Jerusalem was) from the Kingdom of Moab. Bal'mont is looking from the east: Jerusalem lies over the mountains and the Dead Sea.

[36] **mazed** Used in its poetic sense, "confused, bewildered".

[37] **English Jerusalem** In 1920 the League of Nations had mandated, against Arab objections, that Britain take responsibility for what was then known as Palestine (the British "Balfour Declaration" of 1917 having already committed the British to supporting the creation of a Jewish homeland within that territory, a course the British chose partly to secure Jewish support on the Allied side in the Great War). Transjordan was incorporated into the mandate in 1921, which meant that (when its other occupying roles in the region are considered) Britain effectively held dominion over most of the vastnesses of the Middle East and east North Africa throughout the 1920s and beyond.

[38] **Church of the Holy Sepulchre ... Christ laid when brought from the Cross** Also known as Church of the Resurrection, this ancient site is claimed to encompass not only Christ's tomb but also the spot on which he was crucified.

[39] **Alexandria** On Egypt's Mediterranean coast.

[40] **that Odyssey that finally led him to Egypt** Something like the reverse journey of that taken in the Biblical Exodus.

[41] **Westwards and southwards he went, crossing the mountains of Moab ... the jungle swamps of Ludd** If Bal'mont went "westwards" from Jerusalem (as he needs to do to reach Egypt) he would not cross the Mountains of Moab, which are to the east. Nor would he be travelling towards Lod, which is a city northwest of

Jerusalem in a region hardly known for its "jungle swamps". Mitchell was presumably never in charge of navigation while in the army or the RAF.

42 **a pillar of light by night and a pillar of smoke by day** Cf. Exodus 13, 21: "And the Lord went before them by day in a pillar of a cloud, to lead them the way; and by night in a pillar of fire, to give them light; to go by day and night".

43 **the Evening Star** The planet Venus is traditionally both the Morning Star and the Evening Star. Venus is also, of course, the Roman goddess of love.

44 **Transjordania** The Emirate of Transjordan came into being on 11 April 1921 and remained a British protectorate until 1946 (now Jordan). This would seem to confirm that Bal'mont has indeed travelled east, not west, as Transjordan was east of Palestine.

45 **Amman** The capital of modern-day Jordan, confusingly east and north of the Jersualem Bal'mont was said to have travelled "westwards and southwards" from! One's bafflement is compounded by the fact that Mitchell knew this Middle East landscape personally. From Amman Bal'mont goes further east, which is also the wrong direction. Did he get entrammelled in an unspecified side-quest, perhaps?

46 **Kantara on the Suez** Bal'mont then goes back ("north-west") the way he came ("south and east"). Quite how that gets him to the Suez canal is unclear, but perhaps the suggestion is that he has been wandering in some aimless, distressed way. In *Stained Radiance* things are much clearer for his doppelganger: Koupa relates that he spent five years having adventures in "Wahhabi territory" (modern Saudi Arabia) before going "northwards to Sinai, and so, across the desert, to Kantara and Suez" (p. 64). That is, he takes an explicably direct route to the Sinai peninsula and the town on its west side, El-Qantara, which straddles the Suez Canal.

47 **12, Harun-Badrawi, Khalig-el-Masri, Le Caire** "Harun" and "Badrawi" are Arabic male names, here used in designation of an address. "Caire" is French for "Cairo".

48 **the writing of Belshazzar's feast** The biblical Belshazzar's feast (Daniel 5) is sometimes referred to as "the story of the writing on the wall". King Belshazzar, a Babylonian, holds a feast. Unintelligble words are found written on a nearby wall. Daniel is called and explains them thus:

> And this is the writing that was written, Mene, Mene, Tekel, Upharsin.
>
> This is the interpretation of the thing: Mene; God hath numbered thy kingdom, and finished it.
>
> Tekel; Thou art weighed in the balances, and art found wanting.
>
> Peres; Thy kingdom is divided, and given to the Medes and Persians.
>
> (Daniel 5, 25-8)

49 **hereafter is only the dream I built on the so-few facts I sought out later that year** Another sign that the story is not to be taken at face-value: indeed, some of the things Saloney subsequently relates it would be impossible for him to know.

50 **Bulaq Bridge** Mentioned many times in the stories, the Boulak Bridge was completed in 1912, and crossed the Nile in Cairo between Gezira island and the district of Boulak to its east. ("Gezira" simply means island, and is how it is referred

to locally, though the island's official name is Zamalek.) It was demolished in 1998. It extended from what is currently 26 July Street in Boulak and has been replaced by today's 15th May Bridge. It could be opened to permit river traffic to pass through it. The Nile at Boulak was tremendously busy, as it hosted the main quay from which tourists took cruises down the Nile.

51 **beyond Abbassieh, were the Red Hills crowned in fire** Abbassia is a neighbourhood in Cairo's El Weili district, just east of Boulak. The hills are almost certainly the same Mokattam Hills Garland views in *Stained Radiance* (p. 189).

52 **Sunset over Cairo** The effect is potentially to reduce the reality of Bal'mont's "odyssey" to some kind of tourist postcard or painting. Indeed, there is at least one painting called "Sunset Over Cairo" (1904) by Augustus Osborne Lamplough (1877-1930), an example of many he made of the city and the country. It is not included in Lamplough's colour illustrations to the guide-book *Egypt and How to See It 1907-1908* (New York: Doubleday, 1907), but forty-one others are. "Sunset Over the Nile" is reproduced in A. O. Lamplough and R. Francis, *Cairo and Its Environs* (London: Joseph Causton, 1909), unnumbered pages between pp. 90 and 91.

53 **lowe** Warm light.

54 **tramped forth again on his quest** Once more (as in "For Ten's Sake") we have a reversal or negation of the event to which the narrative seems to have been leading up all the while, in this case what would have been a hackneyed romantic reconciliation. But Natasha does not discover that Bal'mont is there and he turns around and walks away. We can only conclude that, for him, life is the very activity of questing ("Key-colour to the kaleidoscope, master-note in the syncopation"), not of securing what is sought. Bal'mont is like the restless hero of one of Mitchell's favourite poems, "Ulysses" (1833) by Alfred, Lord Tennyson (1809-1892), in which Odysseus, returned to Ithaca after years of travel, wishes again to stir and strike out on a new journey. Exit Bal'mont, to reappear enlarged and somewhat metamorphosed as Koupa in *Stained Radiance*.

The Lost Prophetess

1 **The Lost Prophetess** This story was originally entitled "The Road" in *The Cornhill Magazine* version.

2 **Warren strikers** Towards the end of the story we hear of "the lairs of the Black Warrens", and these warrens appear again in "A Volcano in the Moon". But the term is never fully explicated. The suggestion is of very poor neighbourhoods in which sanitation is neglected. The nature of these "warrens" is made much clearer in Mitchell's later novel *The Lost Trumpet*, in which many characters and locations of *The Calends* are revisited: "Down dim dark lanes as the evening came on I had wandered – lanes overhung with crumbling balconies, lanes unknown even to me, dark corridors where the poor and rejected – the maimed and brutalized of this thing that East and West these thousand years have called civilization – lived their dark

and fetid lives, and somehow found still the courage to raise those bursts of laughter that I could hear far in dim, stifling courtyards; still to bring with hope unlessened new life to add to that ferment of pain and want, for children suckled at unshielded breasts in almost every doorway; still to live and lust and seek" (p. 45).

[3] **the Professor of English Literature who fled to join the Whites** Saloney is describing himself.

[4] ***harm* and *soq*** A "*soq*" is a souq or souk; "*harm*" (later in the story spelled "*harîm*") has been absorbed into English as "harem", but it is important to grasp that in Arabic this word traditionally designated the part of a Muslim home reserved separately for women. Mitchell's description equivocates between this meaning and the modern understanding of a group of women kept by a man for sexual purposes. Under the Ottoman Empire, harems could comprise many non-Muslim slaves.

[5] **Khan Khalil** Khan Al Khalili is a major bazaar in central Cairo. See Ola Sieff, *Khan al-Khalili: a comprehensive mapped guide to Cairo's historic bazaar* (Cairo: The American University in Cairo Press, 1993).

[6] **Angora** Ankara, the Turkish capital city (since 1923).

[7] **Sharikhan** Later in the story said to be on the Nile (but then most Egyptian places are); possibly Kawm Sharik, a town between Cairo and Alexandria. However, as Mitchell describes the place, it would appear to be nearer, or indeed within, Cairo.

[8] **the women's regeneration** Presumably this means something like "the resurgence of women" or "women's causes".

[9] **in** "In" (with a capital I) in first edition.

[10] **El-Azhar** Al-Azhar University, in Cairo, founded in the late tenth century, and an important institution in the Islamic world.

[11] **the great train accident** This is almost certainly a reference to the Tay Bridge railway disaster: on 28 December 1879 all fifty-nine passengers died when the bridge collapsed while their train was crossing it. It became well-known in Scotland because the Scots doggerelist William McGonagall (1825-1902) wrote his execrable "The Tay Bridge Disaster" (1880) to commemorate it.

[12] **Pre-Raphaelite Brotherhood** An informal group of English artists and writers founded in 1848. Mitchell often quoted some of its members in his works, and seemed in general favourable towards the movement.

[13] **Ruskin and Morris** John Ruskin (1819-1900), an important English writer on art and architecture, who among other things championed the Pre-Raphaelites. William Morris was also strongly influenced by him.

[14] **The New Age** The concept of a "New Age" in spirituality was prevalent in late-19th century theosophy. The term was politicised by *The New Age* (1894-1938), a weekly Christian socialist magazine which, by 1908, had become more up-to-date and radical, mixing a kind of Guild socialism with Fabian thinking, and at least for a time supported women's causes.

[15] **to demand the freedom and the shedding of the *pushi*** The "Sedra-Pushi" (Persian: "putting on the sedra", a sedra being a type of undergarment) is a ceremonial rite of passage in the Zoroastrian religion in Iran. But if this is what is

being referred to, Mitchell may have misunderstood "pushi" rather than "sedra" to signify the garment. The meaning is clear enough though: Hatoun is agitating politically for and among the women for greater freedom and political rights.

[16] **Women's League of Al-Islam** An organisation which exists only in this Mitchell story.

[17] **Freedom and the Alphabet** That is, political equality with men and access to education.

[18] ***Haj** ... **Jihad*** Hajj is the pilgrimage to Mecca, which all Muslims are expected to make at least once in life. *Jihad* literally means "striving" (especially one's "higher" self struggling against one's "lower") but Mitchell takes it in the more controversial meaning of "Holy War".

[19] **Bey** In the Ottoman Empire a bey was the governor of a province. The word later became a term of respect in Turkish and Arabic, added after the name and equating to "Esq." or "Sir" in English.

[20] **the Khedive** The title given to the viceroy of Egypt when it was controlled by Turkey (1867-1914).

[21] **the Yemen ... Yahya clan** The British had seized the Yemeni city of Aden for use as an entrepôt in 1837. They turned it into a colony and it remained such until 1963, when it was incorporated into the State of Aden within the Federation of South Arabia. The Federation became the People's Republic of South Yemen in 1967, and in 1990 it united with North Yemen to become Yemen. When the Ottoman Empire withdrew from Yemen in 1918, Imam Ahmad bin Yahya Hamidaddin (1891-1962), a religious leader in the territory, declared himself King of Yemen, and for about a decade troubled the British with periodic but unsuccessful military attacks on Aden. Thereafter he too became "an uncertain friend of the English".

[22] **the Muski** Sharia Muski (Muski Street), one of the busiest in Cairo, and then a main thoroughfare between the Khan Al Khalili bazaar and downtown.

[23] **lateen sail** A triangular sail which originated in the Mediterranean in Roman times.

[24] **came merciful release** The suggestion (enhanced a few lines later when we learn that his wife has been "supplanted for a season") is that Shihada Bey has repeatedly raped Jane. In the next section we learn that "he had the orthodox horror of the mad", which we infer is what causes him to desist.

[25] **amulet-clutching silence** The jewellery is likely to have a religious significance.

[26] **eunuch** A castrated man permitted to be in the presence of women in the harem. Those with an interest in the Egyptian dimensions of the subject are referred to Otto Meinardus, "The Upper Egyptian Practice of the Making of Eunuchs in the XVIIIth and XIXth Century", *Zeitschrift für Ethnologie* 94,1 (1969), pp. 47-58.

[27] **Ayesha the Abyssinian and Namlah the Copt** Ayesha is from modern-day Ethiopia (as Abyssinia was renamed after the Second World War); if Namlah is a "Copt" she is either descended from ancient Egyptians or is a member of the Coptic Orthodox Church, an Oriental Orthodox Christian church in Egypt.

[28] **And it seemed to them as they looked that upon that curtain was flung**

a sudden picture This reads very like the biblical episode of Belshazzar's feast already explicitly alluded to in the preceding story.
[29] **zenana** Persian: synonymous with "harem" (in the sense of a part of a house reserved for women).
[30] **thaumaturgist** A magician or sorcerer.
[31] **the first woman Prophet of God, one who superseded Christ and Mohammed** There are female prophets in the Bible (but none has a book named after her). There are arguably none in the Qur'ān, in which Jesus and Muhammad both figure as prophets.
[32] **no record but the fragmentary verbal survives** Yet another sign of the unreliability of the tale.
[33] **our bodies shall be ... temples of the living God** "Know ye not that ye are the temple of God, and that the Spirit of God dwelleth in you? If any man defile the temple of God, him shall God destroy; for the temple of God is holy, which temple ye are" (1 Corinthians 3, 16-17).
[34] ***El Darb*** "Al Darb" literally means "the road" or "the way" (Arabic). In this story, following this "road" becomes Jane's quest.
[35] **The Buddhist Eightfold path, the Aryan Way ...the City of God** These are all offered as analogous practices leading to spiritual enlightenment in Buddhism, Hinduism, and Christianity respectively. In other words, the prophetess has founded a religion.
[36] **those who merely looked and listened and feared** Cf. Psalms 34, 4: "I sought the Lord, and he heard me, and delivered me from all my fears." Even when perhaps not deliberately alluding to the Bible, one can sense it influencing the flavour of Mitchell's prose, sometimes in lexis, sometimes in rhythm, often in both.
[37] **the Paul of the wild, new faith** In Acts 9, the splenetic Saul of Tarsus is travelling to Damascus when he is struck blind for three days by a light from heaven, and God speaks to him. He is miraculously cured and converts to Christianity. By Acts 13 he is referred to as "Paul". He goes on to write several epistles in the New Testament.
[38] **the laying-on of hands** Cf. Luke 4, 40: "Now when the sun was setting, all they that had any sick with divers diseases brought them unto him; and he laid his hands on every one of them, and healed them."
[39] **quarters of the Greeks** There is actually a neighbourhood in Cairo called "Haret el Roum" ("Quarter of the Eastern Christians"). According to the Egyptian census of 1927 there were over 76,000 Greeks living in Egypt (up from 62,000 in 1907), which was the highest official figure recorded. Thereafter it declines, most rapidly after the 1952 nationalist revolution. D. J. Enright's novel *Academic Year*, set in Alexandria just prior to the 1952 overthrow, refers to it as "a city which became less Greek and more Arab every year" (London: Secker and Warburg, 1955, p. 84). The current estimate for Greeks living in Egypt is around 5,000.
[40] **cholera** The fatal bacterial infection, usually caused by drinking infected water, was a constant cause for concern in Egypt. There had been major outbreaks under

the British in 1883 (almost 50,000 deaths), 1895-6 (over 17,000 deaths) and 1902 (almost 35,000 deaths).

[41] **Ragheb Pasha, the Ghazi's friend** There had been a well-known Isma'il Ragheb Pasha (1819-1884), who had been Prime Minister of Egypt for a single summer (64 days, 1882), ending in the very month that the British landed. A Ghazi is a Muslim warrior (Arabic).

[42] **mullahs** Leaders of Muslim mosques (Persian).

[43] **Young Turk** The Young Turks was the name given to an opposition movement which arose in the Ottoman Empire in the last quarter of the nineteenth century.

[44] ***hôsh*** A *hosh* (Arabic) is a courtyard in a traditional Arabic residential building, usually in the centre.

[45] **Kemal** Mustafa Kemal Atatürk (*c.* 1881-1938), founder of the Republic of Turkey and its first president from 1923 until his death.

[46] ***khâtûn*** Lady (Arabic).

[47] **Dirhem** A common name in Turkey.

[48] **and thereon beat the demented women** The syntax renders the action (and the actors) ambiguous. Presumably the eunuchs do not kill the women by beating them against the outside of the door, but the women inside the palace beat on the door in desperation at what appears to be deliberate drowning. The entire description of the "murder", however, seems intentionally obfuscated.

[49] **they** This is a slightly inelegant shift from the "they" of the preceding paragraph, which signified the eunuchs outside the door; the "they" of this paragraph denotes those still alive within.

[50] **that Avalon where Arthur dreams, and sleeps the Danish king** As Arthurian legend has it, King Arthur is taken to sleep on the mythical island of Avalon until he is needed again by his people, at which point he will awake to lead them again. In different versions, Ogier the Dane is taken to Avalon.

Daybreak

[1] **Mantell** A seven-letter surname containing (in the same order) five of the eight letters of Mitchell's own. He is a journalist, as was Mitchell for a brief spell (1917-1919). Mantell is nonetheless an actual English name.

[2] **your Urals** The addressee has already been signalled as Scottish, and the Scottish analogy for the Russian Ural mountains is most likely Mitchell's own much-visited Grampians, a large mountain range that extends from near the north-east coast of Scotland all the way to the west coast, also stretching significantly north and south.

[3] **indistinguishes** One of the occasions when what appears to be an insecure grasp of English deliberately conceals a quite sharp and witty observation.

[4] **Spengler** Oswald Spengler (1880-1936), German author of *The Decline of the West*, originally published in two volumes in 1918 and 1920 (2 vols, tr. Charles Francis Atkinson, London: George Allen & Unwin, 1926 and 1928). Mitchell was to

refer to Spengler, almost always negatively, a great deal. In *The Conquest of the Maya* (London: Jarrolds, 1934), he makes fun of "the full-throated bellow of Dr. Oswald Spengler, assiduously devastating the planet with theories of cyclic catastrophe" (p. 126). In the same year he implied (in the pages of *Left Review*, with an astuteness shown by few other contributors to a well-known literary-political debate) that Communists who believed that contemporary western literature was in a decadent state probably took their historical understanding, ironically, from the right-wing "half-witted Spenglerites" (Bold, *Smeddum*, p. 738). In *Gay Hunter* (London: Heinemann, 1934) the eponymous heroine reflects on "Spengler, with his theories of cyclic catastrophe, of the rise and fall of cultures, inevitable and unceasing. His slick, quack arguments, built of poor reasoning and worse research, had left her unmoved, but how they had moved her contemporary world!" (p. 48). Indeed, from the publication of the first volume of his work Spengler seemed instantly to become all the rage in much European intellectual discussion until the Nazis openly appropriated his ideas in the 1930s.

5 **'Oh, the memory and the ache ... In my ain countree'** The Scottish poet Allan Cunningham (1784-1842) was asked to help collect traditional songs for a collection, but instead passed off some of his own compositions. Two poems in *Remains of Nithsdale and Galloway Song*, ed. R. H. Cromek (Paisley: Alexander Gardner, 1880) contain the refrain "in my ain countrie" ("Hame, Hame, Hame" and "The Sun's Bright in France") but neither of them has a stanza like this. Mitchell is probably quoting one of the later versions of the song, which was often freely adapted.

6 **Eoanthropus** Mitchell, to debatable effect, often allowed his archaeological and anthropological interests to seep into his fiction. *The Calends of Cairo* is notable in that this often distracting habit is kept in check, except on rare occasions, like this one. He is referring to what we more commonly call Piltdown Man (*Eoanthropus dawsoni*: "Dawson's dawn-man"), named after Charles Dawson (1864-1916), who in February 1912 discovered in a river gravel pit close to Piltdown, Sussex, what he claimed were fossil fragments of a skull intermediate in development between apes and humans (though it was at the time dated to half a million years ago, not 200,000). It was not until the 1950s that this was indisputably proved to be a deliberate hoax.

7 **to steal the singer from her hills** Mitchell's Cairo is replete with anecdotes of love (or lust) at first sight, which lead more than once (well, it's only natural) to thoughts or metaphors of kidnap. Shihada Bey has abducted, raped and abandoned Jane Hatoun in the preceding story. Now Mantell wants "to steal the singer from her hills", but the need is obviated by her ready acquiescence to his wishes, which seems so instant that it does not last long enough for Mitchell even to be able to describe it. Mantell loves Dawn at first light, one is tempted to say, and she alights on him.

8 **She detested the poor Spengler** It's handy that the object of Mantell's desire, as well as being alluring and radiant and athletic, keeps up to date with the very latest work in Central European history and sociology. But then, she is ultra-modern.

Nevertheless, one wonders, how long did she wait for *The Decline of the West* to arrive in her local library, and did she have to wait until the local lad o' pairts had finished with it? Mitchell was to repeat this mixing of romantic desire with unlikely intellectual similarity in *The Thirteenth Disciple*, in which Domina (although being a chemist) is vastly read in anthropology and happens to be in complete agreement with Malcom's mistaken historical theories.

[9] **he would hear the sun come audibly** The mind boggles at the acuteness of his hearing. But, of course, the hills are alive with the sound of Dawn.

[10] **'You're out of the hills and the sunrise.'** Yes, she comes from the hills and, yes, her name is Dawn, and yes, the story is called "Daybreak". You have already told us all this, JLM.

[11] **'How can they help it?' said Roger, her lover** Exchanges between courting couples like these were the kind of thing an editor or friend ought perhaps to have advised Mitchell to stop attempting. The embarrassing ineptitude with which he handles them was to be much exacerbated in *Stained Radiance* and *The Thirteenth Disciple*. The reader who comes to this story knowing Mitchell's first two novels may be feeling a little jaded, as both extensively fictionalise Mitchell's courtship of his wife in a Scottish setting. This story was, however, first published before them. There is no doubt that Mitchell was extremely concerned, like D. H. Lawrence, for example, with writing about developing sexual relationships between men and women; but that his writerly talents tended in this direction could be questioned from the clumsiness of his early attempts.

[12] **the thousand a year or only eight hundred** The inflation multiplier for the century 1924 to 2024 is almost exactly fifty, which can thus be used as a rough rule of thumb for converting most of the currency values in the book: £1,000 in 1924 is equivalent in today's money to just over £50,000.

[13] **twinkle-tapers lighting her grey eyes** Mitchell was clearly taken by his idea that women's eyes could be described as containing tapers: he transplants Dawn's tapers into Rita in *The Thirteenth Disciple* (whose peepers are so described six times).

[14] **arm's** "arms" in the first edition.

[15] **little river** The Thames also runs through much of *Stained Radiance* and *The Thirteenth Disciple* as the Nile runs through the Cairo stories, but at 215 miles (346 km) long and with a mean width of about 0.2 miles (0.3 km), it is "little" compared to the mighty Nile (4,100 miles or 6,600 km long, mean width approximately 1.75 miles or 2.8 km).

[16] **his gazette** The newspaper or magazine he works for.

[17] **refractory** Unmanageable, difficult.

[18] **captain of the hosts of the morning** Cf. Joshua 5, 14-15: "And he said, Nay; but as captain of the host of the Lord am I now come." A biblical "host" is an unseen army, usually of angels, defending God. Mitchell's "morning" of course echoes both "Dawn" and "Daybreak".

[19] **erring Germans ... the Defile through which march the hosts that have**

climbed from the beast Mitchell would entitle the War chapter in *The Thirteenth Disciple* "The Defile of the Beast". A defile is a narrow passage or gorge, and a Western Front trench is a kind of "defile", the kind in which a man inevitably becomes a beast. Here, however, "the hosts that have climbed from the beast" (i.e. evolved humans) also appear to live in a "Defile". The "erring Germans" are not Great War soldiers but "half-witted Spenglerites".

[20] **the child born dead... it seemed that Dawn herself would die** Mitchell's wife Rhea, *née* Rebecca Middleton (1901-1978), had had a miscarriage in January 1926, which he would dramatise at much greater length in *Stained Radiance*, in which Thea too almost dies.

[21] **he had found a gazette willing to send him abroad ... to ... write a series-impression of Cairo and the Nile-country** Mitchell often needs to get his characters from one country to another quickly (Garland to the Middle East in *Stained Radiance*, Malcom to Mexico in *The Thirteenth Disciple*) and usually does so by resorting to the most flagrant *deus ex machina*. It is not unknown for truly famous writers or journalists to be despatched for lengthy "international correspondent" duties like this, but why would any publication go to the expense of sending for an entire year a "not too-good journalist" on a junket better writers would kill for?

[22] **So they came to our Polychromata, those two** We now have, literally, a Cairo Dawn.

[23] **Kubbah** In *The Thirteenth Disciple* Metaxa is "the bastard son of an American irrigation official and a Cairene Greek [...] He had been an architect [...] who had helped to design the mud sky-scrapers of Palais de Koubbah" (p. 129). The Koubbeh Palace (as it is now known) is a mid-nineteenth century edifice in Cairo, which became the official royal residence in 1917. It was just south of where Mitchell was stationed with the RASC in 1922-1923. Presumably what is meant here is that Dawn and Roger return to the neighbourhood of the palace, where they are staying temporarily.

[24] **La maison Saniosu** The Saniosu House (French). The word "Saniosu" has no particular meaning in relation to a house, but is rather chosen, or invented, so that the following joke can be made.

[25] **Sans-Sous** "Sans souci" is a common French expression meaning "carefree" but "sans sous" literally means "without sous", i.e. penniless ("sou" being a term for a low-value French coin). Mitchell is being witty, and moreover witty in a foreign language. He himself cannot refrain from deeming it "a great jest".

[26] **khamsin time** The khamaseen is a hot, dry, sandy wind that periodically affects Egypt.

[27] ***Until the day break and the shadows flee away*** From the words of the Bride in Song of Solomon 2, 17: "Until the day break, and the shadows flee away, turn, my beloved, and be thou like a roe or a young hart upon the mountains of Bether."

[28] **the Sphinx** The Sphinx is an enormous reclining statue of a mythological creature

(part human, part animal) which sits near the Giza pyramids, but this name for it is by analogy with the creature of Greek mythology, and not Egyptian in origin.

29 **Philistine** Here used simply in the modern sense of "without taste" or "with no feel for art".

30 **the Riddle of the Sands** The title of a popular espionage thriller, *The Riddle of the Sands: A Record of Secret Service* (1903) by Erskine Childers (1870-1922), though Childers' sands are not of any desert but much colder ones around the Frisian Islands in the North Sea. In Greek myth the Sphinx poses a riddle to her interlocutors, who are eaten if they do not answer correctly.

31 **Mena House** The Mena House Hotel derives its name from King Menes or Mena of the first Egyptian dynasty. It was English-owned and opened in 1886. It acquired Egypt's first swimming pool in 1890. In 1907 it had 200 rooms and added thirty more in 1920. Well-to-do Brits, including royalty, frequently stayed there. It is now the J. W. Marriott Cairo Mena House, glorying in the address 6 Pyramids Road. Reynolds-Ball, *Cairo of to-day* (1898) waxes quite lyrical about it (pp. 27-8).

32 **the Delta** The Nile delta.

33 **brunet** The word originally meant any person with hair of the colour we now refer to when we say "brunette", but this rare spelling now tends to be used (very infrequently, it should be said) as its masculine form; cf. "blond" and "blonde".

34 **long before there was Celt or Saxon or Slav** Saloney is curiously well-versed, like his creator, in European ethnic history. All this phrase means is "a long time ago".

35 **Perhaps it is a memory that has come to you across ten thousand years** In this entire paragraph we witness the shoes of Diffusionism sticking out from under a closed curtain. In some of Mitchell's later works they were regrettably to step from attempted concealment and walk into the middle of the room. Diffusionism (sometimes called "hyperdiffusionism") was the belief – for some like Mitchell an accepted doctrine – that cultural innovations in pre-history spread geographically from a single source, Egypt, which so happened to have the oldest written records and thus is the earliest society in history (as opposed to pre-history). Diffusionist theories, which in themselves lacked a great deal of internal consistency, were definitively destroyed by scientific advances in the dating of ancient artefacts, especially after the Second World War. But they became something of a hobby-horse for Mitchell, who increasingly droned on about them like an acolyte in fictional and non-fictional works, in a manner that is now quite embarrassing, given that they were in retrospect so obviously pseudo-scientific. In this paragraph we hear Saloney invent an entirely spurious Egyptian lineage for a modern Scotswoman. However, there may be (as there often elsewhere is not in Mitchell) a winking irony in this case: after all, Saloney has told us, "I looked at her and wove the fantasy."

36 **the little madame its prophet** But not a lost prophetess.

37 **my Volga lands** Kazan sits on the Volga, the longest river in Europe.

38 **But this is the absurd fatalism** One would be more likely to classify the refusal of medical advice, and thinking of it as "cheating", to be gross stupidity. But what is

unspoken in the text here is the prospect of abortion or hysterectomy. Still, no convincing reason is given for Dawn's refusal, and the plot wobbles. A confident prediction of definite death consequent upon future pregnancy is a gross unlikelihood in any case, but even if we accept it, it is difficult to believe that it was not followed by procedures aimed at ensuring it did not happen.

[39] **Dr Adrian, the English** Who will reappear in some of the stories to come.

[40] **no gynæcologist can be anything but gynæcolatrist** There is no such word as "gynaeolatrist" (indeed, very few English words end in "latrist"), so this recondite *bon mot* requires abilities in or investigation into etymology, and one might well protest that, just as a joke is not funny if it needs to be explained, so a witticism is not funny if it requires one to parse it in an etymological dictionary (in this case *OED*). "Gynaecology" derives from combining *gynaeco-* ("woman") with *-logy* ("knowledge"); but *-latrist* (as in the word "bibliolatrist") derives from Latin ("worshipper"). If "woman-lover" is what is meant, then the drollery is not only unamusingly obscure, but patently untrue as a factual proposition.

[41] **khamsin time** "khamsin-time" in first edition (the hyphen is here removed for consistency with previous usage of the phrase in this story).

[42] **the Barrage ... Heliopolis** The Delta Barrage or Nile Barrage is a dam completed in 1862 on the Nile north of Cairo. It was replaced in the late 1930s by a new dam, but the original construction remains, and is now used as a road bridge. Modern Heliopolis (literally "City of the Sun" in Greek) is now thought of as a suburb of Cairo, 11 miles (18 km) north-east of downtown by road.

[43] **Abu Zabal** Another of Cairo's many modern suburbs, 17 miles (27 km) north-east of downtown by road.

[44] **Ragnarok** The name given in Norse mythology to a series of foretold natural catastrophes in which the world burns and is flooded.

[45] **Grampians sunset** If Dawn had come up she could, paradoxically, have sung a sunset song.

[46] **curlews** Wading birds, native to Scotland.

[47] **Alpha in Centaur** Alpha Centauri, one of the stars closest to our sun.

[48] **Lesdiguières** Not a common name in France, though there was the famous François de Bonne, duc de Lesdiguières (1543-1626).

[49] **limnings** Vague or sketchy outlines.

[50] **a boy** One of the "dawnmen", then, alluded to in this and in the opening of the immediately succeeding story. Rhea Sylvia Leslie Mitchell (1930-2014), the Mitchells' daughter, was born on 17 March 1930, three days after her father was formally discharged from the Royal Air Force. That was many months after the story was written but very close in time to its original publication as the tenth in the "Polychromata" sequence.

[51] **miasmas** A miasma is an unpleasant atmosphere, usually with the implication of it spreading, like a smell or smoke.

The Epic

[1] **The Epic** In a letter to Alexander and Ellen Gray (13 July 1929), Mitchell writes: "I've just corrected the proofs of No. 2 – 'The Epic.' which has lovely spots of writing in it, though I sez it as shouldn't. But there are several crudities in it that now, six months after the original writing, make my hair stand up." This dating would make it one of the earliest stories written for the series, which Mitchell commenced in December 1928. I am grateful to William K. Malcolm for pointing out this letter to me (correspondence TS, National Library of Scotland).

[2] **the dawnmen** Pre-historic humans.

[3] **aliens** Used here in the sense of "foreigners".

[4] **Ismailia, El Musky, El Manakh, Maghrabi, Shiekh Rihan** The Ismailia Desert Road runs all the way from Cairo to the city of Ismailia, about 80 miles (130 km) north-west. Muski Street we have already met in "A Lost Prophetess". Al Manakh and El-Maghraby are frequently mentioned in guides of the time as good streets for shopping, but the latter is not the current Cairo street of that name: it is now called Adly Street. Sheikh Rehan St (the first edition's spelling has not been corrected) is in downtown Cairo, running mostly due east from the Nile.

[5] **him who seeks to interpret Cairo's soul** Deliberately echoing the title of one of the stories, we might think of this as suggesting that the collection itself (and/or the reader, perhaps) is on a quest, as well as Connan.

[6] **I think he had perhaps the Irish blood** Connan (sometimes Conan) is an Irish surname. Sir Arthur Conan Doyle (1859-1930), for example, had Irish parents. But the surname or variants of it are first found in Mitchell's native Kincardineshire as early as the fourteenth century.

[7] **a stoker** Anyone who constantly feeds a fire, as a fireman on a steam train, for example.

[8] **Hotel Continental** According to *Egypt and How to See It 1907-1908*, "The Continental is a large new hotel facing the Opera Square and the Esbekieh Gardens, and offers many attractions to its patrons. The terrace has a most animated appearance. This hotel has the most central position of any, and is conveniently near the best shops and the bazaars; in fact, it is a good starting-point for all the sights of Cairo" (p. 24). This anonymously-authored guide-book, also published in French and German editions and already cited as containing many of Lamplough's illustrations, has an appendix on Egypt's hotels which gives some indication of their size. According to it, the Continental had 400 rooms and 500 beds in 1907 (p. 155). The building was demolished in 2018.

[9] **Dostoievsky** Fyodor Dostoevsky (1821-1881), the great Russian novelist. Connan's jocular point is that the Russians have been so long fighting in the Great War and the subsequent Russian Civil War that it is a marvel any have survived.

[10] **arabiyeh** An *araba* (Turkish: plural *arabas*) is a horse-drawn carriage for passengers. Mitchell's spelling of the word is found only in the works of the English writer Sax Rohmer (1883-1959), whose use of such "local" terms to add exotic colour

to his prose has since been the subject of some controversy.

[11] **smellsome** Not listed in English or Scots lexica, so probably Mitchell's coinage.

[12] **Hichens** Robert Smythe Hichens (1864-1950), English writer and Egypt enthusiast. Henry Denison, the hero of his successful novel *An Imaginative Man* (London: Heinemann, 1895), would not be out of place as a Mitchell character. By p. 68 he has become obsessed with the Sphinx:

> The Sphinx lays a spell upon all. It is too strange to leave no impression upon anybody. But to Denison it had seemed, as he stood before it first, in the burning afternoon and near to the clamouring tourists, the Something he had waited for, wanted, all his life. The immensity of its gaze, the terrible, unrelenting passivity of its attitude, drew him as the hidden vice draws the holy man till he falls.
>
> Had his wife refused to stay at the Mena House, Denison would have forced her to come there.

This was not Hichens' only fiction to use Egypt as a setting, and he also wrote *Egypt and Its Monuments* (New York: Century, 1908), whose frontispiece bore an image of the Sphinx.

[13] **bull-men of Assyria** Lamassu, a god to the Assyrians in Mesopotamia (*c.* 2500 BC- *c.* fourteenth century AD), was often depicted as having a human head and a bull's body.

[14] **I read your poems in Kazan** It's a small world.

[15] **argots** Argot essentially means jargon or slang. But "argot" itself is arguably a recondite jargon word (it is not one that immediately comes to mind) and we may begin to suspect that Saloney's occasional linguistic self-deprecation is just part of his act.

[16] **Kheops, Khefren, and Men-kaura** Three generations of pharaohs. Khefren was Cheops' son and ordered the building of the second largest pyramid in Egypt, also at the Giza site. Menkaura (the text's hyphen is Mitchell's) was the son of Khefren. His is the smallest of the three principal pyramids at Giza.

[17] **comparing its face to that of a notable pugilist** A humorous comparison Mitchell was to repeat very quickly in *Stained Radiance* (p. 188): "Looking up in the battered face, he laughed at sight of the wonder of the ages. For it had the face of an unfortunate pugilist." In the novel the "notable pugilist" was named as "Mr Beckett", to wit English boxer Joseph Beckett (1892-1965), one time British and British Empire heavyweight champion, who ceased competing in 1923.

[18] **the Suq el Fahlamin** It is not clear if Mitchell is referring to a fictional bazaar, but it would be unusual if he were. A real-world original has not been identified.

[19] **El Katal or El Fostat** Al-Qaṭāʾi was once the capital of Egypt, founded in 868. Nothing original survives of it today except the Ibn Tulun Mosque. It was adjacent to Fostat, Egypt's first capital under Muslim rule until it too was destroyed in the twelfth century, and both were absorbed by nearby Cairo, to the north. Fostat is now the historical centre of modern Cairo, sometimes appearing on anglicised maps simply as "Fustat". Saloney calls it "Al Fostat" in "The Gift of the River".

[20] **café of Simon Papadrapoulnakophitos** In the first edition, "café" was

printed without the acute accent all other instances of the word have in the text, so it is here corrected. We have already heard of this "little Simon" in "He Who Seeks" and his "incredible surname" will be noted in "Vernal". It is, however, a cod Greek name coined for purely comic effect ("Papadopoulos" is a common Greek surname). It's possible that Mitchell is aiming at some complex Joycean Greek pun understood only by him. Simon is mentioned or appears in several of the stories, as he seems to run Saloney's favourite watering-hole.

[21] **Sharia Khalig** "Sharia" simply means "street", so this is simply another way of referring to the Khalij al-Misri.

[22] **boyar** A boyar was a member of the highest ranking of the nobility in feudal Russia. Here the word is used tongue-in-cheek to refer to the multitude of diasporic Russians in modern Cairo.

[23] **the street of All Egypt** Rather as the Nile flows through most of the significantly populated parts of Egypt, and in that sense *is* Egypt, so the erstwhile canal which flows through Cairo is similar. The "All" in "All Egypt" is playing on "Al", the definite article in Arabic: "al-Misri" can mean "the Egyptians". There is yet another joke going on here, for the historically-minded Mitchell would know that there was once the notion of "All Egypt" in the period before Lower and Upper Egypt unified in approximately 3100 BC. The creation of "All Egypt", then, was virtually synchronous with the beginning of what we call "the history of the world".

[24] **the Ramesids** The Ramessid royal dynasty in Egypt extended from 1292 to 1189 BC.

[25] **electric tram-car** The electrification of tramcars was well under way in some European cities by the end of the nineteenth century. A sign of Cairo's advanced development is that it had an electric tram system by 1896 (it was owned by a Belgian company, however). By contrast, London United Tramways did not open the British capital's first electric tram service until July 1901.

[26] **the pride of all her days** "The pride of life" is a biblical phrase for a certain kind of sinfulness: "For all that is in the world, the lust of the flesh, and the lust of the eyes, and the pride of life, is not of the Father, but is of the world" (1 John 2, 16).

[27] **all the colours of Moqattam** The "Red Hills" of "He Who Seeks" (which makes Cairo, in the prostitutional analogy, a scarlet lady).

[28] **The Nietzsche, the fascist** Benito Mussolini (1883-1945) had been the Fascist leader of Italy since a seizure of power in 1922. There was no formal Fascist political party in Britain until the founding of the New Party (later the British Union of Fascists) in 1931, but in 1923 an organisation called "British Fascisti" (from 1924 "Fascists") had been established. Mitchell is not accusing the German philosopher Friedrich Nietzsche (1844-1900) of being a Fascist or a Bolshevik. He is just one item in a list of three things seemingly immune to Saloney's romantic whimsy (which makes the Russian seek "the heart of a maid or a sunset"). Not for the first time, Saloney wishes to turn away from (and perhaps wishes to turn us away from) the political realities of 1920s Europe which he has fled to Cairo to escape.

[29] **putting the cattle into tins in Argentina** Argentina's agricultural advantages,

including its huge stocks of cattle, had made it, just before the Great War, one of the ten richest countries in the world measured by per capita income. Britain had been a large importer of Argentinean beef: by 1910 "Argentina was the origin of around 65 percent of the frozen and chilled beef imports into Britain" (Hohn P. Huttman, "British Meat Imports in the Free Trade Era", *Agricultural History* 52, 2 [1978], p. 260). But a military junta took power in 1930 and things deteriorated from there.

30 **his descent from Akhnaton, Cleopatra, and de Lesseps** Saloney spins another of his bogus Diffusionist genealogies. Akhenaten was a pharaoh of the fourteenth century BC; Cleopatra was the last Queen of Egypt before it became a Roman province in the first century BC; Ferdinand Marie, Comte de Lesseps (1805-1894) was a French diplomat who had been involved in the construction of the Suez Canal in the 1860s.

31 **Moses, Mohammed, and the Mamelukes** Moses is the Old Testament prophet; Muhammad the Islamic prophet; and mamelukes were members of military regimes which were established by freed slave soldiers which ruled in Egypt from medieval times until 1812.

32 **Solga Yon, the Tartar who burned the monks in Kiev** What was then the territory of Kievan Rus' was overrun by the Mongol Empire in the thirteenth century. The sack of Kiev took place in 1240. "Solga Yon" is unidentified.

33 **A man who will drink beer ... on Mount Olympus** Cf. "He Who Seeks": "I think the gods must drink of English beer in Olympus these days".

34 **Indian string-bed** Presumably a charpai, an Indian bed constructed by weaving rope on a wooden frame.

35 **the Gozi quarter** Unidentified.

36 **like Wilde's girl with silver-sandalled feet** "The Harlot's House" (1885), a poem by Oscar Wilde (1854-1900), ends with the stanza "And down the long and silent street,/The dawn, with silver-sandalled feet,/Crept like a frightened girl."

37 **the ugliest nigger that ever salaamed outside a Beardsley grotesque** Aubrey Beardsley (1872-1898) was an artist who sometimes illustrated Wilde's works. A salaam is a bow made in greeting someone. The now offensive word "nigger" does not seem to have troubled writers Mitchell liked or who were writing at the time. The short stories of H. G. Wells and W. Somerset Maugham were replete with it, for example, even when non-racial analogies (as here) were readily available.

38 **the unquiet dead** This concept has its source in Icelandic sagas, in which there are real, restless corpses visible to the living.

39 **like worms cut off from the sunlight** Cf. *The Thirteenth Disciple* (p. 77): "All his life the people of the abyss, the cheated of the sunlight, were so to haunt his happiest moments and dreamings".

40 **femme de chambre** Chambermaid (French).

41 **Sudanese ... a harpy** Sudan borders Egypt to the south. In Greek and Roman mythology, a harpy is an ugly creature with the body of a bird and the head of a woman.

42 **with a plague-pitted face** From smallpox, still a real problem in the Africa of

the 1920s. There was an epidemic in 1926 when, according to Ahmad Hilmy-Bey, *Smallpox in Egypt: Its History and Control* (Cairo: Government Press, 1933), only three-fifths of the population of Alexandria was vaccinated.

[43] **Georgian poetasters** Weak poets of the "Georgian" period, which is generally understood as extending from the accession to the throne of King George V (1865-1936) in 1910 to either the beginning or the end of the Great War (1914-1918), after which "Modernism" begins to assume cultural pre-eminence. For example, one landmark series of poetry anthologies, *Georgian Poetry*, published six volumes during the years 1911-1922.

[44] **the Epic of the Khalig** An announcement of intent which immediately assimilates him to his author, who is writing a book in that exact spirit.

[45] **Khawaja** Lord, master (Persian).

[46] **mujik** Peasant (Russian).

[47] **Stone Men** I.e. Stone-Age Men.

[48] **Shelley** The English poet Percy Bysshe Shelley (1792-1822).

[49] **daedal** I.e. intricate, complex.

[50] **emir's** In modern Arabic "emir" equates to "prince" but it was a term given to rulers or leaders of small countries.

[51] **wattle hut** A humble habitation made of wooden strips woven together.

[52] **since the days of Harun** The Old Testament prophet Aaron, brother of Moses.

[53] **bridal** Wedding ceremony.

[54] **east** "East" (with a capital E) in the first edition.

[55] **real ... real ... real** In other words, she is of the unquiet dead, apprehensible by his senses.

A Volcano in the Moon

[1] **they'll be questing the skies from Palais de Kubbah** From "the Kubbah observatory", as the story soon intimates. We are told that it is "an observatory built on the roof of a house in Palais de Kubbah" by Gellion, who has privately imported the telescope. Presumably, then, this private observatory has remained in the world of the story until the time of its telling, and "they" are Flore and Friedrich (of whose astronomical efforts we shall learn). So the observatory is Mitchell's fiction. There is no evidence that the Koubbeh Palace had its own independent observatory. A modern Egyptian observatory had been established in Abbassia (adjacent to Koubbeh, which is to the north) in 1868, but the telescope was moved to Helwand, considerably south of Cairo, in 1904, though the empty building apparently remained until at least 1952. It stood in Midan Radkhana (Observatory Square). Maps of the 1920s mark it as "Old Observatory". The site is now occupied by Ain Shams University Faculty of Arts, on the corner of El-Khalifa El-Maamoon and Al Quaeed.

[2] **the Great Shadow** I.e. the Great War.

[3] **Gellion and Freligrath** Gellion is a rare surname even in France, where most occurrences of it are found. The German surname is surely derived from Ferdinand Freiligrath (1810-1876), German poet and collaborator with Karl Marx (1818-1883).
[4] **Mme** Madame, Mrs (French): his wife.
[5] **the Ardennes** A region in north-east France, bordering Belgium.
[6] ***le bon Dieu*** The good God (French).
[7] **he had been a Martian, a champion of the good canals** That is, he subscribed to the views of the Italian astronomer Giovanni Schiaparelli (1835-1910) that there were straight observable "channels" (mistranslated into English as "canals") on the surface of Mars.
[8] **selenographers** Selenography is the study of the moon's physical features.
[9] **Schroter's Valley** In *Hanno, or the Future of Exploration* (London: Kegan Paul, Trench, Trubner & Co., 1928) Mitchell speculates about the first evening of the first people to land on the moon: "it may be that before sunset, the party will reach the mountains south of Herodotus, in Schroter's valley, where the volcanoes still play and their drifting gases whorl in the thin lunar atmosphere" (pp. 89-90). But there are, as we now know for sure, no active volcanoes on the moon.
[10] **Flore** A female name meaning, predictably, "flower". Cf. the similar name Flora.
[11] **Caliphs' Tombs ... the Ghizeh stones** "The Ghizeh stones" is a dismissive phrase for the Giza pyramids. The Tombs of the Abbasid Caliphs date from the mid-thirteenth century and are located on modern Cairo's El Khalifa Street
[12] **Mme Curie** Marie Curie (1867-1934), Polish discoverer of radium and polonium, who lived for much of her life in France and became a French citizen.
[13] **Mount Wilson observatory** The Hooker telescope operating since 1917 at the Mount Wilson Observatory, California, was not exceeded in aperture size (100 inches or 2.5m) until 1949, when it was dwarfed by the Hale telescope (200 inches, 5.1m) at the nearby Palomar Observatory. Neither is now very significant as far as size is concerned: the Large Binocular Telescope at the Mount Graham International Observatory, Arizona, with two 331-inch (8.1m) mirrors, has been the largest telescope in the world since 2004.
[14] **tow-headed** A towhead has extremely light blond hair, almost white. The term is usually only applied to children.
[15] **when the War broke out** Germany declared war on France on 3 August 1914.
[16] **Bavaria** In southern Germany, bordering on Austria.
[17] **too old for soldiering** This means he is more than forty-five, the upper age limit for men mobilised by France at the beginning of the Great War.
[18] **Liebknecht** "Karl Liebknecht (still one of my heroes: one of the world's great heroes)": *The Thirteenth Disciple*, p. 60. Between 1912 and 1916 Liebknecht (1871-1919) was a Social Democratic Party of Germany representative in the Reichstag. Mitchell wrote an honorific poem on his assassination (Bold, *Smeddum*, p. 200). He had opposed the War. The grammar of the sentence is ambiguous: it could be read as suggesting either that Freligrath was the other "public man" or that a different person was the "other". If we take the second meaning – and assume a man is

specifically intended and not Rosa Luxemburg (1871-1919), Liebknecht's fellow revolutionary – it could be one of several. More than two very notable Germans spoke out against the Great War.

[19] **libration** The slight oscillating horizontal motion of the moon, which sometimes permits us to see at the edge of the disc regions normally hidden on its "dark side".

[20] **volcan-glow** Thus reads the first edition. "Volcan" is French for "volcano".

[21] **Ramadan** Ramadan is the ninth month of the Islamic calendar, during which Muslims fast and pray. It is, importantly, moon-determined: it takes place from the first monthly appearance of the crescent moon and lasts until its next.

[22] **El Azhar** Probably the Al-Azhar Mosque on Nafak Al Azhar.

[23] **M. le Colonel** Monsieur le Colonel (French), a rather respectful form of address.

[24] **when the Nile runs back through Bulaq Bridge** I.e. never, because the Nile flows only in one direction.

[25] **facing a firing-squad** Possibly for desertion. Many national armies in the Great War executed their own in this way.

[26] **Bosche** German (slang, more often "Boche").

[27] **Zeitoun** A district in north Cairo.

[28] **The adventure-soul in man** This kind of sentiment seems a particular tic of Saloney's, but in fact his creator often seemed to share it. Malcom in *The Thirteenth Disciple*, for example, desperately wishes to be part of "the adventure".

[29] **Tennyson** One of Mitchell's favourite poets, Tennyson was being translated into several European tongues, including German, even early in his writing career.

[30] **the mountain-shadow of the War** The War, then, has something in common with the volcano.

[31] **Sharia Kamel** Possibly Al Kamel, a street near The Koubbeh.

[32] **Spartacist** Liebknecht's so-called Spartacist Uprising of January 1919 was a failed attempt to overthrow the post-War German government.

[33] **The seasonal orbit-roll** The moon's orbit is slightly elliptical and its relation to the sun-earth axis is slightly inclined, and so it appears to "roll" over time relative to the earth as it orbits. The "roll" from beginning to end takes about 18.5 years.

[34] **Helwan-les-Bains** A spa town south of Cairo. Its springs were said to have the same chemical composition as those in Aix-les-Bains, France. Reynolds-Ball, *Cairo of to-day* (1898) described it as follows (pp. 26-7): "Helouan is, indeed, the oldest health resort in the world. There are about a dozen sulphur springs similar to those of Aix-les-Bains, but rather stronger. One of its chief merits is that those who have undergone a course at Aix can continue their 'cure' here during the winter and spring, when, of course, the Aix establishment is closed. The atmosphere is remarkably pure and salubrious, and the electrical, tonic influence of the desert climate is felt here in a remarkable degree. There are good hotels here, two resident doctors, and several pensions. The Administration, too, have shown themselves thoroughly alive to the requirements of modern tourists, by providing lawn-tennis courts, laying down golf-links, etc. Hitherto the chief drawback was that the English guests were in a minority, the baths belonging to a German directorate."

[35] **mon** "My" (French).
[36] **Frankish** A western European people of Roman times and the early Middle Ages, originally Germanic, spreading to France.
[37] **au revoir** "See you again"; "goodbye" (French).
[38] **there is no night that may ever blind the flame that lights the wastes** Mitchell struggles to derive a romantic principle from his story.

The Life and Death of Elia Constantinides

[1] **CONSTANTINIDES** We know from Mitchell's correspondence that this was the last story in the sequence to be written. In *The Cornhill Magazine* version of this story this name was spelled throughout as "Constantinidos". The change was doubtless made because "Constantinides" is a common Greek name, whereas "Constantinidos" is not. It derives, of course, from Constantine I (*c.* 272-337), the Roman emperor who embraced Christianity and founded the city of Constantinople.
[2] **Campanella** Tommaso Campanella (1568-1639), Italian author of *Civitas solis* (Latin: "The City of the Sun"), a utopia describing an egalitarian society. Mitchell was to become preoccupied with the idea of a "City of the Sun" as a vague signifier of some possible future utopian freedom. He invokes it repeatedly in his works.
[3] **three** "Three" (with a capital T) in first edition.
[4] **born in Samos, of ... dark Ionian stock** Samos is an island in the Aegean Sea. It had been Greek since 1913. Ionia was a region in the east of modern-day Turkey, south of İzmir, close to Samos.
[5] **since the days of Homer** In other words, since as long as the written word has survived, Homer being the earliest writer whose works we have on record.
[6] **Dr Adrian** The English doctor introduced in "Daybreak".
[7] ***papakes*** *Papak* is Greek for "father".
[8] **'fey'** The word has a range of meanings, but here and later in the story it probably means something like "otherworldly".
[9] ***phantasma*** The word usually suggests a delusion.
[10] **two of his brothers vanished to Athens and the army** Greece remained neutral until July 1917, when it joined the War on the Allied side.
[11] **Vathy** The word (Greek: "deep") is used to name many coastal settlements in the Ionian area. The Vathy on Samos is in the north-east of the island, though on modern maps it is sometimes designated "Samos City".
[12] **the painted lips** Which phrase rather confirms in advance that she is a prostitute.
[13] **eikon** A variant spelling of "icon", in this case a religious image or statuette typical of the Eastern Orthodox Church.
[14] **embrasure ... loggia** An embrasure is an opening in a wall that is splayed or curved on the inside and a loggia is a covered external gallery or corridor.
[15] **Smyrna** Since 1930 the port city of İzmir, in modern Turkey. It had originally been Greek and the Greeks and Turks fought over it in the Greco-Turkish War (1919-

1922); the Greeks were ultimately unsuccessful in regaining it.
[16] **Chios** A Greek island in the Aegean Sea.
[17] **reveille** "Le Réveil" in French (from the verb "réveiller", to wake) is a wake-up call in the military, usually sounded by a bugle or trumpet.
[18] **English guns** Greece was supported in its war against the Turks by Britain and France.
[19] **Manissa** Manisa is a Turkish city, north-east of İzmir.
[20] **white happiness** Presumably the opposite of a black mood.
[21] **Kemal Pasha smote the flimsy Greek lines** Already mentioned in "The Lost Prophetess", Mustafa Kemal Atatürk was a Turkish field marshal during the Greco-Turkish War. He had become famous by leading the Ottoman Empire's victory against the Allies at the Battle of Gallipoli in 1915, and is essentially seen as the heroic founding father of the modern Turkish state.
[22] **westward-pouring** I.e. heading back to Greece.
[23] **Anatolians** Anatolia, often in the past called Asia Minor, is the large region in modern Turkey in which these parts of the story are set.
[24] ***archegos*** "Leader" (Greek). The word occurs four times in the New Testament, usually to describe Jesus. It is not the name of an actual rank in the Greek army: Elia actually becomes a *lochagos*, the equivalent of a captain, so he is at the lower end of the officer class.
[25] **the Peloponnesus** The Peloponnese or Peloponnesus is a peninsular region in the south of Greece.
[26] ***moira*** *Μοῖρα* (Greek) means fate or destiny, and is the singular of *Μοῖραι*, the Greek name for the Three Fates. The Fates were three mythological sisters who made sure that every person reached the destiny thought to be assigned to them.
[27] ***kore loukophotos*** *Kore* (Ancient Greek) means "girl". Mitchell would appear to be aiming at *lykófotos*, meaning "crepuscular" (i.e. dark, like the dusk).
[28] **the Piræus** Piraeus is a port city in Greece, near Athens. The "the" before the word would seem to be one of Saloney's oft-misused definite articles.
[29] **south at Bab el Hadid, down Clot Bey** Bāb al-Ḥadīd (Arabic) means "The Iron Gate" and designated one of the ancient city gates of medieval Cairo (as well as many other Arabic settlements). Until 1955 it was the name given to a square outside Cairo's main railway station (now Ramses Square). Clot Bey was the form of address given to Antoine Barthelemy Clot (1793-1868), a French doctor known for advancing medicine and medical education in Cairo. A long street was named after him which extended south from Bāb al-Ḥadīd to the Ezbekiyeh gardens (now called Al Bostah).
[30] **el Nahassin** Al-Nahhasin Street was part of Al-Mu'izz Street (a grand ancient street in Old Cairo which often appears on contemporary maps as Al Moez Ldin Allah Al Fatmi). This particular souk specialised in metalwork.
[31] **as from the bottom of a canyon** Mitchell was partial to describing passing through the modern metropolis as like walking in a canyon or among cliffs: he does it twice in *Stained Radiance* (pp. 19, 266) and again in *The Thirteenth Disciple* (p. 214).

[32] **khans** In the modern context this simply means "shops" or "marketplaces".
[33] **Citadel** The Cairo Citadel, a medieval fortification which had been the permanent seat of government in Egypt until the nineteenth century (often appearing on modern maps as "Citadel Saladin").
[34] **unconscious** I.e. "unconscious of".
[35] **Kalo** The Greek word *καλό* (*kaló*) means "right" or "good".
[36] **the night the Turks took the city** Atatürk's army seized Smyrna from the Greeks on 9 September 1922.
[37] ***Phantasmata toi helioi*** "Phantoms of the sun" (Greek).
[38] **Salih ibn Muslih** The name of the rescued servant ("ibn" means "son of") contains two Arabic words designating different kinds of goodness: a *salih* is a righteous person while a *muslih* is a reformer who aims to make others righteous. Both Saleh and Muslih appear as named individuals in the Qur᾽ān.
[39] **dervish** A member of a Muslim religious order who dances energetically while at devotion. In the English-speaking world the word has come largely to be applied to persons thought wild or mad.
[40] **carbines** A carbine is a firearm, with a barrel longer than a pistol but shorter than a rifle.
[41] **incomprehensible as that last cry on the Hill of Crucifixion** Mark 15, 34: "And at the ninth hour Jesus cried with a loud voice, saying, Eloi, Eloi, lama sabachthani? which is, being interpreted, My God, my God, why hast thou forsaken me?" The "incomprehensible" cry is actually Christ quoting (in Aramaic) the first line of Psalm 22. Matthew (27, 46) concurs that Jesus speaks thus and dies "about the ninth hour" (i.e. approximately 3pm, the hours of the day being counted from dawn or approximately 6am). Mitchell quotes Christ's words in *Stained Radiance* (p. 230) and, writing as Gibbon, uses the phrase as an epigraph in a later story, "Forsaken", published in 1934 and reprinted in Bold, *Smeddum*, pp. 46-57.

Cockcrow

[1] **Lemnos** A Greek island in the Aegean.
[2] **bucolic** Rustic.
[3] **Shari' Abbassieh** El-Abaseya is a major street that runs across Old Cairo.
[4] **Hadramaut** The Hadhramaut (Mitchell's spelling of the name was common at the time) is a region in modern-day Yemen. At the time Mitchell was writing, much of it was the Aden protectorate, which the British held until 1967. North of it, between Yemen and Oman, was an "empty quarter" (Rub' al Khali), which is the largest area of uninterrupted sand in the world. In 1927 it became part of the Kingdom of Nejd, one of the two kingdoms which were united to form modern-day Saudi Arabia in 1932.
[5] **the sand-cities of the Shiah** Shia Islam is a small branch of the religion (considered globally) after the Sunnis, though it has a majority following in a few

territories, such as Iraq. In Yemen Shias have historically been in a minority, but a sizeable one. As the most readily available building material in the Hadhramaut is sand, many cities in the region (like Shibam in Yemen) have been built using it as a base material.

[6] **the hasting guest** Hurrying to keep up with the striding and self-absorbed Ravelston, that is.

[7] **Marco Polo** Marco Polo (*c.* 1254-1324) was a Venetian merchant famed for his records of his travels to the Far East.

[8] **Phidias ... Hellas ... Aristotle** Phidias (*c.* 480-*c.* 430 BC) was an Ancient Greek sculptor; Hellas is the ancient name for Greece; Aristotle (384-322 BC) the classic Greek philosopher. How this sentence is quite to be understood is not exactly clear as its grammar appears suspect.

[9] **suburban** "surburban" in first edition.

[10] **Red Hills** Presumably the Mokattam Hills again, but if one sees the sun go down behind them one would have to be east of them, which would place you significantly distant from central Cairo.

[11] **un-originative** Lacking the ability to be original.

[12] **the leader of a Polar Expedition ... Knut Hammssen ... Odyssey through the Gobi Desert** In other words, he is a typical Mitchell fantasy figure, like Metaxa in *The Thirteenth Disciple*, who has had the kinds of *Boy's Own* adventures that Mitchell himself was able only to read about. Mitchell clearly revelled in the "man of the world" idea, but in such characters the travels are far-flung and collectively unlikely. Metaxa breezes off on an expedition to Antarctica, for example, then to New Guinea, and later becomes "a fugitive amidst the Wahhabi villages of the Great Dahna" (p. 130), which happens to be a large desert region in modern Saudi Arabia. Indeed, Ravelston is pretty much a sketch for Metaxa, who "passed a year in Kamchatka, six months in the Gobi, and four months in struggling through the mountains of Indo-China, in company with Knut Hammsen, to the safety of a French river-post" (p. 130). The Gobi Desert is in Northern China and southern Mongolia. Knut Hamsun (1859-1952) was a famous Norwegian writer, awarded the Nobel Prize in Literature in 1920. Among his lesser-known works are *In Wonderland* (1903), which details a journey he made from Russia to Constantinople in 1899. But Ravelston's chances of being in his company at any time in the Gobi Desert were zero.

[13] **the Huxley-Haeckel tradition** Thomas H. Huxley (1825-1895) was a biologist who championed the evolutionary theories of Charles Darwin (1809-1882). He was an explorer in his earlier life and also, coincidentally, the father of Mitchell's *Cornhill* editor. Ernst Haeckel (1834-1919) was a German zoologist and also a populariser of Darwin.

[14] **brought fire from heaven** In Greek mythology, Prometheus, one of the Titans, revolts against the gods by stealing their fire and giving it to humans. As a punishment, Zeus has him tied to a rock so that a vulture can peck at his liver.

[15] **the house called Daybreak** That is, the house so named by Dawn, the

protagonist of the story "Daybreak".
[16] **chemic** Simply an obsolete word for "chemical" but Saloney uses it with an old-fashioned wonder that is more redolent of the awe once inspired by alchemy.
[17] **caligraphy** Not a misprint: the word can be spelled with a single or double l (*OED*).
[18] **Lister** Joseph Lister (1827-1912), British surgeon, who advanced antiseptic surgery, among other achievements. The idea of an individual creating a technologically advanced machine or achieving something hitherto undreamt-of (like a cure for a fatal disease) is straight out of H. G. Wells.
[19] **a Republican of your Plato ... a Samurai out of Wells** *The Republic* is perhaps the most famous work by the Greek philosopher Plato (c. 427-348 BC), and puts the case that society ought to be ruled by philosopher-kings. In Wells's *A Modern Utopia* (London: Chapman and Hall, 1905), the "samurai" caste governs the utopia (Wells later referred to them as "New Republicans"). In Wells's novel *Marriage* (London: Macmillan, 1912), pp. 324-5, we have summarised for us "a tattered little pamphlet" called "Proposals for the Establishment of an Order of Samurai": "The order was to be a sort of self-appointed nobility serving the world. It shone with the light of a generous dawn, but cast, I fear, the shadow of the prig. [...] These Samurai, it was intimated, were to lead lives of hard discipline and high effort, under self-imposed rule and restraint. They were to stand a little apart from the excitements and temptations of everyday life, to eat sparingly, drink water, resort greatly to self-criticism and self-examination, and harden their spirits by severe and dangerous exercises. They were to dress simply, work hard, and be the conscious and deliberate salt of the world. They were to walk among mountains. Incidentally, great power was to be given them."
[20] **sarcomata** The plural of sarcoma, a malignant tumour.
[21] **Cairo's leading gynæcologist** A reference to Dr Adrian.
[22] **'Stealthy Terror'** *Stealthy Terror* (London: John Lane/The Bodley Head, 1918) is a thriller by the Scottish Episcopalian minister John A. Ferguson (1871-1952). Ferguson was born in Callander, Perthshire, but at some point moved to England (the epistle dedicatory to *Stealthy Terror* is signed off "FOLKESTONE"; he died in Hampshire). In the novel, set in July 1914, a Scottish doctor studying in Berlin is given a document which contains information vital to Britain, and is consequently hunted from Berlin to Hamburg to Scotland to London and finally to the Kent coast. As this summary alone suggests, the plot is essentially a rip-off of *The Thirty-Nine Steps* (Edinburgh: Blackwood, 1915) by the most fabulously successful Scottish writer of the time, John Buchan (1875-1940). Ferguson wrote much else of a similar kind. Perhaps the "secret jest" of such a phrase for Pamela and Ravelston is that they share a knowledge of Ferguson's novel.
[23] **the violet ray** I think this an example of Mitchell trying to impress when his knowledge is on shaky ground. Violet is on the visible spectrum and is not cut out by glass. Mitchell probably means "ultra-violet radiation", a great deal of, but not all of which, normal glass does also block. We might puzzle over why anyone would want

to expose their home and themselves to harmful radiation, but until the mid-twentieth century heliotherapy (as it was called) was seriously prescribed, particularly for tuberculosis sufferers. While it turns out that Pamela and Ravelston may simply be seeking a tan, the reason so many were doing so by the 1920s, it is also intimated, was on account of the presumed health benefits. D. H. Lawrence's short story "Sun" (1926) begins "'Take her away, into the sun,' the doctors said" (*The Woman Who Rode Away and other stories* [London: Secker, 1928], p. 33).

24 **Sorry** The capital S suggests that Pamela may not be apologising, but rather addressing Saloney archly with a variant of the archaic "Sirrah".

25 **Smeyat'cia, posmeyat'cia** Pamela appears to be declining the Russian verb.

26 **Archangels** The biblical hints about the hierarchy of angels were later elaborated to make it comparable (as it sometimes was in Christian mythology) to an army. An archangel is only one step above the lowest on the ladder, which is the angel: a Lance Corporal, one might say.

27 **Mess Artillery** Saloney has reversed the normal word order, and presumably means a dance at the mess of one of the artillery divisions. A mess is an area where soldiers eat and socialise.

28 **German air-raiders** In the Great War air-raids were conducted by airships and London was the main target. They began as early as 1915 and by the end of the War had accounted for 556 deaths.

29 **Hysteria** Not now considered a serious medical diagnosis, but it would have raised few eyebrows to hear a doctor in the 1920s expressing belief in such a psychological condition.

30 **Pandora** In Greek mythology, Pandora is the first woman created by the gods. She famously opens the jar ("Pandora's box") which contains the many evils of humanity.

31 **carcinomata** The plural of carcinoma, a cancer which can arise in epithelial tissue, like the skin. If this is true then sunbathing is the last thing Pamela should be doing, but in Mitchell's time the link between UV radiation and skin cancer was not firmly established. Ravelston clearly does not recognise it.

32 **the Citadel Hospital** The British had converted part of the Cairo Citadel as an army hospital in 1882. It was to be used through two world wars. Since 1949 it has been the National Military Museum of Egypt.

33 **the European season** I.e. the colder months in Europe (November to April). "The Cairo Season" was a recognisable phrase to the class of Brits who liked to winter there. There would even soon be a German film, *Saison In Kairo* (*Season in Cairo*, 1933) shot on location in Egypt, a romantic comedy with a plot the early Mitchell might easily have conceived.

34 **philanderings** The clear suggestion is that Pamela engages in sexual affairs.

35 **St Peter** Saint Peter is known as one of Christ's apostles, but in popular culture has also become the celestial being who greets souls at the gates of heaven, to which he holds the keys: the detail of "keys" in the following anecdote may thus explain the obscure reference. (Cf. Gault in "The Passage of the Dawn": "I've escaped to heaven

from hell – St Peter himself shook hands with me on arrival"). There are other possibilities: Saint Petersburg was, for example, the pre-War capital of Saloney's Russia, though it was named after a Tsar, not the first Pope.
[36] ***Kak vi pazhivaiete? ... pocmesyaietc'ie*** "How are you?" ... followed by another inflection of the Russian verb "to laugh".
[37] **the Kubbah observatory** The private, residential observatory described in "A Volcano in the Moon".
[38] **flambeaux** The plural of *flambeau*, the French word for a burning torch.
[39] **The future's trust to me** The meaning seems to be that she gave him a feeling of confidence in the future.
[40] **amethyst** A rather "poetic" way of denoting purple or violet, the colour of amethyst quartz. Mitchell was fond of the conjunction: in *Stained Radiance* we get "amethystine night" (p. 35) and then an "amethystine dawn" (p. 128).
[41] **They would waken the dead.** But waking the dead is also a resurrection (a return to behavioural norms, or virtue, in Pamela's case). Once again, as in "For Ten's Sake", we find Mitchell mining the Bible to give resonance to a secular plot, which could also be said to rewrite the biblical story of the Prodigal Son (Luke 15, 11-32) as the Prodigal Wife.
[42] **Judas** In the Gospels, Judas is the apostle who betrays Jesus, takes a cash reward from the Romans, and then hangs himself. Before his execution Jesus predicts that the apostle Peter will deny knowledge of him before the cock crows the following morning, which he does three times. The difference between them which the final lines of the story exploits is that Peter's lie is a betrayal for which he can try to make amends, but Judas's action is beyond rehabilitation (the difference, in Catholicism, between a venial and a mortal sin).

Vernal

[1] **VERNAL** Characteristic of the Spring season (or, metaphorically, of youth).
[2] **eighty-four in the shade** The temperature given is in degrees Fahrenheit (on the Celsius scale equating approximately to 29).
[3] **Spring** The capital S consistently given to "Spring" throughout this story is inconsistent with lower-case use so far in the text (also used for other seasons), but it has been allowed to stand given the centrality of the season to the story, indicated from the beginning in its title. In later stories, where appropriate, lower case is substituted.
[4] **crying through the willows** The Volga provides sustenance to many willow forests, but the point here is the traditional association of willows with weeping.
[5] **There are boatmen singing there** The traditional shanty, "Song of the Volga Boatmen" (with its refrain "Yo, heave-ho!"), is probably the most globally recognised cultural text which mentions the Russian river, recorded in songbooks by the mid-nineteenth century. In March 1922 the Spanish composer Manuel de Falla (1876-

1946) composed his "Canto de los remeros del Volga (del cancionero musical ruso)" ("Song of the Volga boatmen [from the Russian songbook]") for piano, which was dedicated to Russian refugees under the auspices of the League of Nations, then trying to raise funds to deal with an estimated two million displaced Russians (Gonzalo Armero and Jorge de Persia [eds.], *Manuel de Falla: his Life & Works* [London: Omnibus Press, 1999], p. 149).

[6] **In the beginning was God, and He created James Freeman** A parody of the first sentence of the Bible (Genesis 1, 1): "In the beginning God created the heaven and the earth."

[7] **James Freeman served Him all the days of his life** Cf. Psalms 23, 6: "Surely goodness and mercy shall follow me all the days of my life: and I will dwell in the house of the Lord for ever." There is, of course, a potential contradiction in the notion of a "free man" who "serves" another.

[8] **that English Bible** The King James Bible or Authorised Version of 1611.

[9] **Dickens and Trollope** The English Victorian novelists Charles Dickens (1812-1870) and Anthony Trollope (1815-1882).

[10] **Norla** We learn later in the story that this is the name of Freeman's daughter.

[11] **the faith of some church that conforms not to your national belief** I.e. to a nonconformist church, not the dominant Anglican church, and from what we soon learn Freeman appears to be in an evangelical "fire and brimstone" tradition rather than being a happy-clappy peace-and-love merchant.

[12] **veldt** The word used to describe a raised, often treeless flat plain in the southern parts of Africa; what Americans might call a prairie.

[13] **south of France** Consistently printed as "South of France" (with a capital S) in the first edition, herein corrected throughout.

[14] **Helwan** The Helwan-les-Bains of "A Volcano in the Moon".

[15] **Pension Avallaire** A fictional guesthouse. In Mitchell's later novel *The Lost Trumpet*, we learn "'Georgios Papadrapoulnakophitos was cook at the Pension Avallaire, so you may have no doubts as to his culinary skill. He was dismissed from his post but a month ago, and has since then been wasting his talents in the kitchen of the little Simon'" (p. 57).

[16] **the Republic of Plato** This does not mean that Saloney is a "samurai" like Ravelston in "Cockcrow", but simply that he is unmarried (as Plato stipulated his philosopher-kings should be).

[17] **Utopia** The word means "no place" and was coined by Sir Thomas More (1478-1535) for his fictional work in Latin of the same name (1516).

[18] **garden of Esbekiyeh** The Ezbekiyeh gardens were developed in the 1870s before the British occupation, but by Mitchell's time the area had become a significant tourist hangout, with many bars, cafés, theatres and cinemas (and plenty of brothels nearby). The present gardens are much smaller than was then the case.

[19] **Lady of Serenity ... Coptic Church** There was a Cairene Church of the Virgin Mary, built in Zeitoun in 1924, but this was after Mitchell's time in the city. Saloney is referring to Saint Virgin Mary's Coptic Orthodox Church (also known as Sitt

Miriam or the Hanging Church) in Old Cairo, one of the oldest churches in Egypt, dating from the third century. But it would be difficult to find a Coptic church which did not have similar frescoes or paintings of the Madonna, usually with child. These would likely not be to Freeman's devotional taste: Mary is deprecated in most forms of protestant Christianity and seldom seen as an object of devotion.

[20] **the friendship** They have a "Platonic" (i.e. sexless) relationship. The name derives from the discussion of love in Plato's *Symposium*.

[21] **a dragoman to the boot** One of Saloney's more humorous misuses of the definite article (the correct phrase is "to boot" meaning "as well").

[22] **Gamaliyeh bazaar** The Khan Gamaliyeh in the Gamaliyeh ("camel drivers") quarter, close to the Khan Al Khalili.

[23] **from the Red Sea lands** The Red Sea divides Africa from the Middle East in the region, so this effectively means "from lands to the east of the Red Sea".

[24] **attar of roses** An essential oil, usually distilled from the petals of the damask rose.

[25] **Do you think she would allow me?** That is, to draw her.

[26] **the Museum** The Museum of Egyptian Antiquities, built in 1901, in Tahrir Square.

[27] **an old Greek myth** A pigeon belongs to the same family of birds as a dove, and in some versions of myth the Greek goddess of love, Aphrodite, was born using the blood of a sacrificed dove. Many representations of her show her holding a dove.

[28] **Dubara, down past el Roda** The Cairo district of Dubara now tends to be assimilated to Garden City on many modern maps. It is opposite Gezira island. Rhoda Island, or Manial al-Roda, is another island in the river, to the south of Gezira.

[29] **the valley of the Avalon** Avalon was a delightful mythical island in Arthurian legend. Mitchell refers to it often, for example in *Hanno* (pp. 30, 60), in *Stained Radiance* (p. 249) and in *The Thirteenth Disciple* (p. 152).

[30] **downstream** On the Nile this generally means in a northerly direction. They are returning to their point of origin.

[31] **the Bab-el-Futtuh** Bab al-Futuh is one of three surviving gates in Old Cairo's city wall, dating from the tenth/eleventh centuries.

[32] **freed harems** Various pieces of legislation, beginning with the Anglo-Egyptian Convention for the Abolition of Slavery (1877), had led in Egypt to the banning of the import of slaves and sale of existing slaves. Eventually slaves were granted the right to apply for freedom. Slavery, though much reduced, still continued in Egypt in Mitchell's time, however.

[33] **little Jew-men of the blue serge and yellow boots** Some Hasidic Jews traditionally wear a long coat (a "kapote") but their preference would usually be black, so neither blue serge nor yellow boots is entirely explicable to the present editor. There had been considerable anti-semitism in Egypt historically, and it was on the rise after the War when the British were granted a Mandate in Palestine, which was (correctly) viewed as Allied support for the Zionist cause. It must be said that "little Jew-men" sounds casually contemptuous, and Mitchell himself was not

above expressing such contempt towards Jews in his own voice. In a letter to Naomi Mitchison of 10 August 1933 he refers to "little Jew-boys of the Sunday newspapers" (National Library of Scotland correspondence TS.).

34 **called himself Utro – of the Morning** "Утро" is Russian for "morning". He thus claims to be a Cairo Dawn.

35 **ex-aristo** One of the aristocrats dispossessed by the 1917 revolution.

36 **in the civil war hoisted the Black Flag of Anarchy** Anarchist groups and parties traditionally bear a red or black flag (now often combined) as their ensign. Many anarchist organisations and publications called themselves Black Flag. There was left-wing as well as right-wing opposition to the Bolsheviks. In Ukraine, for example, the anarchist Makhnovshchina movement fought the Russians in the Ukrainian War of Independence (1917–1921).

37 **Green** So-called Green armies were local militias opposed to both the Red and White armies.

38 **Lunacharsky and the Department of Education and Culture** Anatoly Lunacharsky (1875-1933) became head of the People's Commissariat for Education in the first Soviet administration, a post he held until 1929.

39 **a gigantic Palace of Music** Mitchell's fleeting references to places and events are usually rooted in fact, but it is not clear if he has in mind a Soviet building that had actually been constructed. Perhaps what is more notable is that here we have yet another of the incredibly accomplished *übermensch* who ludicrously litter Mitchell's early work. We have already met one, Ravelston, in "Cockcrow". There are arguably three in *The Thirteenth Disciple*: Metaxa, Malcom and Domina. Only in *Stained Radiance* are we obviously meant to view Koupa's amazing achievements ironically, not least because he appears to be the only source of their report.

40 **the Cheka** The Cheka was the colloquial name for the All-Russian Extraordinary Commission for Combating Counter-Revolution, Speculation, Sabotage, and Misuse of Authority. It was a secret police organisation established by Lenin within weeks of the October revolution. In *Stained Radiance* Koupa is "appointed to a post on the 'Tcheka in Petrograd" (p. 62). Its repression of dissenting views and actions was unforgiving. See George Leggett, *The Cheka: Lenin's Political Police* (Oxford: Clarendon Press, 1981).

41 **the Black Bands** Possibly a translation into English of the more commonly named "Black Guards" of the Russian anarchist movement.

42 **Gladkov** Feodor Gladkov (1883-1958), Russian and Soviet writer. His socialist realist novel *Cement* (1925) had just been published in English (tr. A. S. Arthur and C. Ashleigh, London: Martin Lawrence, 1929). It was a "reconstruction" novel about post-revolutionary Soviet society.

43 **an obscenity of suspicion ... goes with the dark old sacrifice-cults** This echoes the earlier description of James Freeman, who "Since the age of twenty [...] had preached and believed the ancient, cruel god of sacrifice".

44 **a story-plot in which I figured as the false clue** Mystery and crime narratives often include one or more "red herrings" to mislead the reader into

suspecting motives or actions which turn out not to be pertinent and distract attention away from the truth. In this escapade Norla has deceived her father by leading him to think that she is merely going with Saloney (who is thus the "red herring" or false clue) to paint, when in fact her intention is to have an assignation with Alexandr.

[45] **Sashka** Sashka (in Russian) is the short, more intimate form of "Alexandr".

[46] **looked at her not either** I.e. he avoids looking at her as she avoids looking at him.

[47] **that calling that Solomon heard ... and set for ever in words undying** "I sleep, but my heart waketh: it is the voice of my beloved that knocketh, saying, Open to me, my sister, my love, my dove, my undefiled" (Song of Solomon 1, 15). Solomon was the name given to the anonymous author of the biblical Song of Solomon, a collection of love poems spoken alternately by a man and a woman.

[48] **consulate marriage** Consular marriages still take place, because the marriage is thus registered under the law of the country whose consulate it is. There was no Soviet ambassador to Egypt between October 1917 and October 1943, so presumably the British consulate is the one envisaged.

[49] **'M'sieu' –'** The odd-looking punctuation here is in fact accurate, as the apostrophes in "M'sieu'" indicate the dropping of letters from "Monsieur".

[50] **an ague** A fever.

[51] ***'Mary!'*** The name of his wife who absconded with a Russian artist when Norla was five but also the name of the mother of Jesus and yet again of Mary Magdalene, a follower of Jesus often said (though not in the Bible) once to have been a prostitute.

[52] **an old priest** I.e. James Freeman.

[53] **Presbyterian Church** St Andrew's, the Scottish Presbyterian Church, founded in 1909, now St Andrew's United Church of Cairo, on 26 July Street.

[54] **the Gate of Spring** "Gate of the Spring" is the English name given to Pēgē Gate in the ancient city walls of Constantinople (modern Istanbul, visited by Mitchell on RASC service in October and November of 1921).

[55] **We called her the Sitt Miriam** One presumes that Freeman, when he sees this woman, mistakes her for his absentee wife. Mitchell is certainly flirting with the idea that she may indeed *be* his wife (she is "an Englishwoman", after all, but she is also "fair and young", so the idea may be that her looks *remind* him of her when she was with him). She is a vision of "Spring" (renewal, resurrection, rebirth, beauty, energy) and her vernal spirit at death seems by metempsychosis to transfer into Norla.

Yet she lives in "the street of shame" and is presumably a prostitute and, for all her seeming radiance, dies inexplicably a few hours after being introduced. Mitchell actually has Metaxa – not very probably – encounter his own wife working in a brothel in Paris in *The Thirteenth Disciple* (p. 158). Mitchell is relying for shock value on contemporary moral panics about what was called "White Slave Traffic". There was actually a film called *Fighting the White Slave Traffic* (1926) and the League of Nations promulgated an International Convention to Combat the Traffic in Women and Children in 1921. International cities like Cairo were exactly the kinds of places such fears might turn into reality. For example, many of the Cairo locations in this story are centred on the Ezbekiyeh area. Its Wagh El Birket red-light district had become especially notorious because of a mass riot which took place there on 2 April 1915, initiated by thousands of Australian and New Zealand troops waiting to be shipped to the Gallipoli Front. The riot itself was sparked after an English soldier discovered his own "white slave traded" sister working there.

This was, however, a very rare occurrence, and the energy expended on the problem of the "white slave trade" was out of all proportion to its size: "As for prostitution, though there were as many as 100,000 prostitutes in London alone during the mid-Victorian era, the records of occupied Egypt point to a very limited number of prostitutes who were British. Out of 280 police raids on 175 brothels in 1914, not one British prostitute was found. Similarly, out of the 931 women minors in the white slave trade who were arrested at disembarkation in the same year, only seven were British" (Lanver Mak, *The British Community in Occupied Cairo, 1882-1922*, unpublished Ph.D. thesis, School of Oriental and African Studies, University of London, 2001, p. 142; available at https://eprints.soas.ac.uk/29227/1/10731322.pdf).

The story's ending leaves the reader with a number of unresolved questions. Is it news of the woman's death that leaves Freeman "broken and frightened", as if it were some kind of sign from God? But Saloney does not say if he tells him of her death or not. Then again, is it his subjective vision of his wife, now free of him, insouciant and happy, that causes in him some kind of moral epiphany and volte-face? Whatever the fine grain of the conclusion may be, the broad brush is clear: as in "For Ten's Sake", another puritanical zealot seems to have been redeemed.

East is West

1 **above Heliopolis** An aerodrome was established in Heliopolis in February 1910. During the War the British built another airfield close to it, which became RAF Heliopolis in 1918. This is where John Garland appears to be stationed in *Stained Radiance* (p. 188). Neither exists these days but the Almaza Airbase now occupies the approximate site.

2 **Dædalus of the East – of Crete and Crete prehellenic** Daedalus is a figure in Greek mythology. Born in Crete, he invented (among other things) wings that he and his son Icarus used to attempt to escape imprisonment on the island. The two important phases of Greek civilisation before the Hellenes are the Minoan (approximately 2600-1400 BC) and the Mycenaean (1600-1100 BC). Minoan culture originated on Crete.

3 **La Manche** The French term for the English Channel (literally "the sleeve").

4 **The Icarian Sea lies not in Western Europe** Icarus ignored Daedalus's warnings and flew too near to the sun. His waxen wings melted and he plummeted to his death. The Icarian Sea is thus the name given to the Mediterranean in the area

where he fell (south of Samos).

[5] **East is East and West is West** This mantra-like phrase, often quoted by the British to emphasise that fundamental racial and cultural differences should be maintained, originates in "The Ballad of East and West" by Rudyard Kipling (1865-1936), a narrative poem which begins:

Oh, East is East, and West is West, and never the twain shall meet,
Till Earth and Sky stand presently at God's great Judgment Seat;
But there is neither East nor West, Border, nor Breed, nor Birth,
When two strong men stand face to face, tho' they come from the ends of the earth!

One can see that the first line (the one most used to emphasis cultural difference) is in fact contradicted by lines 3 and 4 (which abjure not only cultural but also social and class differences) in a spirit which appears too confrontational to be termed brotherhood-of-man but which, if omitted, gives quite a misleading view of Kipling's meaning – making it into a "heresy", as Saloney says. The poem was first collected in *Barrack-Room Ballads and other verses* (Leipzig: Heinemann & Balestier, 1892, pp. 85-94); the italics are in the original. According to J. I. M. Stewart, this collection "was to be for a generation the most popular and widely-selling of all volumes of English verse" and "was to be reprinted some fifty times in the course of the succeeding thirty years" (*Rudyard Kipling* [London: Gollancz, 1966], pp. 83, 102). By 1926 Methuen was in fact issuing a fifty-ninth reprint of its British edition. Even in 1929 Kipling was a massively popular contemporary writer, having won the Nobel Prize in Literature in 1907, though like Wells his heyday was over. He was an active anti-communist in the 1920s. Mitchell's library contained Kipling's *The Naulahka: a story of West and East* (Leipzig: Heinemann & Balestier, 1892), a mostly forgotten novel set in India which Kipling wrote with Wolcott Balestier (1861-1891). In *The Thirteenth Disciple* the young Mitchell surrogate, Malcom, finds Kipling to be a writer "whom he could not abide" (p. 37).

[6] **pre-Copernican** The Polish astronomer Nicolaus Copernicus (1473-1543) proved that the Earth goes round the sun and not the reverse.

[7] **numbered with symbols evolved in the East two thousand years ago** I.e. Arabic numerals.

[8] **aeronauts** A very literary word for pilots, probably taken from Wells, who used it liberally in futuristic works written before the advent of aeroplanes or during their early development.

[9] **the winged crests of ancient Egypt** The bullion wing patches worn by RAF pilots display a winged design which is indeed reminiscent of many of the ancient Egyptian royal crests. Saloney is amassing examples of how East and West "merge and flow".

[10] **jingo men** A jingo is a chauvinistic patriot, in this context one who would strongly adhere to the binary rule "East is East and West is West".

[11] **Nordic ... Mongolian ... pre-Aryan ... Cambodia** This kind of thing was to become a tic of the early Mitchell: packing recondite references into what is

effectively a list intended primarily to demonstrate the author's erudition. Did Mitchell have in mind a real raising of "here the banner Nordic and there the flag Mongolian", an editor naturally wonders? He usually does, but the editorial explication seldom enhances the context other than to demonstrate our author's vaunted knowledge of literature, or world affairs, or languages, or whatever it may be. The Norwegian Roald Amundsen (1872-1928) had planted "the banner Nordic" in the South Pole in 1911. Mongolia had achieved its freedom from Chinese occupation in 1921 (incidentally with the aid of the Russian White Army). "Aryan" here means a people of Indo-Iranian origin, originating around 1500 BC. Cambodia was a French possession from 1867 until 1953. I cannot identify specific "symbols obscene" that may have originated there, but Mitchell obviously has in mind something like the process whereby the original (beneficent) Eurasian religious symbol the "sauwastika" was appropriated by the German Nazi Party when it adopted it as its official symbol around 1920. The Nazi swastika is mentioned at the end of the story.

12 **a mongrel Ainu** The Ainu are an indigenous people of northern Japan, who ethnically precede the modern Japanese.

13 **the design first graved on the ancient stones of Cuzco** Cuzco is a city in modern Peru. It was the capital of the Inca Empire between the thirteenth and sixteenth centuries.

14 **troglodyte** Technically a cave dweller, but here it means what it generally still means, a clumsy or unsophisticated person.

15 **King Oonas** The Egyptian pharaoh Unas, who ruled from around 2345 until 2315 BC. Little is known about him. Reynolds-Ball, *Cairo of to-day* (1898) quotes from an inventory in the National Museum catalogue of 1896: "Some *membra disjecta* of the mummy of King Oonas, which are quaintly labelled with a touch of grim humour, 'Fragments of King Oonas'! This was found in the Pyramid of Oonas at Sakkarah. It is probably the most ancient mummy in existence" (p. 79).

16 **whorling** A favourite word of Mitchell's. "Whorl", "whorls", "whorled", "whorling" or "whorlings" appear twice in *The Calends*, twice in the (very short) *Hanno*, no less than nine times in *Stained Radiance*, and once in *The Thirteenth Disciple*. The word simply means a spiral or concentric-circular pattern (and is related to "whirl").

17 **nullah** The name given to many kinds of watercourses like streams or river beds in India; the Arabic equivalent would be "wadi".

18 **ornithopter** In *Hanno*, Mitchell mentions the future possibility of helicopters and ornithopters in the same breath (p. 19). The ornithopter was based on the principle of flapping wings rather than rotating blades and, unlike the helicopter, never really took off as Mitchell envisaged. Some experimental ornithopters did function reasonably for short periods or distances, and models worked better than those built to a human scale.

19 **cambered planes** Curved surfaces, as on the wings. While it is Saloney who speaks this paragraph, his creator (ironically a member of the RAF until 14 March

1930) shared his dim view of the aeroplane. It is clear from *Hanno* that he thought it might evolve "into helicopter or ornithopter" and thereafter, presumably, be dispensable (p. 19). He goes further (pp. 27-8):

> For purposes of northern exploration the aeroplane has been much over-praised. It is no more an instrument of exploration than Herr Amundsen is an explorer. The trans-Arctic flights early in the present decade achieved nothing; they were mere exuberances of ignorance favoured by inexuberance of climate. As a scouting and general survey instrument it has its uses under favourable conditions. [...] But neither aeroplane nor airship is the last word in aircraft. Their mastery of the air is scarcely beyond the level attained in the mastery of the water by the catamaran of the dawn-savage. The time is probably very near when the Wright invention, with its pitiful inability to achieve vertical ascents or descents, its clumsy and continuous stalling dangers and general untrustworthiness, may be superseded by craft that will indeed transform normal land exploration; craft capable of hovering (i.e. of being maintained in the air with the propulsion screw shut off) are almost within the inventor's view. The autogiro has pointed the way.

History one, Mitchell nil? Or was he just being contrarian? While at the time of his writing the aeroplane was barely a quarter-century old, it had developed rapidly enough for reasonably widespread international commercial travel to begin, and no other flying machine was to come near it in terms of world-transforming effect. There was plenty of evidence that this would be so: for example, Charles Lindbergh (1902-1974) had flown from New York to Paris non-stop over two days in May 1927. Advances in aeroplane design and capacity were happening pell-mell, were constantly in the news, and were considered a modern sensation. Few of Mitchell's readers are likely to have agreed with his downbeat view.

[20] **pterodactyl** The carnivorous flying pterosaur of prehistoric times.

[21] **half-caste sing-song** Thus begins a stretch of narrative which most readers today would consider gratuitously racist. However, this was an age when respectable writers were openly racist, usually under the guise of "Eugenics". H. G. Wells was a staunch eugenicist. Mitchell's *Cornhill* editor Leonard Huxley, indeed, was President of the British Eugenics Society, and had published his Conway Memorial Lecture, *Progress and the unfit: delivered at South Place Institute on May 27, 1926* (London: Watts & Co., 1926), which now reads like a tract in fascist social engineering. Whereas Mitchell's racism is sporadic and casual (and it is clear from even this story that he was entirely accepting of interracial mixing and procreation), in Huxley it is organised, consistent and virulent. Huxley observes that the British Empire is rather like the Roman, and that we should take note of the reasons why an empire like Rome fell, and guard against a similar thing happening again. One of the ways we should do so is forcibly to prevent the "feeble-minded" or physically or racially degenerate from procreating. Indeed, the idea of there being "lesser breeds" was in large part what the justification of empire had always been based on. Nonetheless, what are we to make of a Mitchell who seems happy to reproduce such reactionary prejudices? It

can be a shock if, coming from his later work, one has understood him to be an enlightened socialist. A socialist he certainly was but, as we see from *The Calends*, this was a socialism with some blind spots regarding colonialism and racism. Mitchell was, it should be said, hardly alone in encompassing such contradictions. They can be found in the writings of many radicals and liberal intellectuals of his time. One could attempt to argue that Mitchell establishes this apparently unquestioned "racist" framework only to dismantle it later in the story, or that it is Saloney (not necessarily Mitchell) who seems to share in the seemingly axiomatic white supremacy, but the present editor is not disposed to be so generous. Mitchell does indeed end on an anti-racist note, but only after treating us to a lot of unreflective racist blether before we get there. There need be no doubt that this kind of racist talk was entirely common in British-controlled Cairo and the rest of the empire, but that is not the point: verisimilitude is not the same as ideological innocence.

22 **Goanese half-caste ... Jaffa** His grandfather was from the state of Goa, in India, and was of mixed race. Jaffa is a port city in modern-day Israel (British-controlled Palestine in the 1920s). From the mid-nineteenth century it has had a significant orange-growing industry.

23 **Lyons** An antiquated, not incorrect, spelling of Lyon, the city in southern France.

24 **Legion** During the Great War the French decorated 55,000 combatants, including airmen, with the *Légion d'honneur*, the country's highest military and civil honour. The *Légion d'honneur* has five grades, so "a high Legion decoration" is entirely plausible.

25 **lynched ... anti-colour pogrom** This sounds like the American south, so one might imagine that the city is St Louis, Missouri, home since 1917 to The St Louis Aircraft Corporation, which made planes for the Americans in the Great War.

26 **an indemnity** Compensation.

27 **yellow boots** This phrase recalls the "yellow boots" worn by the Jewish men in "Vernal", but the exact import of the utterance, never mind the putative humour, remains opaque. Is the idea that "yellow boots" refers to dark-skinned persons who go barefoot?

28 **I, who love types and so seldom find them** He invents them instead.

29 **Aryans ultra-bred** "Aryans" now has a changed meaning in the text: it designates Nordic or white peoples, the "Aryans" of Nazi racial theory.

30 **'without the Law'** I.e. outside or above the law. Saloney is alluding to a biblical passage: "now the righteousness of God without the law is manifested, being witnessed by the law and the prophets" (Romans 3, 21).

31 **keel** The ornithopter has already been likened to a boat, whose keel is a beam running the entire length of the underside of the vessel, from bow to stern.

32 **we'll never have ornithopters** Never say "never", but her brother's prediction about the ornithopter has been pretty accurate so far. His views on the helicopter have proved pessimistic: in 1927 the German Engelbert Zaschka (1895-1955) made a model with vertical rise and descent and hovering ability, and in 1928 the

Hungarian Oszkár Asbóth (1891-1960) constructed a prototype that vastly bettered Zaschka's design. As a civilian conveyance the helicopter was established by the arrival of the American-made Bell 47 at the end of 1946.

[33] **the old Frost ornithopter in the London Science** E. P. Frost (1842-1922) was an English ornithopter pioneer. A wing from the first craft he got to leave the ground (in 1904) is still displayed in London's Science Museum.

[34] **English Aero Club's pilot certificate** The Aero Club of Great Britain, which was founded in 1901 and became the Royal Aero Club in 1910, from which date it also began issuing Aviators Certificates, which were recognised under the Fédération Aéronautique Internationale.

[35] **Egremont and Lilienthal** Otto Lilienthal (1848-1896), a German sometimes referred to as "the father of aviation", who had significant engineering success with gliders, making over 2,000 successful flights until one stalled and he fell to his death. In H. G. Wells's novel *Tono-Bungay* (London: Macmillan, 1909) the narrator George Ponderevo becomes an experimental aircraft builder and discusses this pursuit at some length with Beatrice Normandy (p. 362):

> I told her something of my experimental work. She had never heard of the soaring aeroplane, and was excited by the thought, and keen to hear about it. She had thought all the work so far had been a mere projecting of impossible machines. For her Pilcher and Lilienthal had died in vain. She did not know such men had lived in the world.

Of an Egremont connected to aviation I know nothing, and indeed there may be none, because it was not beyond Mitchell sometimes to throw in an incongruous name for the sake of now lost comic effect.

[36] **Sharia Kamil** Sharia Kamel (now El-Gomhoreya), on the western edge of the Ezbekiyeh gardens.

[37] **is** "Is" (with a capital I) in first edition.

[38] **Seen anything of the Melforts there? ... Malta** The British Empire was obviously a very small world for those who could move easily in it. The islands of Malta were part of the British Empire from 1814 until 1964, an important strategic entrepôt located, like Cyprus (a British colony from 1925, but in British control long before), between Gibraltar and Egypt. These island possessions gave the British enormous dominance of the Mediterranean, the Suez Canal, and the route to India and the Far East.

[39] **certificates of departure** I.e death certificates.

[40] **snub-man** Presumably a man who snubs.

[41] **a disposition to pronounce what as hwaw** In other words, that of a member of the British upper classes (or of one pretending to be).

[42] **squadron leader** From 1919 the RAF had its own ranks (having before that used army ranks). Squadron Leader is a commissioned rank, higher than a Flight Lieutenant but lower than a Wing Commander.

[43] **forming fours** On the assumption that "the latest wonder of science" is an aeroplane, it is not forming the shape of the number 4 in the air. Rather, "forming

fours" is a military drill formation in which soldiers march in groups of four. The implication seems to be that Reginald is experimenting with flying several planes in synchronized fashion. These were as yet still early days in military aviation.

44 **inspecting engines to see if they're properly shaved** The word "shaved" (now, at least) has a technical meaning with respect to engines (it means removing the engine, smoothing out the metal inside the engine bay, and concealing exposed wires and connections) but Mitchell possibly intends simply the idea of inspecting to check that engines are clean and regularly maintained.

45 **Brahmin** The highest caste in Hindu society.

46 **sahib** In colonial India, a word used by the British and Indians to indicate respect for another man ("memsahib", used for a woman, occurs later in the story).

47 **Miocene** The Miocene epoch in geology is between 23 million and 5 million years ago.

48 **bandy authorities** I.e. argue about scholarly matters.

49 **a Gypsy adventurer** Saloney is not, I think, saying that Joyce is actually Romany: he is using the word "Gypsy" merely to express his idea of Joyce's "exotic" and romantic nature.

50 **the seven gates of Egypt** According to the so-called Book of Gates (an ancient Egyptian funerary text) the soul passes to the underworld through a series of gates. Excavations have revealed depictions of such gates in many of the more notable burial sites. The Temple of Osiris at Karnak near Luxor has a wall carving showing seven gates.

51 **the doctor of Chaumont** Chaumont is in north-east France, and became the general headquarters of the American army in July 1917 once it entered the Great War. In October of that year the Americans established the temporary Chaumont-sur-Aire Airdrome. Quite what Adrian means when he refers to an "air-ambulance" is not clear, but it is probably much more primitive than our modern idea of an ambulance. There are recorded uses of aircraft being used to evacuate injured victims in the Great War. It would appear that Adrian has met Mogara before, perhaps in one of them.

52 **study brown** A brown study is a mood in which a person is somewhat lost in their own thoughts and not particularly aware of surrounding things.

53 ***Per ardua ad astra*** "Through adversity to the stars" (Latin): the official motto of the RAF.

54 **a bee in his bonnet** I.e. an obsession (idiomatic).

55 **anachronism** Mogara already feels that the aeroplane is an obsolete machine.

56 **Hope springs eternal** The phrase has now become almost proverbial. "Hope springs eternal in the human breast" is its fuller form, which is a line from *An Essay on Man* (first epistle, 1733), a long philosophical poem by Alexander Pope (1688-1744).

57 **Waken up!** It looks as if Mitchell's Scots linguistic habits have intruded here: one hears "waken up" used as an imperative in Scotland quite regularly, but an English person like Joyce would most likely say "Wake up!"

[58] **pringling** I.e. tingling.
[59] **Always there's the Adventure** In *The Thirteenth Disciple* Malcom and Domina talk frequently of "the Adventure".
[60] **whitely** A rare adverb in English, but it means what it says. Something like "pale-facedly" is the surface import, but the accompanying hint may be that he is behaving the way a white person would find acceptable.
[61] **the Mountains of the Moon** A mountain range of legend, believed to be at the source of the Nile.
[62] **'white mulatto'** The feminine form is actually "mulatta". Like "half-caste", the word is now considered offensive or inappropriate by most anglophone speakers, and has largely passed out of currency. A mulatto is a man of mixed race, usually with one white and one black parent, as was sometimes the case in colonial Africa (usually a white European father and a black African mother). A "white" mulatto is simply lighter-skinned, and in some cases may pass for caucasian. In short, therefore, there is no such thing as racial purity in the modern world; white is not necessarily white or black black; we are all mongrels. This closing homily is clumsily didactic, and it betrays the young Mitchell's rudimentary abilities in integrating politics and fiction. The attempt is nonetheless significant. It tells us that Mitchell did not consider the Nazis ignorable, even as early as 1929. There had been Federal elections in Germany in May 1928 and the Social Democrats remained the largest party, with 153 of 491 seats. The Communists secured 54 seats. The Nazis took only 12. This hardly suggested that the Nazis were a serious Parliamentary threat, although they may have been considered a potentially insurrectionary or actually subversive one. It was the election of September 1930 (more than a year after Mitchell had completed the "Polychromata") that seemed to suggest a profound change in things: the Nazis took 107 seats.

Gift of the River

[1] **Landward** A real surname, though by the 1920s most of the people bearing it would be American. There are no records of this name ever having been found in Scotland.
[2] **the Egyptian Gazette** The oldest English-language newspaper in the Middle East, founded in 1880, and still publishing.
[3] **the Greek Institution** We will learn that this is "a Greek Institution for the destitute".
[4] **Heloise ... Abelard** Peter Abelard (*c.* 1079-1142), a French scholar, had a passionate relationship with and eventually married Héloïse d'Argenteuil (*c.* 1100-1163/4), a French nun. Their romance became the basis for several famous stories and poems in European (including English) literature.
[5] **Paolo** The love story of Paolo and Francesca is told in *The Divine Comedy* (1308-1321) by Dante Alighieri (1265-1321). Francesca da Rimini was murdered by

Giovanni Malatesta, her husband, when he discovered she was in love with Paolo Malatesta, his brother. Dante meets Francesca and Paolo in *Inferno* canto V. The pair were the subject of a painting, *Paolo and Francesca da Rimini* (1855), by one of Mitchell's favourite pre-Raphaelites, Dante Gabriel Rossetti.

6 **Nileward** Overlooking the river.

7 **one who waits and weeps Leander** The story of Hero and his lover Leander derives from Greek mythology. All of these comparator stories involve a degree of tragedy (frequently the death of one or both lovers) or the suffering of unfulfilled desire.

8 **lung-wasting** Tuberculosis was a fatal disease until treatments with antibiotics proved successful after the Second World War. A hot, dry climate was often recommended to sufferers. Reynolds-Ball, *Cairo of to-day* (1898) had an entire chapter on "Cairo as a Health Resort" (pp. 24-34) but its author was sceptical:

> Cairo itself cannot be unreservedly recommended as a health resort pure and simple. The Egyptian climate is undeniably admirably suited for a winter residence, and in most respects it is superior to that of any health resort in the South of France – the world's great winter sanatorium. But the city of Cairo possesses too many factitious drawbacks, which militate against its use as a climatic health station. Now that other health resorts, such as Luxor, Assouan, Helouan, etc., are getting better known and developed, medical men are beginning to realise that hygienically speaking Cairo is not Egypt. Its enormous population and limited area for one thing does not commend it to medical men as a winter residence for their patients. An over-crowded city of over 400,000 inhabitants, with its unsatisfactory hygienic conditions and appallingly primitive and unsanitary system of drainage – if system it can be called – the occasional visitation of cholera, etc., seems indeed the last place to which the health-seeker, as distinct from the mere tourist or pleasure-seeker, should be sent. It is true that the sanitation of the Continental, Shepheard's, Ghezireh Palace, and other fashionable hotels is beyond reproach, but then the visitor is not likely to spend the whole time in his hotel. Besides, the innumerable social gaieties and dissipations of this fashionable winter-city offer too many temptations to the invalid to neglect his health (pp. 24-5).

9 **Majorca** The Balearic island of Mallorca was not at this time the British holiday excursion purgatory it was later to become, but it is quite a good post-Second World War example of how, even after colonialism, commercial demand could turn a foreign place into something incongruously anglified.

10 **Esperanto** A language invented by L. L. Zamenhof (1859-1917) with the aim of creating an international language. Insofar as there was major enthusiasm for it, the 1920s was its heyday. It was looked upon benignly by anti-nationalists (such as anarchists and communists) because it prospectively would reduce the global power of the national languages associated with colonialism, mainly English, French and Spanish. It was viewed with hostility by many others, including national governments, for precisely the same reason.

[11] **World-Speech** In H. G. Wells's novel *Mr Britling Sees It Through* (London: Macmillan, 1916) Herr Heinrich "confessed two principal ambitions. They varied perhaps in their absolute dimensions, but they were of equal importance in his mind. The first of these was, so soon as he had taken his doctorate in philology, to give himself to the perfecting of an International Language; it was to combine all the virtues of Esperanto and Ido. 'And then,' said Herr Heinrich, 'I do not think there will be any more wars – ever'" (p. 422).

[12] **that Celtic fringe that is now denied by your historians** Explication of this statement would require more space than the passing remark merits, but the reader interested in the claim is referred to Steven G. Ellis, "Why the History of 'the Celtic Fringe' Remains Unwritten", *European Review of History—Revue européenne d'Histoire* 10, 2 (2003), pp. 221-31.

[13] **crematorium** Cremation was not a tradition in Egypt, as destroying the body was thought to make impossible the passage of the soul to the next life. It had been opposed in many countries for the same religious reasons, but the practice had been growing in Britain. It was regulated by the Cremation Act 1902. Mitchell himself was cremated in February 1935.

[14] **that strange burial-service of your Church** The Order for The Burial of the Dead in the *Book of Common Prayer* of the Anglican church.

[15] **a national fête** A national holiday.

[16] **the domed house of the Freligraths** The observatory of "A Volcano in the Moon".

[17] ***Quelle honte!*** In context the French Flore means something like "What a shame!"

[18] **with the stars** I.e. in heaven.

[19] **Ribaddi** Mitchell appears to have filched this unlikely name from Rib-Addi (variously spelled), king of the Phoenician city of Byblos in the fourteenth century BC. Many letters from him to the Egyptian pharaoh of the time have survived.

[20] **the Venus transit** The rare but visible passage of Venus on a course between the Earth and the sun (or one of the larger planets), first observed in 1639. No one could have seen such a thing in the 1920s. A transit had not occurred since 1882 and would not take place again until 2004. When it did occur in colonial times many European countries sent massive expeditions to good vantage points on the globe to observe it. The transit usually lasts for only a few hours.

[21] **From too much love of living ... somewhere safe to sea** A stanza from "The Garden of Proserpine" (1866) by Algernon Charles Swinburne (1837-1909), a poet Mitchell admired and frequently quoted.

[22] **carved mushrabiyeh work** A mashrabiya is a bay window (usually with only a framework but no glass) with carved wood decoration, found projecting from the upper floors of buildings in Islamic countries.

[23] **set the hammer** I.e. he cocked the pistol, preparing to fire it.

[24] **like a Greek out of Wilde** The complaint seems to be that a Greek woman in a work by Wilde would be unrealistically aestheticised or idealised.

[25] **a *koré* of the vases** *Kore* (the word does not have the accent it is given in the first edition) was a form of Greek sculpture depicting young women, but hardly ever naked. Sometimes the head alone was worked into the stone of a vase. Thea in *Stained Radiance* is described as being "like a nude Greek koré of the Athenian vase-makers" (p. 78).
[26] **Hades** I.e. hell (from the name given to the Greek underworld).
[27] **just as idiotic as in English** The statement is doubly "idiotic" or inapposite: firstly, while it is grammatically acceptable, in regular conversation one would say, "It's me", but secondly, "It is I" is always true whoever says it and in this situation fails to identify the speaker as intended.
[28] **his protégée in ... an unnecessary state of negligée** Mitchell clearly could not resist this euphonous innuendo. A protégée is a female pupil or student, a négligée a woman's light nightgown. In French these words literally mean "protected" and "neglected" respectively. But "négligée" is being used, as it often was, for titillating purposes: the girl is wearing hardly anything or, indeed, nothing at all.
[29] **starvation and worse send scores south from Smyrna and the Archipelago** The archipelago is the Greek islands, and the dire circumstances hinted at are the consequences of the Greco-Turkish War, which ended in 1922 but was followed by reprisals and persecution.
[30] **to the modern Romaic as Virgil to ... the little d'Annunzio** The Romaic is the modern Greek vernacular, which has simpler grammar and pronunciation than ancient Greek. Virgil, or Publius Vergilius Maro (70-19 BC), was the author of the epic Latin poem *The Aeneid*. Gabriele D'Annunzio (1863-1938) had gained some reputation as a writer in his native Italy but after the War wrote little and was most noted for being a vigorous nationalist.
[31] **Kora** From her likeness to the *kore* vase images. It is also another name for Persephone, who was abducted by Hades and became queen of the underworld in Greek mythology.
[32] **Greek is the oldest and purest of the Aryan dialects** No it isn't, which definitively blows out of the water Mitchell's strained attempt to make his linguist sound professional and credible. "Aryan" is not a language with dialects, and there is no such thing as an "Aryan" family of languages.
[33] **some unlicensed house** An illegal brothel.
[34] **the cornflowers** Her eyes have already been likened to sunflowers. Persephone's mother, Demeter, was a corn goddess, with power over the growth of crops.
[35] **Thibaut August** The Freligraths' son.
[36] **the lover steadfast** Saloney puns on the dog's name.
[37] **drab** "A dirty or untidy woman" (*OED*) with overtones in this case of prostitution.
[38] **catapault** A variant spelling of "catapult".
[39] **Kora in Eleusis** In ancient Greece initiation rites were held by the cult of Persephone and Demeter at Eleusis. Persephone was believed eventually to have escaped Hades and been reunited at Eleusis with her mother, Demeter, who henceforth allowed crops to grow again. It would appear that, somehow or other,

Kora has been assimilated to Joan Landward, or that Joan is inexplicably resurrected in her form.

It is Written

[1] **First sunset after Ramadan** Because Ramadan involves fasting and other observances, its end would be greeted with some relief or, going one step further, much "painting the town red".

[2] **In all the Forest of Faith is a rending and overthrow** The phrase sounds biblical but no particular biblical passage presents itself as a model. Rather "rend" in biblical terms means to tear or split apart, and usually refers to clothing, because the tearing of outer garments in some cultures or communities signified the strength of one's emotions. "Overthrow" means what it still does, and the general sense is that there is much turbulence for the religious in the modern, atheistic world.

[3] **future generations who excavate in the strata carboniferous** I.e. many millions of years hence (strata dating from the carboniferous period in geology having been formed at least around 300 million years ago).

[4] **the Thirteenth Disciple** The title of Mitchell's second novel, published in January 1931, six months before *The Calends of Cairo* but six months after the periodical appearance of the last of the "Polychromata" stories.

[5] **you'll have to forgive him his lemonade** It would appear that Steyn is a teetotaller.

[6] **Wadi Faregh** This watercourse is located in the Western Desert of Egypt, part of the larger Sahara Desert. It to the west of Cairo, near the Qattara Depression (not to be confused with the different Wadi Faregh in Libya).

[7] **Polyorthes, a Hellenised Egyptian** Fictional.

[8] **a Lost Testament, in the handwriting of our Saviour Himself** As close to a Holy Grail as one can get, then.

[9] **chemic** An antiquated word simply meaning "chemical".

[10] **Basrah** Basra was the name of a region and city in southern Mesopotamia (now Iraq) and was held by the Ottomans until the Battle of Basra in November 1914, when it was occupied by British and Empire troops. It was mostly Moslem with, before the War, about 4,000 Jews and 6,000 Christians in a population of about 200,000.

[11] **jungle-walls across the Shatt-el-Arab** The Shatt al-Arab is a river formed by the meeting of the Euphrates and Tigris rivers in the Basra region. The "jungle-walls" are the vegetation along its banks.

[12] **Within twenty ... another mirage** By November 1915, then, if he arrived in March 1914.

[13] **Shelley in a world of Anarchs** The poetic reference is to "The Masque of Anarchy" (1819), a famous poem by Shelley much beloved by radicals.

[14] **an agony Gethsemane-like** In the gospels, Jesus's "agony in the garden" before his crucifixion occurs in the garden of Gethsemane in Jerusalem.

[15] **a super-ape bending in amusement** The depiction of god as a super-ape has a certain satirical edge because the metaphor is drawn from atheistic evolutionary theory.

[16] **without country or home or mandatory power ... Chaldeans, Armenians, unprosperous Jews, Nestorians** Chaldea was a small country in ancient times but was absorbed into Babylonia by the sixth century BC; Armenia was part of the Ottoman Empire and in Anatolia the Turks, fearing that the unhappy Armenians were supportive of the Russians, committed genocide against them between 1915 and 1917, forcibly driving many out of the territory; Jews, often subject to persecution, were famously peripatetic; a Nestorian believed in the doctrine of theologian Nestorius (d. *c.* 450), which stated that Christ himself was two persons (one human, one divine) loosely united, but this view was deemed heretical and there was a schismatic diaspora of Nestorians to Persia.

[17] **1925** One of the few specific dates in the volume.

[18] **the mountains beyond Lake Van** The largest lake in Turkey, in the east, in the Armenian highlands. Several monasteries, or their ruins, survive in the area.

[19] **Nicolaos of Corinth** Fictional.

[20] ***the heathen Mani*** Mani (216-274/7) was an Iranian prophet who founded the religion of Manichaeism. Manichaeism assumes a primeval conflict between the forces of light (good) and dark (evil).

[21] ***the Fathers*** The "Church Fathers" or early theologians who established Christian church doctrine.

[22] **Trebizond ... the south Black Sea** Now Trabzon, a city and region in Turkey on the south-east corner of the Black Sea.

[23] **Mevr** "Merv" in the first edition, but Mitchell is surely invoking the "Mevr" of "For Ten's Sake".

[24] **Christian Mysteries ... Council of Nicaea** The Christian mysteries are those elements of God or his workings which seem supernatural and inexplicable but are considered real. The First Council of Nicaea (now İznik in modern Turkey) convened in 325 and settled many theological disputes in the early Christian church as a means to establishing doctrine.

[25] **Three million lie and rot in France** As a result of the Western Front fighting in the Great War.

[26] **Ministry of the Interior ... Ordnance Survey** The "Ministry of the Interior" is what in Britain is called the Home Office. Ordnance Survey (OS) is Britain's national mapping agency, established in the mid-eighteenth century. I have used an historic map of Cairo prepared by OS in editing this volume (reproduced along with many others at https://www.oldmapsonline.org).

[27] **rowelled** A rowel is a spiked disc at the end of a spur, used by a rider to drive on a horse. The meaning here is simply of a landscape scarred with a river bed, as if created by a giant rowel.

[28] **Ave of Rossetti's ... Against the fervid sky** Mitchell also quotes "Ave" by Dante Gabriel Rossetti in *The Thirteenth Disciple* (p. 248). There is no doubt that

Mitchell did think Rossetti's poem "very beautiful" but few modern readers are likely to share his view. Its antiquated language and conventional poeticisms make it read poorly now.

[29] **that picture of the Virgin** Mary, mother of Jesus. The "picture" of her in "Ave" is not the only one Rossetti created: he painted her as well, in *The Girlhood of Mary Virgin* (1849).

[30] **anthropomorphism** The attribution of at least some human characteristics to a god.

[31] **sky-whelming** "Whelm" is a verb little used on its own, and is seldom coupled with anything other than in the word "overwhelm". It simply means to turn upside down.

[32] **Gillyflower Arnold** A gillyflower is one of several types of plant, like carnations, stocks and wallflowers.

[33] **light a lantern for me** Gillyflower alludes to Matthew 25, 1-15 (the parable of the virgins and the lamps). It may seem a strange thing for an atheist to do, but then Mitchell was an atheist forever nodding to the Bible as well.

[34] **hog-back** In geology a hogback is a sharp ridge with steeply sloping sides.

[35] **tortoise-shell glasses** The name given to a pattern overlaid on certain materials (her glasses are not made from actual tortoise-shell).

[36] **the little madame who once lived at Daybreak House** Dawn in "Daybreak".

[37] **exploring and mapping the putative oil-centres in the Bahaira** The Bahariya Oasis in the Western Desert of Egypt, about 230 miles (370 km) west of Cairo. The idea that in the 1920s an American oil company would send a single young woman to Egypt to explore for oil is, of course, one of the most unrealistic plot elements imaginable, Mitchell's sheer fantasy.

[38] **we haven't got a world board of control yet** The analogy is taken from the Board of Commissioners for the Affairs of India (known as the India Board or the Board of Control), founded in 1784, which between 1784 and 1858 was the part of the UK government that managed British interests in India. Gillyflower imagines some such Wellsian outfit managing the world. Being a female character in a fiction by the young Mitchell, we should not be surprised that she is interested in exactly the issues Mitchell was, and has read exactly the authors Mitchell has. The early Mitchell is often at his eye-rolling worst when trying to delineate female characters, as here. Who could have guessed that his greatest novel would centre on an extremely well-created heroine?

[39] **the last Ice Age** The last glacial period on Earth is thought to have begun around 115,000 years ago and lasted about 100,000 years.

[40] **We also have come to fight the Darkness** A Manichaean point of view.

[41] **Stone Age shaman ... breaks on a billiards table** A shaman was a man considered spiritual in primitive communities, with powers of prophecy and healing. The Stone Age is a vast historical span of 3.4 millions years, ending between 4000 and 2000 BC. It was preceded by the Palaeolithic period, mentioned in the next line. Billiards, by contrast, has been known in Europe since at least the fifteenth century:

a "break" is a period of continuous scoring of points in the game.

42 **pre-Adamic ... mumbo-jumbo of the carrion caves. Saints and ministers!** Adam, according to Genesis, was the first human created by God. "Mumbo-jumbo" denotes nonsense. In his *Travels in the Interior of Africa* (1795) the Scottish explorer Mungo Park (1771-1806) depicts "Mumbo Jumbo" as an actual village official among Mandingo peoples, a kind of family mediator: "This strange minister of justice [...] disguised in the dress that has been mentioned [a sort of masquerade habit, made of the bark of trees], and armed with the rod of public authority, announces his coming (whenever his services are required) by loud and dismal screams in the woods near the town. He begins the pantomime at the approach of night". Mitchell paraphrases this episode in his essay on Park in *Nine Against the Unknown* (London: Jarrolds, 1934), p. 235. Carrion caves are caves in which animals have died and their decaying flesh provides nutriment to other species. "Saints and ministers!" is possibly echoing Hamlet's "Angels and ministers of grace, defend us!" upon seeing the ghost of his father in *Hamlet* (1601; I.iv.43) by William Shakespeare (1564-1616).

43 **when a young woman comes five thousand miles to dig in the earth for weapons to fight that same Darkness** Who knew that exploring for oil could be viewed as a positive part of a cosmic Manichaean struggle? Steyn, who appears to be the kind of obsessive Saloney specialises in meeting, sees it in everything.

44 **Neanderthal** *Homo sapiens neanderthalensis* were an extinct humanoid species living in Eurasia until about 40,000 years ago.

45 **Christ – the great Captain** There were many cultural images of Christ as some kind of captain (usually of a ship of faith, but sometimes as a fighter). For example, there was a popular hymn, "Christ, our mighty Captain, leads against the foe" (1908) by the American Carrie Ellis Breck (1855-1934).

46 **he had grown the mutual charge** The implication, soon confirmed, is that he has developed loving feelings for Gillyflower rather like hers for him.

47 **the passage was of the shortest. Within eighteen feet of the entrance** Something seemed to go very awry with the proofreading or textual corrections at this point, as three typographical errors occur within eleven words: the first edition reads "the passag' was of the shortest. Within eighten feet of the entrancee".

48 **kist** A chest (Scots), usually for storing clothes.

49 **son of Thi-Hetep ... the light of Ormuzd ... Ctesiphon ... Ahriman** Thi (or Tiye) was the wife of the pharaoh Amenhotep III (fourteenth century BC). Ormusd (variously spelled) is the creator deity and sky-god in the ancient Iranian religion of Zoroastrianism (in which Ahriman is the evil spirit, a kind of devil-equivalent). Ctesiphon was an ancient Iranian city, about 22 miles (35 km) south-east of modern Baghdad (where Mitchell had been stationed, March-September 1920, before his year in Cairo).

50 **the Rodin Thinker** "Le Penseur", a famous sculpture by the French artist Auguste Rodin (1840-1917).

51 **perhaps it was God, not Satan, who was overthrown in the beginning**

of time: "And there was war in heaven: Michael and his angels fought against the dragon; and the dragon fought and his angels, And prevailed not; neither was their place found any more in heaven. And the great dragon was cast out, that old serpent, called the Devil, and Satan, which deceiveth the whole world: he was cast out into the earth, and his angels were cast out with him" (Revelation 12, 7-9).

[52] **'Why, I've been blind! ... *Gillyflower!* ...'** The original story as published in *The Cornhill Magazine* had a thirteenth section of two paragraphs which Mitchell cut from the book. It read (Bold, *Smeddum*, p. 402).:

> I turned about and walked away, and left them there with the coming starshine. I climbed to a Faregh brow, and sat and smoked the pipe, with below me the murmur of their young voices. And beyond the hills and sands – Cairo – Egypt – the world that has known so many creeds and faiths, where the young have sat and talked and debated through a million evenings, loving and hating and questioning the gods who shine and pass ...
>
> Yet perhaps indeed scripts and gods, faiths and fears – they matter nothing if the Message that is written endures.

The laboured explanation is obviously consonant with the Christian Socialism implied by "For Ten's Sake": God may not exist or even be malevolent, but what is important are the moral principles that humans have developed under the banner of Christianity.

The Passage of the Dawn

[1] ***bersím ... jinni*** Berseem (also called Egyptian clover) is popular as animal-feed. A jinni is a supernatural spirit (more commonly, "genie").

[2] **the fairy mountains of Mesheen** Unidentified, probably (like "the Kablurz Beg" of "He Who Seeks") a fictional mountain range.

[3] **it is your last Egyptian night** Reader, it is also your last Egyptian story in this book.

[4] **'Abbas Pasha** The opening apostrophe is in the first edition. Abbās Ḥilmī Pāshā (1874-1944) was the last Khedive, the Ottoman Empire's rule in Egypt ending with the War. Until after his death what is now Ramses Street was called Abbas Street.

[5] **Abu Zabal** A Cairo suburb already mentioned in "Daybreak".

[6] **the company Trans-Saharan Transport** Fictional.

[7] **far beyond Kufra, regions where the oases ceased ... raiding Tuareg of Air and Tibesti** Kufra is a group of oases in south-east Libya, bordering Egypt. The Tuareg people are nomadic Berbers in the Sahara. The Aïr Mountains are in northern Niger, the Tibesti mountains mainly in northern Chad. Virtually all of this indicated area was then French West Africa.

[8] **stars!'** In the first edition a single horizontal line space separated this paragraph from the next. It has here been omitted.

[9] **caterpillar automobiles** The American Caterpillar Tractor Company was

created in 1925 from a corporate merger. It established its first African dealership in Tunisia in 1926, but the vehicles were used mainly in construction rather than for transport.

[10] **Algiers to Timbuctoo** The capital of modern Algeria and the ancient city in modern Mali respectively.

[11] **jazz and uplift** Both, in the 1920s, were associated with African Americans. The 1920s and 1930s were retrospectively to be called by some The Jazz Age. "Uplift" has not survived so well as a term, though the idea of African American spiritual improvement it describes also gave birth to the musical culture of hymns and spirituals.

[12] **Monkeyville trials** In 1925, a Tennessee high school teacher named John Scopes (1900-1970) was charged with the crime of teaching his pupils about evolution. The Scopes Monkey Trial, as it became known, was the first to be broadcast by radio. The trial was held in the small town of Dayton, which became referred to colloquially as "Monkeyville". Scopes was found guilty and fined $100, but won his appeal.

[13] **nasalisation** Another scornful remark about the American accent (hatred of "nasal Americanisms" has already been expressed in "Gift of the River").

[14] **Hassanein Bey** Ahmed Hassanein Bey (1889-1946), an Egyptian explorer, had made an expedition through Libya in 1923, discovering mountains and water sources. He published *The Lost Oases: being a narrative account of the author's explorations into the more remote parts of the Libyan desert and his rediscovery of two oases* (1925).

[15] **the articles thirty-nine of your Church** The Thirty-nine Articles of Religion, formulated in 1571, encapsulate the doctrines and practices of the Anglican Church and can be found in the *Book of Common Prayer*.

[16] **Webley** A revolver, standard issue for military throughout the British Empire at the time, manufactured by the company Webley & Scott.

[17] **settle the hash of** I.e. silence (colloquial).

[18] **potted** Tinned.

[19] **clad in sin and shining raiment** In Mark 9, 3 Jesus's "raiment became shining", which befits him as a king. Elsewhere in the Bible splendid raiment is associated with luxury. Cf. Matthew 11, 8: "But what went ye out for to see? A man clothed in soft raiment? behold, they that wear soft clothing are in kings' houses."

[20] **chucked my billet** Resigned.

[21] **the camel gave a ping ... and doubled up** I.e. it died.

[22] **the beach at Mustapha ... Frankfort** The beach is in Alexandria (the Mustafa Pasha British barracks in Alexandria were nearby). "Frankfort" is a spelling of "Frankfurt" actually preferred by some Germans.

[23] **your Mr Wells an incarnation of Akhnaton** In "The Epic" Saloney has already convinced a customer of his "descent from Akhnaton".

[24] **beyond Siwa – he was in Cairo and staying at Shepheard's Hotel** The Siwa Oasis is about 350 miles (560 km) west of Cairo. Shepheard's Hotel was the most famous and luxurious hotel in Cairo, founded as the "Hotel des Anglais" in

1841. It was situated north-west of the Ezbekiyeh gardens, not far from the Continental, and was destroyed by fire in 1952.
[25] **the cut of my drill** "Drill" is the name given to a coarse form of cotton or linen, hence, by extension, the impressiveness of his dress.
[26] **Kyrilovich** The first time we learn of Saloney's patronymic.
[27] **gay commissar** The Princess transfers the idea of *The Gay Hussars* (1909), an operetta by the Hungarian Emmerich Kálmán (1882-1953) which celebrates the joyousness (not the homosexuality) of Hungarian cavalrymen, to the Soviet context.
[28] **In Cairo for nine of them?** This dates this meeting of Saloney and Pelagueya to 1929 at the earliest, 1930 at the latest. In "He Who Seeks" Saloney has told us that he was at the siege of Perekop in November 1920.
[29] **she who had been the Princess Pelagueya Bourrin** Which is presumably why she left revolutionary Russia. She reappears in *The Lost Trumpet*. Pelagueya is the name of a female character in "The House with the Mezzanine (A Painter's Story)" by Anton Chekhov (1860-1904), *The House with the Mezzanine and other stories,* tr. S. S. Koteliansky and Gilbert Cannan (New York: Scribner's, 1917), pp. 1-28.
[30] **the soldier-groom, Budenni** Semyon Mikhailovich Budyonny (1883-1973), a Soviet military commander during the Russian Civil War. He was the founder of the Red Cavalry, which fought Deniken's (also Saloney's) White troops in 1919.
[31] **South** Capitalised by Mitchell because "South Russia" was the name given to the White territorial stronghold in 1919-20 (almost as if it were a separate state).
[32] **a Ural river** The Ural river, so-called because its source is in the southern Ural mountains.
[33] **nouveaux riches** "Newly rich" people (French).
[34] **a passage to Egypt** Mitchell could hardly be unaware that E. M. Forster (1879-1970) had a few years before published the novel *A Passage to India* (London: Arnold, 1924).
[35] **to sell myself as advantageously as possible** Not exactly as a prostitute but not, what from she tells us, as a wife either: more a "paid escort".
[36] **canaille** Common people, the rabble (French in origin).
[37] **this** "This" (with a capital T) in the first edition.
[38] **last testament** His will, from which Gault benefited.
[39] **palanquin** A box with poles, covered to conceal the distinguished passenger, carried by servants holding the poles: a mode of transport usually reserved for royalty.
[40] **the Zulu in Versailles** Zulu people are natives of Southern Africa. The British had fought a successful colonial war against them in 1879. By the time of the Treaty of Versailles and the Paris Peace Conference (1919-20) which produced it, many such former enemies were present as Empire representatives, making their national claims. These included, for example, South Africa, although no Zulu spoke for it. Saloney uses the example simply to capture the surprising variety of interracial and inter-ethnic encounters in the post-War world.

[41] **wigs and patches and gibbets and powder** A gibbet is a gallows-like structure from which the dead bodies of criminals were publicly hanged as a deterrent to others. The last public execution in Britain was in 1868. Essentially this is a short list of once seemingly fixed customs which have now been abandoned (wearing wigs, eye patches and face powder being the others).
[42] **his face a satyr's** Satyrs are the drunken and lustful gods of the woodland in Greek mythology.
[43] **Pharillon** Oddly enough, E. M. Forster had also published *Pharos and Pharillon* (London: Hogarth Press, 1923) a couple of months after Mitchell sailed back to Britain from Egypt. It was a short series of essays, articles and stories about Alexandria, where he had been stationed with the British Red Cross during the War. Pharos and Pharillon are the names of the two lighthouses in Alexandria harbour.
[44] **massif** A word used to denote a mountain range or a part of one.
[45] **Terra incognita** Unknown territory (Latin).
[46] **a cul-de-sac** A dead-end.
[47] **floriferous** A word of which Mitchell seems unduly fond. He is looking for a better term than "flowery" but "floriferous" does not mean quite the same thing. It is used to designate a plant that produces many flowers, not anything that has a merely "flowery" appearance. Mitchell was to use the ungainly word again (this time of handwriting) in *The Thirteenth Disciple* (p. 283) and in *Nine Against the Unknown* (p. 55) of sculpture.
[48] **Waken up** The second time this Scotticism has occurred in the book.
[49] **beatification** A slightly blasphemous way of describing his new-found wealth (beatification is the first step on promotion to the status of a saint by the Catholic church).
[50] **an old Turkish castle out in Abu Zabal** The older name of Abu Zabal was al-Quseir (Arabic: 'small castle').
[51] **the off-side wheels of the car** Those furthest from the kerb.
[52] **halcyon** Idyllically happy.
[53] **waxed** I.e. advanced.
[54] **the world's sanction we've forgone and she refuses** She has turned down the idea of marriage, which would be the mark of society's approval of their relationship.
[55] **Sollum** Sallum, a town on the Egyptian coast near the Libyan border.
[56] **this is the last of the Saloney stories** Not so, as Mitchell was to have Saloney narrate his novel *The Lost Trumpet*, similarly set in Cairo and the Middle East, and using many of the same characters. The novel is in many ways an immediate sequel, in which Saloney has been ten years an expatriate dragoman.

L'Envoi

[1] **L'Envoi** The Envoi is usually the short concluding part of a work in which the

writer bids farewell. In old French "l'envoy" also meant "sending forth", and so the two notions are combined: the writer bids farewell to the work and sends it forth to the public.

2 **the great steel bridge** The Boulak Bridge.

3 **Connan** "Connon" in first edition.

4 **Arthur John Hall** An Australian Army friend of Mitchell in Cairo. He was to be the joint dedicatee of Mitchell's *The Lost Trumpet*. As William K. Malcolm draws to my attention, Mitchell's library contains a copy of Palgrave's *Golden Treasury*, signed "Arthur J. Hartnell Hall, Cairo 1922" and "Leslie Mitchell, 1922", and *The Poetical Works of Percy Bysshe Shelley, Vol. I: Lyrics & Shorter Poems*, signed "From Arthur Hall to Leslie Mitchell, October 1922, Abbassia".

Printed in Dunstable, United Kingdom

64412502R00150